Beyond Data Protection

Noriswadi Ismail • Edwin Lee Yong Cieh
Editors

Beyond Data Protection

Strategic Case Studies
and Practical Guidance

Editors
Noriswadi Ismail
Quotient Consulting
London
United Kingdom

Edwin Lee Yong Cieh
Christopher Lee & Co
Petaling Jaya
Malaysia

ISBN 978-3-642-33080-3   ISBN 978-3-642-33081-0 (eBook)
DOI 10.1007/978-3-642-33081-0
Springer Heidelberg New York Dordrecht London

Library of Congress Control Number: 2013931209

© Springer-Verlag Berlin Heidelberg 2013
This work is subject to copyright. All rights are reserved by the Publisher, whether the whole or part of the material is concerned, specifically the rights of translation, reprinting, reuse of illustrations, recitation, broadcasting, reproduction on microfilms or in any other physical way, and transmission or information storage and retrieval, electronic adaptation, computer software, or by similar or dissimilar methodology now known or hereafter developed. Exempted from this legal reservation are brief excerpts in connection with reviews or scholarly analysis or material supplied specifically for the purpose of being entered and executed on a computer system, for exclusive use by the purchaser of the work. Duplication of this publication or parts thereof is permitted only under the provisions of the Copyright Law of the Publisher's location, in its current version, and permission for use must always be obtained from Springer. Permissions for use may be obtained through RightsLink at the Copyright Clearance Center. Violations are liable to prosecution under the respective Copyright Law.
The use of general descriptive names, registered names, trademarks, service marks, etc. in this publication does not imply, even in the absence of a specific statement, that such names are exempt from the relevant protective laws and regulations and therefore free for general use.
While the advice and information in this book are believed to be true and accurate at the date of publication, neither the authors nor the editors nor the publisher can accept any legal responsibility for any errors or omissions that may be made. The publisher makes no warranty, express or implied, with respect to the material contained herein.

Printed on acid-free paper

Springer is part of Springer Science+Business Media (www.springer.com)

Foreword

The motivation and inspiration to publish this book were triggered in October 2011 when data protection charted Malaysia and certain member states of the Association of Southeast Asian Nations' (ASEAN) media headlines and marketplace talks. It has been a "hot cake" and "buzz word" to date. Global developments on data protection have pushed the needs to ASEAN and some other Asian contours to having a legislation that complements or replaces their existing sector specific data protection legislation, self-regulated rules, guidelines and code of practices. Undeniably, it is a gigantic task due to their different cultures, demography and values. When this book was written, stakeholders in Malaysia and ASEAN have been questioning on how the laws, regulations and guidelines are to be implemented effectively? What are the impacts towards their businesses? What about their compliance obligations to reach the level of adequacy to the most comprehensive data protection laws in the world—the European Data Protection Directive 95/46/EC? And what is the way forward for Malaysia and ASEAN? There are too many questions, instead of, answers due to the embryonic stage of data protection laws in this particular region.

The typical sentiment by the marketplace is that data protection is purely legal, thus, a lawyer's job; assign and delegate the task to the lawyers, hence, they will navigate it! At best, this should be avoided in totality. Data protection is everyone's responsibility, whether one is a member of parliament, an owner of a start-up business, investor, chief executive, auditor, company secretary, human capital advisor, chief financial officer, chief marketing officer, teacher, engineer, doctor, nurse, banker, insurer, plumber, driver, chief technology officer, chef, fashion designer, singer and even to a layman out there. It is indeed a 360-degree subject matter, ranging from one's personal life, professional life and to the period of death. It is indispensable to appreciate data protection as much as one appreciates life to the fullest. Caveat.

To disseminate and diffuse the building blocks of data protection is a collective leadership and responsibility. In order to achieve this for Malaysia and ASEAN, we are humbled and elated to have had leading experts who contributed to this handy and practitioner's based masterpiece. Drawing and combining from their breadth of experience that spans more than ten decades in total, readers may find their respective chapters to being their look, feel and passion in data protection. It is written by way of their strands in pragmatic and practical manner so that the given answers for such questions could potentially be tailor-made in your respective organisations, businesses, outfits, institutions, even, at your home too! Ideally, this masterpiece complements the powerful authority of Professor Abu Bakar Munir and Associate Professor Siti Hajar Mohd Yasin's treatise: *Personal Data Protection in Malaysia, Law and Practice*, published by Sweet & Maxwell Asia in 2010. It is neither competing nor prevailing over the views of these leading academics. Rather, it provides insightful strategies and way forward for readers to approach data protection via best practices from the editors and contributing authors' experience. In turn, we hope the readers are able to translate their thoughts into reality and practice.

As cliché as it may sound, this masterpiece would not have been possibly published and given its birth without the diversity of talents, experts, partners and friends that we are particularly indebted to, in a non particular order; Quotient Consulting Founder and Co-Founder, Mujahid Abdul Wahab and Azli Mohamed; Hjh Nur Jalila Taslim, Ajit Dhal Pasha, Men, Sherry and beloved family; Lee Chiew Kee, Khong Ah Hoay and beloved family; Dato' Mohd Hilmey Mohd Taib, Executive Chairman of HeiTech Padu Berhad; Wooi Huen (Alden) Yap; Dr. Priti Parikh; Khaeruddin Sudharmin; Abu Hassan Ismail, Director General of Department of Personal Data Protection Malaysia (Ministry of Information Communications and Culture Malaysia); Professor Dr. Ida Madieha Abdul Ghani Azmi; Professor Datuk Dr. Khaw Lake Tee; Associate Professor Dr. Juriah Abdul Jalil; Assistant Professor Dr. Sonny Zulhuda; Dr. Federico Ferretti; Majlis Amanah Rakyat, Kuok Foundation Berhad; Kuok Yew Chen of Christopher Lee & Co; Eva Rose Rahim; Indirani Viknaraja; Eduardo Ustaran; Michelle A. Farber; Philipp E. Fischer; Dan Manolescu; Rosman Mustafa Kamar; Muhammad Nizam Awang; Ezakry Mohd Hada; Dr. Satirah Zainal Abidin; Aidil; Kong Lim Chan & Soon Mee Lai; Muhammad Dahlan Berhan; Ramizan Ramly; Subra; Eskandarian Samsudin; Thomas Sadler; Vinodhini Kumarasamy of SPi Global, Manuela Schwietzer and Dr. Brigitte Reschke of Springer.

Most importantly we hope readers are pleased with this masterpiece, the first of its kind in Malaysia and ASEAN, equipped with global insights' leading experiences and practices.

8 July 2012
London
Kuala Lumpur

Noriswadi Ismail
Edwin Lee Yong Cieh

Contents

1 Introduction 1
  Noriswadi Ismail

2 Personal Data Protection and Privacy Law in Malaysia 5
  Edwin Lee Yong Cieh

3 Personal Data Protection Act 2010: An Overview Analysis 31
  Edwin Lee Yong Cieh

4 Limitations of the Personal Data Protection Act 2010 and Personal Data Protection in Selected Sectors 65
  Edwin Lee Yong Cieh

5 Technology and 'Actors' in Data Protection 99
  Noriswadi Ismail

6 Selected Technologies' Appraisal from the PDPA's Lens 111
  Noriswadi Ismail

7 Acclaiming Accountability. Preaching Best Practices 125
  Noriswadi Ismail

8 The Scope of Application of EU Data Protection Law and Its Extraterritorial Reach 135
  Eduardo Ustaran

9 Information Security in the Internet Age 157
  Eva Rose Rahim

10 Data Protection and Local Authorities in the United Kingdom ... 187
   Indirani Viknaraja

11 Data Protection Enforcement: The European Experience—Case Law 217
   Dan Manolescu

12	**Data Protection Audit: The German Experience** 233
	Philipp E. Fischer
13	**Concluding Remarks** 261
	Noriswadi Ismail and Edwin Lee Yong Cieh

About the Editors and Contributing Authors 265

Contributors

Philipp E. Fischer SuiGeneris Consulting, Gernotstr. 4, Munich 80804, Germany, pfischer@suigeneris-consulting.com

Noriswadi Ismail Quotient Consulting, 29 Duffell House, Loughborough Street, London SE11 5PX, UK, noris@qconsultant.com

Dan Manolescu E-crime expert, Rue du Noyer 230, Ap.3, Brussels 1030, Belgium, dmanolescu@gmail.com

Eva Rose Rahim Demand QC Global Ltd., 52 Penderry Rise, London SE6 1HA, UK, Miss.raz.rahim@gmail.com

Eduardo Ustaran Partner, Field Fisher Waterhouse, 35 Vine Street, London EC3N 2AA, UK, eduardo.ustaran@ffw.com

Indirani Viknaraja Southend on Sea Borough Council, Civic Centre, Victoria Avenue, Southend-on-Sea, Essex SS2 6ER, UK, IndiraniViknaraja@southend.gov.uk

Edwin Lee Yong Cieh Christopher Lee & Co, 25-2, Block B, Jaya One Section 13, Petaling Jaya 46200, Malaysia, edwin@christopherleeco.com

Introduction

Noriswadi Ismail

> *The fantastic advances in the field of electronic communication constitute a greater danger to the privacy of the Individual*
> Earl Warren, 14th Chief Justice of the United States
> (19th March 1891-9th July 1974)

Abstract

This introductory chapter provides the macro overview on how this book works and its interrelationship between the chapters. It is the 'starter' before readers will further proceed to the 'main course' and the 'dessert'. The diversity of contributions could be seen through practical discussions, analysis, examples, case studies and opinions of the editors and the contributing authors. They derive these from their exposures, observations and interactions with diversified stakeholders across the globe (ranging from Europe, Middle East, Africa, Southeast Asia, Asia Pacific, East Asia, Americas and to the rest of the world). Appropriately, the editors and the contributing authors have had this collective mission: leading data protection through knowledge sharing and capacity building.

As at Quarter 1 of 2012, eight Asian countries are ranked within the top 20 countries with the highest number of Internet users. Out of these, three ASEAN countries have made it into the list; Indonesia is ranked 8th, the Philippines and Vietnam are ranked 17th and 18th, respectively. Overall, China dominates the ranking with a total of 513.1 million Internet users, followed by the United States—245.2 million Internet users and India—121 million Internet users (see http://www.internetworldstats.com/top20.htm. Accessed 1st July 2012). In Malaysia, the penetration rates, at a glance, is divided into broadband, cellular

---

N. Ismail (✉)
Quotient Consulting, 29 Duffell House, Loughborough Street, London SE11 5PX, UK
e-mail: noris@qconsultant.com

phone and Direct Exchange Line. Based on the recent statistics issued by the Malaysian Communications and Multimedia Commission (MCMC), as at Quarter 1 of 2012, the broadband penetration rate per inhabitants (for every 100 inhabitants) is 19.6 % and per households (for every 100 households) is 62.9 % (see http://www.skmm.gov.my/attachment/Statistics/PR_glanceQ12012.pdf. Accessed 2 June 2012). These numbers indicate a healthy growth and it may be exponentially grow within the next decade.

1.1 The Masterpiece's Offerings for Malaysia

The actors representing the above numbers are the data subjects, data users and data processors. These are amongst the terms used in the Malaysian Personal Data Protection Act (PDPA) 2010. Prior to understanding how the terms apply, readers will be able to appreciate the infancy development of privacy law in Malaysia and the legislative rationale for the PDPA 2010, to which, is comprehensively addressed by Edwin Lee Yong Cieh (Edwin) in **Chap. 2**. Readers may learn that this chapter firms up the conceptual understanding on privacy development in Malaysian courts. The beauty of this chapter is that it heralds the historic milestone of Malaysia's journey towards the PDPA 2010 and the influences, which shaped it.

1.1.1 The Concepts in the PDPA 2010

Like any other data protection legislation, the PDPA 2010 starts by outlining the seven personal data protection principles; general, notice and choice, disclosure, security, retention, data integrity and access. This is further elaborated in **Chap. 3**. Exemptions of these principles, the rights of data subjects as well as criminal offences and liabilities of data users are also explained in an easy-to-read table form. **Chapter 4** suggests constructive appraisals of the PDPA 2010. At the time of this publication, the PDPA 2010 regulations/guidelines have not been published/gazetted in the Parliament yet. Alas, stakeholders are awaiting the gazetted enforcement date in anticipation. It is predicted that these will be taking place by end of 2012 or within the first quarter of 2013. Whilst this is quite uncertain, Edwin has gregariously put his practical thoughts on certain limitations of the PDPA and cross-referred its descriptive analysis with other sector-specific legislation that deal with data protection, albeit on a piecemeal basis.

The first three chapters formed the required fundamentals of this book. After having gone through these, it is pertinent to look into how the PDPA 2010 is addressed by way of issues-based. I take the task to illustrate, in plain English, the relevance of technology as an enabler in data protection. Substantially, the who's who in Malaysia and potential ASEAN member states which may embark on the similar move (the Philippines, Singapore and Indonesia). The illustration is further supported by the data protection 'bubble' between the government, businesses and consumers, which concludes **Chap. 5**. Perhaps, the focus of issues-based that are linkable to the application of the PDPA 2010 within the context of Radio Frequency Identification (RFID) technology, associated with the Internet of Things (IoT) and the Cloud Computing (the Cloud) and Closed Circuit Television (CCTV) may make the readers potentially intrigued. **Chapter 6** offers practical guidance, considerations and pointers, as opposed to, lengthy analysis and criticism. It does not, however, explain the technical sophistication of the Cloud as seen in **Chap. 9**, written by Eva Rose Rahim (Eva) who details this succinctly. The value proposition is that, technology and business should and must not be the bar towards data protection. Likewise, data protection should not be the bar towards technology and business.

Acclaiming Accountability. Preaching Best Practices. These are the two key 'X factor' tips that I implore. Strategic consideration ranging from company, organisation, institution to governments are illustrated for potential adoption. The tone of **Chap. 7** is very much depending upon leadership, accountability and sustainability. It is a collective priority for all and what matter most are implementation, enforcement, review and reform—a potential roadmap for the PDPA 2010 subsequent to its enforcement and implementation.

1.2 The Masterpiece's Offerings from the Global Practices

Eduardo Ustaran (Eduardo) leads the strategic tips on the scope of application of the EU data protection law and its territorial reach. As mentioned in the foreword, the DPD 95/46/EC (DPD) is the world's leading and most comprehensive model, and by far, the 'controversially' best. The take home tips that readers will appreciate are the practical implications of the existing DPD rules, its proposed changes and how it affects the future of data protection.

The focus on **Chap. 8** puts detailed analysis on the criteria for the applicability of the current DPD, the need for change and the proposed criteria for the EU Data Protection Regulation. Readers are able to apprehend the complexity faced by, and the criticisms against, the proposed EU Data Protection Regulation. And Eduardo, who is the so-called 'authority' leads us to explain in this chapter.

A different dimension is designed for readers in this masterpiece—the interaction between data protection and freedom of information—how it is being governed and managed in the government. Indirani Viknaraja (Rani) articulates this by sharing with us her hands on public sector experience through case studies and guidance. This is supplemented by customised toolkit, which is informative, productive and authoritative for Malaysian and ASEAN governmental officials to consider its adoption. **Chapter 10**, by itself, is a stand-alone chapter that is beyond the PDPA's application (which exempts Federal and State governments). Due to this, it is convinced that Rani's thought leadership will potentially provide some headway for Malaysia and ASEAN member states.

Information Security. A topical issue tops most governments, businesses and organisations' priority. Almost every seconds and within the blink of our eyes, one's data is hacked, tampered, shared, transferred, deleted, archived and aggregated. The Cloud evolution adds to the complexity and the technical attributes of technologies that are linkable and integrated between one to another poses compliance complexity and business challenge. Eva, through her technical acumen, illustrates on the information security in the Internet age. She relates this by way of technical solutions that are data protection-friendly. Readers will appreciate the comprehensive concerns and solutions in **Chap. 9**.

1.2.1 Audit and Enforcement Approaches

Germany, is perhaps, the first country in the world that introduces data protection auditor certification. Readers are given the rare privilege to appreciate the guidance, tips, dos and don'ts shared by Philipp E. Fischer (Philipp), who is a certified data protection auditor. In **Chap. 12**, he guides us through to explore the ins and outs of data protection audit and the challenges whilst auditing. To complement this chapter, Dan Manolescu (Dan) ends this masterpiece by narrating the data protection enforcement from the EU's experience in **Chap. 11**. This narration is particularly useful to data protection authorities in Malaysia and ASEAN member states. Dan's experience will help the readers to navigate the lessons learned from the European contour. The combination of Philipp and Dan's chapters, in a way, are inter-related due to non-compliance, lack of governance and supervision by the data controllers and data processors. It takes into account the previous chapters' insights on; Eva's information security writing in (**Chap. 9**): Edwin (**Chaps. 2–4**); mine (**Chaps. 5–7**); Eduardo (**Chap. 8**); and Rani (**Chap. 10**). Collectively, the diversity of chapters provide a very handy and practical insight into data protection law that span across several jurisdictions, and this itself, presents a very novel and unique approach for the readers' reading pleasure, and it's the first of its kind in Malaysia and ASEAN.

The title of this masterpiece: *'Beyond Data Protection: Strategic Case Studies and Practical Guidance'* is the first humble move to answer the questions for Malaysia and ASEAN. It may not be able to answer all (completely). To this end, it is hoped that it will be the beginning of a data protection journey from this part of the world.

Personal Data Protection and Privacy Law in Malaysia

Edwin Lee Yong Cieh

Issues related to personal data protection have been dabbled with for a long time in this part of the world. The Personal Data Protection Act 2010 is one of the cyber legislation aimed at regulating the processing of personal data in commercial transactions

(Excerpt of Datuk Seri Dr. Rais Yatim's speech, Minister of Information, Communications and Culture, 9th February 2012, during the official opening of the Personal Data Protection Department)

Abstract

Personal data protection is increasingly gaining its popularity and legal recognition in many jurisdictions around the world including Malaysia. In June 2010, the Malaysian Parliament finally enacted the Personal Data Protection Act 2010 ('PDPA'), after a long wait of more than 10 years since the late 1990s. The PDPA will have significant impacts on how personal data is processed by organisations and business entities. In the first part of this chapter, the author explains the rationale for having a personal data protection law in Malaysia, and makes a conclusion as to whether the PDPA has addressed most of the rationale cited in this chapter.

Data protection, also known as data privacy in certain jurisdictions, forms one of the four facets of privacy law. The right to privacy is not expressly enshrined under the Federal Constitution of Malaysia or any specific legislation in Malaysia. In the absence of specific legislation, one has to resort to the common law approach in seeking recognition and protection under the common law right to privacy. Interestingly, the Malaysian courts have taken two different approaches towards recognising the 'right to privacy' in Malaysia. A few cases have been brought to courts in the recent years, which have shed some lights as to whether the right to privacy is recognised and protected under the Malaysian laws. The author examines these cases, in detail, in the second part of this chapter.

E.L. Yong Cieh (✉)
Christopher Lee & Co, 25-2, Block B, Jaya One Section 13, Petaling Jaya 46200, Malaysia
e-mail: edwin@christopherleeco.com

2.1 Personal Data Protection and Privacy Law in Malaysia

2.1.1 Introduction

The rapid growth of digital technology and the proliferation of the Internet have made it easier for anyone to collect, process, transmit and store information from anywhere in the world. The rapid development of technology over the last few decades has witnessed the emergence of several new legal and ethical issues. Unfortunately, the laws have not kept up with the pace of technological development, leaving significant gaps in addressing many issues that arise from the use of these technologies.

It has always been said that technology is a double-edged sword: it brings enormous benefits in terms of its efficiency and productivity; however, it also gives rise to concerns that the widespread use of technology may result in loss of privacy—especially data privacy. Technologies such as surveillance cameras, digital cameras on mobile phones, satellite-based user location computation technology such as Global Positioning Systems (GPS), smart tags, bio-metric or radio-frequency identification (RFID) were not originally invented for invasion of privacy, but they have been used to achieve that purpose.[1] Valuable information such as the personal data of individuals can now be collected, processed, and stored on a large scale at minimal costs. Individuals are increasingly concerned about the harmful consequences that may arise from the misuse of their personal data.

Personal data can easily be accessed from a variety of sources and can also be combined with other databases to generate a new set of databases (known as 'data mining'). With the use of cookies on Internet browsers, data can even be monitored, gathered, profiled and manipulated (known as 'data profiling') in such a way that an individual's behaviour, patterns and preferences can be traced. The prevalent use and pervasive nature of data mining and data profiling have raised concerns that these activities may amount to an invasion of privacy. It makes matters worse when these technologies are, more often than not, invisible to the individuals, which means that the individuals have no control whatsoever as to when and to what extent their data is being collected and processed.

Meanwhile, the Government is also actively engaged in processing our personal data. Large volume of personal data is collected, stored and processed by different government departments for a multitude of reasons and purposes from the moment we are born until we are dead. The processing of personal data has therefore become a key activity within the private and public sectors. In the words of Perri, 'Personal information has become the basic fuel on which modern business and government run'.[2]

---

[1] Ahmad (2008), p. 10.
[2] Perri (1998), p. 23.

Furthermore, the expansion of the high-speed broadband on the Internet has enabled companies, governments and individuals to transfer a vast amount of data within a matter of minutes/seconds. The widespread use of the Internet has also transformed the way we communicate with each other and the way we carry out commercial transactions. People (particularly the younger generation) are disclosing their personal data and sharing their daily activities on blogs and social networking sites, such as Facebook and Twitter, to just about anyone without realising the implications of doing so. As Lilian Edwards puts it, 'The Internet has created a world in which data can be accessed ubiquitously and flows untrammelled across political frontiers'.[3]

2.1.2 The Concept of Privacy

The right to privacy was originally described as the 'right to be left alone' by the US Judge Thomas M. Cooley in 1888.[4] Shortly afterward, the concept of privacy was further articulated and made famous by two Harvard scholars, Warren and Brandeis, in their most celebrated and widely cited article, 'The Right to Privacy'.[5] The learned authors at that time had already recognised that, with the emergence of new technologies in printing press and photographs, the right to privacy had become a form of valuable social interest, which ought to be explicitly protected by the law.

The concept of privacy differs from one country to another. Due to the distinct concept of privacy, it has no universal definition. Privacy has been described as 'the interest that individuals have in sustaining a personal space, free from interference by other people and organization'.[6] Professor Alan Westin argues that privacy is 'the claim of individuals to determine for themselves, when, how and to what extent information about themselves is communicated to others'.[7] Privacy can therefore be said to involve the right to control one's personal information and the ability to determine when and how that information should be processed and used.

The concept of privacy law can further be divided into four main facets, namely data privacy (which concerns an individual's right and interest to control the processing of his personal data being held by another); physical privacy (which involves the protection of an individual from physical interference against his will); communications and surveillance privacy (which concerns an individual's right to have privacy protection from being monitored, be it in the form of surveillance or interception in communications), and territorial privacy (which involves the

---

[3] Edwards and Waelde (2009), p. 449.

[4] Cooley (1888), p. 29.

[5] Warren and Brandeis (1890).

[6] Clark (1997).

[7] Westin (1970), p. 7.

protection of an individual from having unlawful intrusion into his or her private space or workplace). This book is mainly concerned with the first facet i.e. data privacy, which is also referred to as data protection/information privacy.

Different jurisdictions may view data protection differently. Data protection is seen as a fundamental human right for individuals in Europe, while the US treats data protection as a private and consumer protection matter. Due to the differences in their perception towards data protection, it has been treated differently both in Europe and the US. In Europe, comprehensive data protection laws have been drawn up to protect their citizens' personal data. On the other hand, the US prefers a sectoral, self-regulatory approach to data protection, where a range of statutes have been enacted to regulate specific forms of data protection.[8]

In Malaysia, legislation governing personal data protection had been advocated since the late 1990s. The first draft of the country's Personal Data Protection Bill ('PDP Bill') was released for public consultation in 2000. A series of road shows was also held throughout the country to explain the rationale and importance of the PDP Bill. The response from the public, especially those from corporations, consumer associations, non-governmental organisations, and individuals, was overwhelming.

However, due to its potential far-reaching implications, which had raised many concerns,[9] the Government withdrew its plan to table the PDP Bill until further study was completed. The first draft of the PDP Bill had since been redrafted to reflect the concerns raised by various stakeholders as well as the Government's attitude towards personal data protection, particularly after a series of terrorist attacks that took place all over the world in recent years.[10]

The redrafted PDP Bill was tabled for first reading on 19 November 2009 and passed by the Malaysian Parliament on 5 April 2010. It received Royal Assent and was gazetted in June 2010. The Personal Data Protection Act 2010 ('PDPA') will come into force on a date to be announced by the relevant Minister. At the time of writing, the date of the PDPA coming into force has yet to be announced, although it has been reported that it may come into force by the end of 2012.[11] With the enactment of the PDPA, Malaysia has become the first country in the region of South-East Asia to have enacted a comprehensive data protection law.

---

[8] Some major US sectoral approach legislations on privacy are such as the Fair Credit Reporting Act 1970, Electronic Communications Privacy Act 1986, Privacy Act 1974, Family Education Rights and Privacy Act 1974, Right to Financial Privacy Act 1978, Video Privacy Protection Act 1998, Children's Online Privacy Protection Act 1998, PATRIOT Act 2001, Children's Internet Protection Act 2001 and Sarbanes-Oxley Act 2002.

[9] For the potential implications, see Khaw (2002), p. 2.

[10] The general perception is that the Internet and other forms of electronic communications have assisted the terrorists in launching attacks. For this reason, governments all over the world have changed their attitude towards privacy, placing heavy surveillance in the name of national security.

[11] Loh (2011).

2.2 The Rationale for Personal Data Protection Law in Malaysia

2.2.1 The Advancement of Technology

Personal data has been collected, stored and transferred since time immemorial. In the words of Earl Ferrers, 'The collection of personal data is as old as the society itself. It may not be the oldest profession but it is one of the oldest habits'.[12] Traditionally, personal data has been collected, stored and used for many purposes. As personal data was being collected manually, the process was very cumbersome, expensive and time-consuming. This data was kept in manual filing systems such as physical files and filing cabinets. One may have to go through a lengthy process in retrieving the relevant data. This data may not have been kept updated, and may have been easily misplaced or lost. However, with the advancement of technology, personal data can now be easily collected, stored, retrieved, disseminated and even manipulated.

According to Khaw Lake Tee, the idea of having a data protection law in Malaysia was first mooted in 1996. In a report entitled 'Laws and Policies Affecting the Development of Information Technology'[13] prepared for the National Information Technology Council of Malaysia, it was envisaged that, with the increasing use of computers, the public and private sectors would eventually replace their manual filing systems with computerized storage systems. Having recognised the fact that the widespread use of these technologies may have serious impact on the privacy of individuals, the report therefore recommended a data protection law to be enacted to confer protection to personal data of the individuals; to give these individuals some form of control over the use of personal data collected; to encourage free flow of information and to stimulate the growth of the data processing industry.

Following the report, a series of cyber laws had also been developed in response to the challenges brought by technological advancement.[14] It was envisaged at that time that further legislation would be enacted to deal with the convergence of the information, communications and technology ('ICT'). One of the legislation was the data protection law. This has been reiterated in the opening speech of the Minister of Information, Communications and Culture Dato' Seri Utama Dr. Rais

---

[12] Ferrers (1993).

[13] The report was subsequently used as a basis for the formulation of the legislative infrastructure and regulatory framework (the so called 'cyberlaws') for the Multimedia Super Corridor (MSC). The learned author, Khaw Lake Tee was commissioned by the Government of Malaysia to prepare the report and subsequently played significant role in developing and shaping the cyberlaws in Malaysia.

[14] Digital Signature Act 1997 (Act 562), Computer Crimes Act 1997 (Act 563), Telemedicine Act 1997 (Act 564), Copyright Act 1987 (Act 332), Communications and Multimedia Act 1998 (Act 588), Communications & Multimedia Commission Act 1998 (Act 589), Electronic Commerce Act 2006 (Act 658), Electronic Government Activities Act 2007 (Act 680).

Yatim ('Minister')[15] in moving the second reading of the PDP Bill in Parliament. According to the Minister, the aims of the PDP Bill are to create a secure electronic environment; to build confidence amongst consumers and users of both networked and non-networked environment; to accelerate the uptake of electronic transactions; and to contribute to the development of the ICT industry, which in turn will attract investments from local and foreign investors to develop the said industry in Malaysia.[16]

The implication of loss of privacy as a result of the advancement in technology has also been recognized by the courts. Lord Hoffmann in the House of Lords case of *R v Brown*[17] acknowledged that:

> My Lords, one of the less welcome consequences of the information technology revolution has been the ease with which it has become possible to invade the privacy of the individual. No longer is it necessary to peep through keyholes or listen under the eaves. Instead, more reliable information can be obtained in greater comfort and safety by using the concealed surveillance camera, the telephoto lens, the hidden microphone and the telephone bug. No longer is it necessary to open letters, pry into files or conduct elaborate inquiries to discover the intimate details of a person's business or financial affairs, his health, family, leisure interests or dealings with central or local government. Vast amounts of information about everyone are stored on computers, capable of instant transmission anywhere in the world and accessible at the touch of a keyboard. The right to keep oneself to oneself, to tell other people that certain things are none of their business, is under technological threat.[18]

However, the idea of protecting data privacy as a result of the advancement of technology does not seem to garner much support from the technology companies. Scott McNealy, the CEO and co-founder of Sun Microsystems, Inc, infamously made the remarks that, 'You have zero privacy anyway, get over it'.[19] When Eric Schmidt, the then-CEO of Google, was being asked whether people should be treating Google as their most trusted friend, he replied, 'If you have something that you don't want anyone to know, maybe you shouldn't be doing it in the first place, but if you really need that kind of privacy, the reality is that search engines including Google do retain this information for some time'.[20] Mark Zuckerberg, the co-founder of Facebook, also claims that privacy is an outdated concept and is no longer a social norm as 'people have really gotten comfortable not only sharing more information and different kinds, but more openly and with more people'.[21]

The views by some of these technology companies do not rest well with the demand from consumers and Internet users, who have expressed that privacy is a grave concern to them when they are online or using any of these aforementioned

---

[15] The Ministry of Information, Communications and Culture is the ministry that in charge with the responsibility for the protection of personal data in Malaysia.

[16] Parliamentary Debates, House of Representatives (2010), p. 110.

[17] [1996] 1 All ER p. 545.

[18] [1996] 1 All ER pp. 555–556.

[19] Sprenger (1999).

[20] CNBC documentary interview (2009).

[21] Johnson (2010).

technologies. It is a misconception that just because people are putting more information online, they do not care about their privacy. In response to growing demands from consumers, in February 2012, the Obama Administration in the US unveiled its proposed 'Consumer Privacy Bill of Rights', which seeks to improve consumers' privacy protections online and ensures that the Internet remains an engine for innovation and economic growth. The Bill of Rights, once passed, will give Internet users more control over how their personal data is used on the Internet and help businesses maintain consumer trust.[22]

2.2.2 The Emergence of Data Protection Law at the National and International Level

At the international level, two important legal instruments dealing with data protection were formulated in the 1980s, namely, the Council of Europe's Convention for the Protection of Individuals with regard to Automatic Processing of Personal Data 1981 ('Council of Europe's Convention') and the Organisation for Economic Cooperation and Development Guidelines Governing the Protection of Privacy and Trans-border Flows of Personal Data 1980 ('OECD Guidelines'). These legal instruments were amongst the earliest that formulated the form of general principles in relation to the collection, storage, use and disclosure of personal data to what it is today.

The purpose of the Council of Europe's Convention is to achieve greater unity between the signatory states and to extend the safeguards for individuals' rights and fundamental freedom, in particular, the right to respect for privacy, taking into account the increasing transfer of personal data undergoing automatic processing across national borders. It was the first legally binding international instrument in the area of data protection. It differs from the OECD Guidelines in that it requires signatories to implement in their domestic legislation the principles laid down in the Council of Europe's Convention.

The OECD[23] recognises that there is a danger that disparities in national law could hamper the free flow of personal data across the member countries. Restriction on these flows could cause serious disruption in important sectors of the economy such as banking and insurance. For this reason, the OECD Guidelines were developed to help harmonise national legislation on data protection. The OECD Guidelines represent a consensus on basic principles that can be built into existing national law or serve as a basis for legislation in those countries that have yet to have data protection law. Unlike the Council of Europe's Convention, the

---

[22] Office of the Press Secretary, the White House (2012).

[23] The OECD currently has 30 member countries: Australia, Austria, Belgium, Canada, Chile, Czech Republic, Denmark, Estonia, Finland, France, Germany, Greece, Hungary, Iceland, Ireland, Israel, Italy, Japan, Korea, Luxembourg, Mexico, Netherlands, New Zealand, Norway, Poland, Portugal, Slovak Republic, Slovenia, Spain, Sweden, Switzerland, Turkey, the United Kingdom, and the United States.

OECD Guidelines have no legal force. The OECD Guidelines were drafted in the form of recommendations which set out the minimum standards as guidelines. The member countries are of course free to adopt stronger data protection laws than the OECD Guidelines suggest.

In 1995, the European Commission ('EC') enacted the European Community Directive on the Protection of Individuals with regard to the Processing of Personal Data and on the Free Movement of Such Data ('EU Data Protection Directive') with two main objectives, namely, the protection of the fundamental rights and freedoms of natural persons and in particular their right to privacy with respect to the processing of personal data; and the prevention of barriers to the free flow of personal data across the community by virtue of reasons connected with the above protection.[24]

The EU Data Protection Directive sets out data protection principles for the 27 European Union ('EU') member states[25] to incorporate into their own national law. One of the most significant features of the EU Data Protection Directive is that it promotes and encourages the free movement of personal data within the European Economic Area (which consists of the 27 EU member states together with Iceland, Liechtenstein and Norway) by harmonizing national data protection law while protecting the rights and freedoms of individuals when their personal data is processed. It also requires the EEA countries to ensure that transfer of personal data to a country outside the EEA may only take place if the country in question has an adequate level of data protection, unless one of the exceptions applies.[26] This indirectly exerts pressure on countries that wish to engage in data transactions with the EEA countries to provide an adequate level of protection.

The EU is one of the largest trading partners of Malaysia, and therefore lack of data protection law in Malaysia might impede international trade between Malaysia and the EU member states. Due to the significant differences in the ways the EU member states have implemented the EU Data Protection Directive, coupled with the new challenges arising from the technological progress and globalisation, the EC decided to revamp and modernise the EU Data Protection Directive to respond to these new challenges. A draft General Data Protection Regulation was published in January 2012, which would replace the EU Data Protection Directive once it is passed by the EC.

While the EU's approach to data protection is centred on the data privacy as a form of fundamental human rights, Asia's approach focuses more on the impact of privacy in terms of economic and social development.[27] In the Asia Pacific

---

[24] Art 1 EU Data Protection Directive.

[25] The 27 EU member states are as follows: Austria, Belgium, Bulgaria, Cyprus, Czech Republic, Denmark, Estonia, Finland, France, Germany, Greece, Hungary, Ireland, Italy, Latvia, Lithuania, Luxembourg, Malta, Netherlands, Poland, Portugal, Romania, Slovakia, Slovenia, Spain, Sweden, and the United Kingdom.

[26] Art 25 EU Data Protection Directive.

[27] See Bygrave and Pounder where the authors state that the APEC Privacy Framework is unlikely to provide an adequate level of protection as required by the European Data Protection Directive.

region, the Asia Pacific Economic Cooperation Privacy Framework ('APEC Privacy Framework')[28] was adopted in 2004 by the 21 APEC members.[29] The APEC Privacy Framework, which aims at promoting electronic commerce throughout the Asia Pacific region, is intended to provide guidance and direction to its members in implementing data protection law. It claims that it is consistent with the core values of the OECD Guidelines, although it has been criticized by those who say it does not even meet the OECD standard.[30] It contains a set of nine APEC privacy principles dealing with most of the principles commonly found in international or national data protection law, namely, collection, quality, security, use, access, and correction of personal information. The APEC recognises the differences in social, cultural, economic and political backgrounds of each APEC members and therefore it allows each member to voluntarily implement the principles in their domestic data protection regime according to their needs through legislative, administrative, industry self-regulation or a combination of them.[31]

Further development on international instruments continues. The Madrid Resolution 2009 was approved by more than 50 countries at the 31st International Conference of Data Protection and Privacy Commissioners. It constitutes the basis for drawing up the International Standards on the Protection of Personal Data and Privacy, which represents the first step towards a binding international instrument. The call for adoption of a global privacy standard continued in the Jerusalem Declaration 2010 and Mexico Declaration 2011. At the 19th APEC Economic Leaders' Meeting in November 2011, the 21 APEC members approved the Honolulu Declaration, which gears towards a seamless regional economy. The members have agreed that one of the commitments to further open up markets and facilitate regional trade is to implement the APEC Cross Border Privacy Rules System ('CBPRs'). The APEC CBPRs will reduce barriers to information flows, enhance consumer privacy and promote interoperability across regional data privacy regime.[32]

---

[28] The Asia Pacific Economic Cooperation (APEC) Privacy Framework was developed during 2003–2004 by APEC Economic Commerce Steering Group Privacy Sub-Group. The Asia Pacific Economic Cooperation (APEC) is an international organisation consists of 21 members, which is predominantly concerned with trade and economic issues, with members engaging with one another as economic entities.

[29] The 21 members are as follows: Australia, Brunei Darussalam, Canada, Chile, People's Republic of China, Hong Kong, Indonesia, Japan, Republic of Korea, Malaysia, Mexico, New Zealand, Papua New Guinea, Peru, The Philippines, Russia, Singapore, Chinese Taipei, Thailand, The United States and Vietnam.

[30] Greenleaf (2005).

[31] Kuner (2009).

[32] The Honolulu Declaration—Toward a Seamless Regional Economy, the 19th APEC Economic Leaders' Meeting, 12–13 November 2011.

In terms of national law, it is said that Germany and Sweden were amongst the earliest countries to enact a national data protection law in 1970[33] and 1973[34], respectively. The United Kingdom implemented its first Data Protection Act in 1984, which has since been repealed by the Data Protection Act 1998. Most of the countries in Europe and North America have had their data protection laws implemented over the past two decades. In Asia, countries such as Australia, New Zealand, Japan, South Korea, Hong Kong, Taiwan, and Macau have also had their data protection laws since 1990s, although some are of limited scope. Malaysia was already years behind these countries in enacting a data protection law and calls for the introduction of a data protection law had been long overdue.

In the last 2–3 years, the Association of Southeast Asian Nations ('ASEAN') member countries have been very active in enacting data protection law in their respective countries. Malaysia finally enacted the PDPA in 2010, after a long overdue of 10 years. Singapore, the Philippines, Thailand and Indonesia are in the midst of drafting or tabling their data protection law to their respective legislatures. It should be noted that the ASEAN member countries have committed to developing best practices/guidelines on data protection by 2015 as part of their commitment to establish an integrated ASEAN Economic Community by 2015. It is likely that many of these ASEAN member countries will have enacted their very own data protection law by 2015. China and India, two of the world's most populous countries, with two of the largest economies, are also in the midst of developing their data protection law. It has been reported that as of 2012, 89 countries have enacted data protection laws, and the number is still increasing.[35] Graham Greenleaf describes data protection laws as 'come to stay' across the Asia Pacific, although in many different forms. The learned author argues that 2011 may in hindsight be recognized as a 'watershed' year for data protection in Asia.[36]

As a result of globalisation and liberalization of trade and commerce, many laws that have impacts on cross-border transactions have been harmonised to a large extent. Integration of economies between countries is the key driver to the success of globalisation. Such integration involves the harmonisation of laws. As far as data protection is concerned, the free flow of personal data from one country to another is essential as many businesses are now trading on a global basis and many countries, especially the EEA countries, which require that personal data can only be transferred to countries that provide an adequate level of data protection. In the event an EU member state has decided to block a transfer on the basis of inadequacy, this decision will apply to all other member states. It is for this reason that Malaysia recognised the need to enact a comprehensive data protection law, as

---

[33] Germany Hessen Data Protection Act 1970.
[34] Sweden Data Act 1973.
[35] Greenleaf (2012).
[36] For further reading about the analysis of the data protection law in the Asia Pacific, see Greenleaf (2011).

failure to have one may hamper the transfer of personal data, create possible trade barriers and disrupt cross-border transactions.

2.2.3 The New Way of Doing Business via Electronic Commerce and the New Way of Dealing with the Government via Electronic Government

The use of technology has become part and parcel of daily life to many people. Our personal data is transmitted and stored in different databases whenever we do online transaction. It is believed that electronic commerce ('e-commerce') will expand significantly in the coming years. A survey by IDC Malaysia shows that, in 2009, amongst 16 million Internet users in Malaysia, half of them had at least performed one online transaction, which indicates that the e-commerce market in Malaysia is growing healthily.[37]

The Internet has increased the volume of data available to businesses. Whenever the users perform online transactions, they are required to provide a great deal of personal data. There are fears that businesses may collect and mine data, which could then be sold, traded or shared with a third party without the knowledge or consent of the users. Some businesses even mine email addresses from indirect sources such as messages posted on mailing lists, newsgroups or domain name registration databases and use the data collected to send unsolicited emails or advertising materials to these individuals.[38] Every time we use our credit, debit or loyalty card, our purchase is recorded and the retailers will have the records of our personal data and purchase transactions. The information would enable retailers to analyse, assess and build a detailed picture of us, which could then be sold to a third party.

While e-commerce offers many benefits to consumers, such as convenience, easy access to a wide range of goods and services, and the ability to gather and compare information about goods and services, the fear of possible misuse or abuse of personal data has been identified as one of the major constrains to the development of the e-commerce market.[39] According to a consumer behaviour study conducted by Visa International, 64 % of respondents expressed their view that the theft or loss of individuals' personal or financial data in doing online transaction was their biggest fear that held them back from actively engaging in e-commerce.

There is an urgent need to have a proper legal framework to regulate the collection, storage, process, and dissemination of personal data so as to ensure there is a reliable, secure and effective system in place to safeguard personal data. Such protection is indispensable as it gives consumers the requisite assurance and confidence that their personal data will be safeguarded, which in turn builds trust in

---

[37] Abstract from the IDC Malaysia Report on 'Malaysia Internet and eCommerce 2009–2013 Forecast and Analysis'.
[38] O'Neill (2008), p. 32.
[39] Bernama.com (2009).

doing online transactions and establishes a more balanced relationship between online traders and consumers.

The Government also collects and stores massive amounts of her citizen's personal data. For example, the National Registration Department processes most of our personal data, and citizens and permanent residents are required to carry a national ID card. The Inland Revenue Board processes our income tax return, which contains detailed records of our financial affairs and sources of income. The Social Security Organisation maintains records of millions of employees in Malaysia. In 2009, the Parliament passed the controversial Deoxyribonucleic Acid (DNA) Identification Act 2009, which enables the Government to keep and maintain DNA profiles in the DNA Databank for the purposes of human identification in relation to forensic investigation.[40]

The Government also actively promotes the use of e-Government services and has enacted the Electronic Government Activities Act 2007[41] to give legal recognition and facilitate all electronic dealings between the Government and the public. It was reported in the newspaper recently that the Government aims to make 90 % of all its services available online by 2015 as part of a move towards the smart government program.[42] It is no doubt that the Government is one of the biggest data collectors in the country and this alone warrants the development of a proper legal framework to govern the processing of personal data by the Government and to address the far-reaching implications arising from the processing of personal data. Regrettably, the PDPA explicitly excludes the Federal and State Governments from the application of the PDPA.

2.2.4 Lack of Comprehensive Data Protection Law

The right to privacy has long been recognised as a fundamental human right at the international level as enshrined in Article 12 of the Universal Declaration of Human Rights 1948 ('UDHR') and Article 17 of the International Covenant on Civil and Political Rights 1966 ('ICCPR').[43] Despite the fact that Malaysia is a signatory to the UDHR, the right to privacy is not explicitly recognised in

---

[40] The DNA Act 2009 (Act 699) provides for the government to obtain DNA from any person suspected or convicted of a crime and drug users. It is a criminal offences for refusal to provide DNA.

[41] The Electronic Government Activities Act 2007 (Act 680) provides for legal recognition of electronic messages in dealings between the Government and the public, the use of electronic messages to fulfill legal requirements and to enable and facilitate the dealing through the use of electronic means and other matters connected therewith.

[42] Sipalan (2012).

[43] Article 12 of UDHR and Article 17 ICCPR provide that, 'no one shall be subjected to arbitrary or unlawful interference with his privacy, family, or correspondence, or to unlawful attacks on his honour and reputation. Everyone has the right to the protection of the law against such interference or attacks'.

Malaysia. According to the Privacy International's report in 2007, out of 47 countries, Malaysia, Russia and China were amongst the lowest ranking countries in terms of privacy protection, which had been categorised as the 'endemic surveillance societies'.[44]

The Malaysian Federal Constitution is also silent on the issue of data privacy. Although Articles 5–13 of the Federal Constitution spell out the fundamental liberties of an individual, none of the said Articles mention anything about the right to privacy. However, the position seems to have changed recently where the Federal Court, which is the supreme court in Malaysia, held that Article 5(1) of the Federal Constitution, which guarantees that 'no person shall be deprived of his life or personal liberty, save in accordance with law', encompasses the right to privacy.[45]

Prior to the introduction of the PDPA, Malaysia adopted the sectoral approach in protecting personal data. Legislation, rules, regulations, guidelines, and codes of practice have been developed to regulate the collection, use, and dissemination of personal data in specific sectors, such as the banking and financial institutions sectors,[46] healthcare sector,[47] insurance sectors,[48] as well as the telecommunication and multimedia sectors.[49] However, they cover only a piecemeal portion of the issues on data protection. Khaw Lake Tee has rightly pointed out that personal data protection is inadequate if protection can only be found in piecemeal legislation.[50] It is submitted that there is a need to have a comprehensive legislation to cover all aspects of personal data protection. Khaw Lake Tee also emphasises that personal data protection law is not a law relating to general privacy or freedom of information. It does not prohibit the collection, holding, processing or use of personal data; rather it merely requires the data user to comply with the personal data protection principles and other related provisions of the data protection law.[51]

---

[44] The 2007 International Privacy Ranking (2007).

[45] Sivarasa Rasiah v Badan Peguam Malaysia [2010] 2 MLJ 333.

[46] See Banking and Financial Institutions Act 1989 (Act 372); Guidelines on the Provision of Electronic Banking (e-banking) Services by Financial Institutions (BNM); Guidelines on Data Management and Management Information System (MIS) Framework (BNM).

[47] See Code of Medical Ethics adopted by the Malaysian Medical Association, Guidelines on the Medical Records and Medical Reports issued by the Malaysian Medical Council and Confidentiality Guidelines issued by the Malaysian Medical Council.

[48] See Insurance Act 1996 (Act 553); Code of Ethics and Conduct (Second Edition, February 1999) issued by the Life Insurance Association of Malaysia.

[49] See General Consumer Code 2003 drawn up by the Communications and Multimedia Commission; Computer Crimes Act 1997 (Act 563); the Malaysian Communications and Multimedia Content Code ('Content Code') developed by the Communications and Multimedia Content Forum of Malaysia.

[50] The Star (2009).

[51] Khaw (2002), p. 8.

2.2.5 The Growing Problems of Misuse of Personal Data

Personal data such as customer database is now being treated as a commodity where it can be traded just like any other goods or services. Database marketing, especially in the US, is a multibillion-dollar industry. Companies such as data mining, data analytics and credit reference agencies make money by selling consumer data comprising personal data, financial data, health data, buying preferences, web and mobile habits to corporations who use the data for targeted marketing for their goods and services. For example, Acxiom Corporation, one of the largest data mining companies in the US, processes more than 50 trillion data transactions a year and claims that its database contain information about 500 million active consumers worldwide, with about 1,500 data points per person.[52]

In the last few years, the number of complaints over the misuse of personal data has been on the rise. Many people have complained about the nuisance caused by unsolicited phone calls, text messages and spam e-mails. It was reported that the officers from the Ministry of Higher Education had sold students' personal data to private colleges to enable them to solicit students,[53] although this allegation was denied by the Ministry.[54] It was also reported that a list of 1,000 entries containing names, phone numbers, types of credit cards owned and issuing banks and even place of work can be bought for a mere RM100.[55] A list containing the personal data of Datuks and Tan Sris can be bought for RM4 for each individual.[56] It is even more rampant in the real estate industry, where it had been alleged that developers of housing projects and real estate agents engaged database companies to draw up lists of potential property buyers.[57]

Many people are also concerned with the processing of their credit information by credit reporting agencies where credit information is discreetly collected by these agencies without individuals' consent. Previously, there was no legislation governing the activities of these agencies in collecting information regarding the creditworthiness of individuals. These agencies usually collect, store, arrange, organise, and then sell the credit information to banks and financial institutions to assist them in approving loans, credit cards, hire-purchase facilities and other credit-lending related services.

The agencies had no legal obligation to verify the accuracy of the individuals' credit information, resulting in people being unjustly blacklisted or refused loans without a valid reason. It was reported that some individuals who had settled their loans were still being blacklisted as loan defaulters because the credit reporting

---

[52] Singer (2012).
[53] Gomez (2005).
[54] The Star (2005).
[55] Loh and Bedi (2009a).
[56] Loh and Bedi (2009b).
[57] Fernandez and Cheah (2005).

agencies had failed to update their databases.[58] The Government recognised the seriousness of this problem and had to pass the Credit Reporting Agencies Act 2010 ('CRAA') to address this problem. Further discussion on the scope and application of the CRAA is explained in Chap. 3 of this book.

2.2.6 Has the PDPA Addressed Most of the Rationale Cited Above?

According to the explanatory statement of the PDP Bill:

> The Personal Data Protection Act 2009 [now known as the PDPA] as proposed by this Bill seeks to regulate the processing of personal data of individuals involved in commercial transactions by data users so as to provide protection to the individual's ('data subject's') personal data and thereby safeguard the interests of such individual. New technologies and changing market trends are contributing to the increasingly important role of information in the global market economy. This information, in particular the personal data of individuals involved in commercial transactions, has become a valuable commodity. This in turn has created mounting pressure to regulate the processing of personal data so as to increase consumer confidence in the current global market.

From the language of the explanatory statement, it appears that most of the rationale behind the push for a data protection law in Malaysia have been addressed in the PDPA, namely, due to the technological development and the changing market trends, personal data of individuals have become a valuable commodity and as such, there is a pressing need to regulate the processing of personal data, especially in the global market. However, it is also noted that there was no explicit or implied reference made to recognise the general right to privacy and the need for compliance with the EU Data Protection Directive. Therefore, it can be concluded that the major push for the data protection law in Malaysia is more on the economic and social needs, rather than from the political or judicial pressure.

2.3 Privacy Law in Malaysia

2.3.1 Introduction

The Federal Constitution is the supreme law in Malaysia. However, unlike the constitutions in some other countries, the right to privacy is not expressly enshrined in the Federal Constitution. Having said that, it is noted that Gopal Sri Ram FCJ, whilst sitting in the Federal Court in the case of *Sivarasa Rasiah v Badan Peguam Malaysia*,[59] observed that Article 5(1) of the Federal Constitution, which guarantees that 'no person shall be deprived of his life or personal liberty, save in accordance with law', encompasses the right to privacy.

---

[58] The Star (2007).
[59] [2010] 2 MLJ 333.

The question then arises as to whether the Federal Constitution, in particular, Article 5(1), can be interpreted so broadly as to include the right to privacy. In the Court of Appeal case of *Tan Tek Seng v Suruhanjaya Perkhidmatan Pendidikan*[60] the then Court of Appeal judge, Gopal Sri Ram JCA, held that:

> The expression 'life' appearing in Article 5(1) does not refer to mere existence. It incorporates all those facets that are an integral part of life itself and those matters which go to form the quality of life. Of these are the right to seek and be engaged in lawful and gainful employment and to receive those benefits that our society has to offer to its members. It includes the right to live in a reasonably healthy and pollution free environment. For the purposes of this case, it encompasses the right to continue in public service subject to removal for good cause by resort to a fair procedure.

In this case, the right to livelihood and the right to work were held to be guaranteed under the Federal Constitution. Gopal Sri Ram JCA went on to say that, 'Judges should, when discharging their duties as interpreters of the supreme law, adopt a liberal approach in order to implement the true intention of the framers of the Federal Constitution.' Similarly, in *Sugumar Balakrishnan v Pengarah Imigresen Negeri Sabah*,[61] the Court of Appeal construed the expression 'personal liberty' in Article 5(1) in a broad and liberal fashion to include the right of an aggrieved person to go to court and seek relief. Gopal Sri Ram JCA again said that this right was one of the many facets of the personal liberty guaranteed by Article 5(1) of the Federal Constitution. In *Hong Leong Equipment Sdn Bhd v Liew Fook Chuan*,[62] it was held that the Federal Constitution was a living document and the concept it housed in broad and liberal language must be interpreted broadly and liberally in accordance with the particular needs of a developing society.

These cases reflect that the courts are not hesitating in construing the Federal Constitution so broadly to include the basic human rights so as to give effect to the spirits and intention behind the Federal Constitution. As such, with the Federal Court finally recognising the right to privacy as one of the facets of Article 5(1), it is submitted that the right to privacy is guaranteed under the Federal Constitution of Malaysia.

2.3.2 Protection of Privacy in Malaysia: Case Studies

As the right to privacy is not explicitly enshrined or provided under the Federal Constitution of Malaysia or any specific Act of Parliament, we shall now examine whether the Malaysian courts recognise such a right.

---

[60] [1996] 1 MLJ 261.
[61] [1998] 3MLJ 289.
[62] [1996] 1 MLJ 481.

In *PP v Lee Sin Long*,[63] which is believed to be the earliest case where the court first spoke about the term 'privacy', Callow J held that:

> The privacy of a person in his home must be respected, and cannot be disturbed unless first shown to proper authority that reasonable cause for interference is warranted. Without a warrant the householder might be justified in refusing admission to a police officer.

Subsequent cases have also provided some useful insights as to the courts' attitudes in recognising whether privacy right is recognised in Malaysia. In *Nasib Singh v Jamilah*,[64] the issue was whether the inspection of a moneylender's account book containing the details of other debtors' accounts amounted to an invasion of privacy. The Federal Court was of the view that a moneylender was entitled to refuse to disclose the names and accounts of third party debtors other than the defendant who was the debtor in this case. However, if something was revealed in the defendant's account itself that made it necessary, in the interest of justice, to find out whether the other accounts bear out the contention of the debtor or the explanation of the moneylender, then inspection of other debtors' accounts was desirable and justified. The court also emphasised that it was essential that all courts should be vigilant in exercising their discretion to see that the right of the debtor to pry into his creditor's credit affairs was not abused in an oppressive manner, that the names of third party debtors should never be bandied about in open court and financial affairs of the third party debtors should never be disclosed publicly.

Interestingly, the High Court in *Larut Consolidated Bhd & Anor v Khoo Ee Bee*[65] viewed that a Mareva injunction must balance on the one side the need to freeze the assets in question and gain information required against the restrictions to protect the defendants from misuse of information gained or an unwarranted invasion of privacy. Another High Court in *HMO Pacific Sdn Bhd v Dr. Johari bin Muhamad Yusup*[66] also recognised that the drastic nature of an Anton Piller order could invade the right to sanctity and sanctuary to the privacy of one's own home and therefore should be used sparingly.

The High Court in *Makonka Electronic Sdn Bhd v Eletrical Industry Workers' Union*[67] held that an Anton Piller order is intrusive in nature as the party being served with the order is subjected to entry, search and seizure, and such an intrusive order amounted to an invasion of privacy. As such, it was imperative that the applicant for an Anton Piller order prove to the courts that it had complied with all the undertakings, terms and conditions of the order before it can enforce the order against the other party. In *Maxisegar Sdn Bhd v Indera Management Services Sdn Bhd*,[68] the High Court held that the plaintiff, by raiding the defendant's office

---

[63] [1949] 1 MLJ 51.
[64] [1972] 1 LNS 98.
[65] [1997] 5 CLJ 307.
[66] [1997] 1 LNS 550.
[67] [1997] 1 LNS 86.
[68] [2005] 1 LNS 203.

and removing the defendant's documents without a proper court order constituted theft, trespass to land as well as invasion of privacy.

It appears from the aforementioned cases that Malaysian courts do recognise the right to privacy in one way or another. Unfortunately, the courts in those cases did not seize the opportunity to further elaborate on the right to privacy, leaving much uncertainty as to whether that right forms an actionable cause of action entitling a party to sue for invasion of privacy.

2.4 Two Schools of Thought

2.4.1 First School of Thought

The first school of thought taken by the courts is that the right to privacy is not recognised in Malaysia due to the inherent nature of the Malaysian legal system, in which the system is still heavily influenced by the English Common Law. It is said that until the English Common Law explicitly recognises the right to privacy, the Malaysian courts will still follow the traditional approach taken by the English courts.

It was only in 2004 that the High Court, in the landmark case of *Ultra Dimension Sdn Bhd v Kook Wei Kuan*,[69] finally had the opportunity to clarify the state of privacy law in Malaysia. The background of this case is as follows:

The staffs and agents of the appellant had taken a photograph of a group of kindergarten pupils including the respondent at an open area outside the kindergarten. The photograph was said to be published in an advertisement in *The Star* newspaper and *Sin Chew Jit Poh* newspaper, which carried the theme 'Bonus Link Share Your Points'. The respondent sued the appellant on the ground that the appellant's action in supplying the said photograph for the purpose of advertisement amounted to an invasion of the respondent's privacy. The appellant argued that the respondent's claim should be struck out because the right to privacy pleaded by the respondent was not recognised under Malaysian laws.

Faiza Tamby Chik J held that:

> I am of the opinion that invasion of privacy will only give rise to a cause of action provided that the facts fall within the boundaries of an existing and recognised tort. For example, defamation, infringement of copyright and nuisance. In this case, it is clear that the facts of the respondent's case does not fall within the boundaries of any recognised tort.
> **Defamation** – The appellant did not do anything which lowered the reputation of the respondent/plaintiff. Thus, tort of defamation is not applicable.
> **Infringement of copyright** – The respondent does not own the copyright of copyright the said photograph. The copyright of the said photograph belongs to the appellant. Thus, there is no infringement of copyright.

---

[69] [2004] 5 CLJ 285.

Nuisance – The appellant did not unlawfully interfere with the respondent's use or enjoyment of the land or some right over, or in connection with it. Thus, tort of nuisance is not applicable.

... I am of the view that it is clear that English Common Law does not recognise privacy rights and it therefore follows that invasion of privacy rights does not give rise to cause of action. As English Common Law is applicable in Malaysia pursuant to Section 3 of the Civil Law Act 1956, privacy rights which is not recognised under English Law is accordingly not recognised under Malaysian law. Thus, the respondent does not have the right to institute an action against the appellant for invasion of privacy rights. It is noteworthy that invasion of privacy rights via taking and publication of photographs (as in the facts of the instant appeal) is also not recognised in countries such as Australia and the United States of America.

The court went on to say:

... A cause of action may only arise if the photographs are highly offensive in nature and show a person in an embarrassing position or pose. On the facts of the instant appeal, I think the said photograph is not offensive in nature at all because it is merely a photograph of a group of kindergarten pupils in cheerful mood taken at an open area outside the kindergarten, and there was no publication of any information relating to the respondent in the said advertisement. The said photograph was used for a decent purpose which was for an advertisement for Bonuslink card. The said photograph did not picture the respondent in an embarrassing position, and the said photograph does not intrude into the private rights of the respondent. Furthermore, the said photograph was taken at a public place which was an open area outside the kindergarten which anyone present would be free to see and take photographs of the children there. I am of the view that the taking of photographs at public places where there are many passersby and the publication of such photographs in newspapers, brochures and other reading materials does not give rise to a cause of action.

In the High Court case of *Lew Cher Phow @ Lew Cha Paw v Pua Yong Yong*,[70] the plaintiffs applied for an interlocutory injunction to stop the defendants from installing CCTV cameras that faced towards the plaintiffs' house. The plaintiffs claimed that the CCTV cameras had intruded into and affected their private and daily life and as a result of that, they had suffered damages and losses. The defendants, on the other hand, argued that they had installed the CCTV cameras for purposes of home surveillance and security. The defendants also produced computer print-outs of images recorded by the CCTV cameras and the images showed that the plaintiffs' house was only seen as a background image.

Having considered the submissions from both parties, the court rejected the plaintiffs' application and held as follows:

1) There was no evidence to show that the CCTV cameras had intruded into nor affected the private and daily life of the plaintiffs. The plaintiffs had not submitted any evidence to show that the defendants' CCTV cameras had recorded every single move or action by the plaintiffs or that the CCTV cameras were non-static that could be used to record every single activity of the plaintiffs;

---

[70] [2009] 1 LNS 1256.

2) the defendants had the right to install CCTV cameras for purposes of home surveillance and security;
3) there were evidence to show that the plaintiffs applied for the injunction as an act of revenge against the defendants as the defendants had made a complaint to the local authority that had resulted in legal action being taken against one of the plaintiffs, and hence the application was filed in bad faith;
4) if the court were to grant the injunction, it would bring a huge implication to the society as CCTV cameras are nowadays quite commonly installed by residents or businesses to protect the security of their homes or business premises;
5) it was not clear whether installation of CCTV cameras constituted a valid ground for an injunction to be granted under the Specific Relief Act 1950 (Revised 1974);
6) an injunction should only be granted in cases where the facts of the cases are unusually strong and clear in that a similar injunction would probably be granted at the trial on the ground that it would be just and equitable that the plaintiffs' interest be protected by immediate issue of an injunction, otherwise it would result in irreparable injury and inconvenience to the defendants; and
7) the High Court in Ultra Dimension Sdn Bhd v Kook Wei Kuan[71] had decided that the right to privacy is not recognised under Malaysian laws.

In the High Court case of *Dr. Bernadine Malini Martin v MPH Magazine Sdn Bhd*,[72] the plaintiff was a government medical officer attached to the General Hospital of Kuala Lumpur. The first defendant was the publisher of a female magazine, the second defendant ran a bridal gown shop/boutique and the third defendant ran a photo studio. The defendants published a photograph of the plaintiff in a bridal gown in a bridal gown promotion-cum-advertisement in the first defendant's magazine without the plaintiff's consent. The plaintiff sued the defendants for defamation on the grounds that the publication portrayed her to be a woman of loose morals and an unsuccessful doctor who had to resort to do part-time modelling to supplement her income.

The High Court found that the plaintiff's photograph as a bride was not sexually provocative and did not portray her to be a woman of low character. The words appearing on the photograph 'A Special Night' when read together with the plaintiff's photograph, were appropriate and had nothing to suggest that the plaintiff engaged in any immoral activity or lack of virtues. It was too far-fetched for anyone, upon seeing the photograph, to think that the plaintiff had to resort to part-time modelling or that she was not a successful doctor. The concept of the photograph had been blown out of all proportion.

While the plaintiff did not sue on the ground of invasion of privacy, Hishamudin Yunus J made the following remark:

---

[71] [2004] 5 CLJ 285.
[72] [2006] 2 CLJ 1117.

... To my mind, it was unethical and morally wrong for the first and second defendants to have published the plaintiff's photograph for the purpose of their commercial promotion without her consent. it was an unwarranted invasion of the plaintiff's privacy. It is unfortunate for the plaintiff, that the law of this country, as it stands presently, does not make an invasion of privacy an actionable wrongdoing.

It is humbly submitted the above-cited cases were not entirely correct. Due to the influence of the European Convention on Human Rights and the UK Human Rights Act 1998, the English courts have recognised the right to privacy within the expanded scope of the common law doctrine of breach of confidence to protect invasion of privacy in the form of disclosure of private information.[73] However, these cases were unfortunately not discussed and the courts still referred to the older cases where English courts refused to recognise the invasion of privacy as an actionable cause of action. Had these cases been discussed, perhaps the courts would have come to a different conclusion altogether.

2.4.2 Second School of Thought

On the other hand, the approach taken by some other courts in the recent years seems to suggest that there is another school of thought that is more inclined to recognise the right to privacy in Malaysia.

In *Lee Ewe Poh v Dr. Lim Teik Man*,[74] the court, for the first time, departed from the traditional approach as taken by other courts, and explicitly stated that the right to privacy is a recognisable cause of action under Malaysian laws. The background of this case is as follows:

The plaintiff was suffering from haemorrhoids and had consulted the defendant, who is a surgeon in a specialist centre. A procedure was conducted by the defendant and with that the plaintiff's haemorrhoids were successfully removed. The plaintiff was discharged after the procedure. A few days after the procedure, the plaintiff called the specialist centre to inquire about exactly what had happened during the procedure. The plaintiff was shocked to learn from the nurse that the defendant had taken photographs of her private parts during the procedure while was she was under the anaesthesia. The plaintiff was outraged as photography was not in the agenda of the procedure and she was not duly informed. She sued the defendant on the grounds of invasion of privacy and/or dignity. The defendant admitted that he had taken two photographs of the anus of the plaintiff but contended that what he did was in accordance with accepted medical practice and he did not disseminate the photographs but kept them as his medical records to facilitate easy explanation to the plaintiff after the procedure.

The defendant, relying on *Ultra Dimension* case and *Lee Cher Phow* case, submitted that invasion of privacy is not a recognised tort or a cause of action in

---

[73] See Douglas v Hello! Ltd [2001] QB 967, Ashworth Security Hospital v MGN Limited [2002] 4 All ER 193, Campbell v MGN Limited [2004] 2 All ER 995, Murray v Express Newspapers plc [2008] EWCA Civ 446.
[74] [2011] 4 CLJ 397.

Malaysia. The plaintiff, however, relying on the Court of Appeal's case of M*aslinda Ishak v Mohd Tahir Osman*,[75] and contended that the Court of Appeal has recognised and affirmed invasion of privacy as a recognisable cause of action.

In *Maslinda* case, the appellant was arrested by members of the RELA[76] during an operation. The appellant was put into a truck. During the journey, the appellant asked for permission to use the toilet facilities, but was disallowed. She was asked to urinate in the truck. As she was in quite a state, she asked her friends to shield her by encircling her with a shawl in order for her to ease herself. The defendant suddenly opened the door of the truck, rushed in, pulled down the shawl and proceeded to take numerous photos of the appellant in a squatting position urinating. The appellant was thoroughly humiliated with the whole incident and sued the defendant on the ground that her privacy had been invaded, resulting in humiliation, trauma and serious mental anguish.

The defendant was also convicted under Section 509 of the Penal Code, which provides that it is a criminal offence to insult the modesty of any person, utter any word, make any sound or gesture, or exhibit any object, or intrude upon the privacy of such person. The High Court found for the appellant and departed from the old English Common Law that invasion of privacy is not an actionable tort. The Court of Appeal indirectly endorsed such cause of action when the pleadings were specifically referred to and the Court of Appeal did not overrule invasion of privacy as a cause of action.

Applying the *Maslinda* case, Chew Soo Ho JC held that:

> Drawing an analogy of this Court of Appeal case, I am inclined to hold the view that since our courts especially the Court of Appeal have accepted such an act to be a cause of action, it is thus actionable. The privacy right of a female in relation to her modesty, decency and dignity in the context of the high moral value existing in our society is her fundamental right in sustaining that high morality that is demanded of her and it ought to be entrenched. Hence, it is just right that our law should be sensitive to such rights. In the circumstances, plaintiff in the instant case ought to be allowed to maintain such claim.

Similarly, in *Chong Chieng Jen v Mohd Irwan Hafiz Md Radzi*,[77] the High Court took the view that:

> ... an execution of a search warrant by the police will definitely result in the invasion of the privacy and property of the owner of the premises so named and may even result in the confiscation of his property. A person's privacy and the right to his property are very basic rights of a man ...
>
> The role of a magistrate when faced with an application for search warrants is an onerous one. He has to delicately balance the rights of a person to his privacy and the exclusive enjoyment of his property with the need of the police to gather evidence for the prosecution of offences by the state against an individual.
>
> ... a search warrant is a tool which legalize the invasion of a person's privacy, his property and may even lead to the confiscation of his property.

---

[75] [2009] 6 CLJ 653.

[76] RELA is a paramilitary civil volunteer corps formed by the Malaysian government. It has the authority to deal with situations like policemen, such as raiding suspected streets or premises. The members are also tasked with security works.

[77] [2010] 1 CLJ 355.

From the trend of the recent cases, it is observed that the Malaysian courts are increasingly willing to recognise the right to privacy, *albeit* in a limited scope and circumstance. As the Federal Constitution is silent on this issue, the hope is now placed on the courts to uphold the right to privacy as they are, in the words of Lord Wilberforce, 'The guardians of the citizens' right to privacy.'[78] Nevertheless, there is no single Malaysian case overruling these conflicting cases. It is unfortunate that, in all of these cases, the case of *Sivarasa Rasiah v Badan Peguam Malaysia*,[79] which held that the right to privacy is encompassed under Article 5(1) of the Federal Constitution, was not mentioned nor debated at all either by the courts or by the counsels. Unfortunately, therefore, the question as to whether the right to privacy forms a recognisable cause of action remains and continues to be uncertain and debatable.

References

Abstract from the IDC Malaysia Report on Malaysia Internet and eCommerce 2009–2013 Forecast and Analysis. http://www.idc.com/getdoc.jsp?containerId=MY202110S. Accessed 30 Apr 2012

Ahmad N (2008) The right to privacy and challenges: a critical review. Malayan Law J 5(cxxi):10

Bernama.com (16 July 2009) Personal Data Protection Bill to be tabled in Dewan Rakyat. http://www.bernama.com/bernama/v5/newsgeneral.php?id=425714. Accessed 30 Apr 2012

Clark R (1997) Introduction of Dataveillance and Information Privacy, and Definitions of Terms. http://www.rogerclarke.com/DV/IPrivacy.html. Accessed 4 Apr 2012

CNBC documentary interview, Inside the Mind of Google. Aired on 3 December 2009. http://www.youtube.com/watch?v=A6e7wfDHzew. Accessed 5 May 2012

Cooley T (1888) A treatise on the law of torts, 2nd edn. Callaghan & Co, Chicago, p 29

Edwards E, Waelde C (2009) Law and the Internet, 3rd edn. Hart Publishing, Oxford, p 449

Fernandez F, Cheah E (10 August 2005) Database firms selling name lists. The Star, reproduced with permission in the National House Buyer Association's website. http://www.hba.org.my/news/2005/805/database.htm. Accessed 23 Mar 2012

Ferrers E (1993) HL Debs Vol 349, Col 37. In: Rowland D, MacDonald E (2005) Information Technology Law, 3rd edn. London, Cavendish Publishing Limited, p. 299

Gomez G (6 August 2005) Colleges use confidential info to get students, The Star. http://thestar.com.my/news/story.asp?file=/2005/8/6/nation/11685313&sec=nation. Accessed 23 Mar 2012

Greenleaf G (2005) The APEC Privacy Framework – a new low standard. Privacy Law Policy Rep 11(5):121

Greenleaf G (2011) Major changes in Asia Pacific Data Privacy Law: 2011 survey. Privacy Laws Bus Int Rep (113): 1, 5–14. http://papers.ssrn.com/sol3/papers.cfm?abstract_id=2001820. Accessed 1 May 2012

Greenleaf G (2012) Global data privacy laws: 89 Countries, and Accelerating. Privacy Laws & Business International Report, Issue 115, Special Supplement, Queen Mary School of Law Legal Studies Research Paper No. 98/2012. http://papers.ssrn.com/sol3/papers.cfm?abstract_id=2000034. Accessed 1 May 2012

Johnson B (11 January 2010) Privacy No Longer a Social Norm, says Facebook Founder. The Guardian, UK. http://www.guardian.co.uk/technology/2010/jan/11/facebook-privacy. Accessed 6 May 2012

---

[78] R v IRC, Ex P Rossminster [1980] AC 952.

[79] [2010] 2 MLJ 333.

Khaw LT (2002) Towards a personal data protection regime in Malaysia. J Malays Comp Law 29:11, http://www.commonlii.org/my/journals/JMCL/2002/11.html. Accessed 28 Apr 2012

Kuner C (2009) An International Legal Framework for data protection: issues and prospects. Comput Law Secur Rev 25:307–317, http://ssrn.com/abstract=1443802. Accessed 24 Apr 2012

Loh FF (22 November 2011) Personal Data Protection Act to Be Introduced Next Year, The Star. http://thestar.com.my/news/story.asp?file=/2011/11/22/nation/20111122122708&sec=nation. Accessed 12 Mar 2012

Loh J, Bedi R (3 May 2009a) Beware, your data's on sale, The Star. http://thestar.com.my/news/story.asp?file=/2009/5/3/focus/3818877&sec=focus. Accessed 10 May 2012

Loh J, Bedi R (3 May 2009b) Your personal details can be bought for just 10 sen, The Star. http://thestar.com.my/news/story.asp?file=/2009/5/3/nation/3822236&sec=nation. Accessed 10 May 2012

O'Neill J (2008) Big Brother – Who is Watching You? Pocket Issue. London, p. 32

Office of the Press Secretary, the White House (23 February 2012). We Can't Wait: Obama Administration Unveils Blueprint for a Privacy Bill of Rights to Protect Consumers Online. http://www.whitehouse.gov/the-press-office/2012/02/23/we-can-t-wait-obama-administration-unveils-blueprint-privacy-bill-rights. Accessed 10 May 2012

Parliamentary Debates. House of Representatives. Twelfth Parliament. Third Session. First Meeting. (5 April 2010), p. 110

Perri (1998) The future of privacy volume 1: private life and public policy, London: Demos, p. 23. In: Rowland D, MacDonald E (2005) Information Technology Law, 3rd edn. London, Cavendish Publishing Limited, p. 300

Pounder C. Why the APEC Privacy Framework is unlikely to protect privacy. http://www.out-law.com/page-8550. Accessed 5 Jan 2012

Singer N (16 June 2012) You for sale: mapping and sharing, the consumer genome. The New York Times. http://www.nytimes.com/2012/06/17/technology/acxiom-the-quiet-giant-of-consumer-database-marketing.html?_r=1&pagewanted=all. Accessed 16 Jun 2012

Sipalan J (2012) The Star, 90% of government services to go online. http://thestar.com.my/news/story.asp?file=/2012/7/4/nation/11597219&sec=nation. Accessed 4 Jul 2012

Sprenger P (26 January 1999) Sun on privacy: get over it, Wired Magazine. http://www.wired.com/politics/law/news/1999/01/17538. Accessed 15 Mar 2012

The 2007 International Privacy Ranking (28 December 2007) http://www.privacyinternational.org/article.shtml?cmd[347]=x-347-559597. Accessed 2 Feb 2012

The Star (11 August 2005) Ministry denies UPU link in sale of student list. http://www.thestar.com.my/news/story.asp?file=/2005/8/11/nation/11738735&sec=nation. Accessed 10 May 2012

The Star (24 February 2007) Still blacklisted 18 years after paying debts. http://thestar.com.my/news/story.asp?file=/2007/2/24/nation/16961912&sec=nation. Accessed 10 May 2012

The Star (3 May 2009) Little Protection under the Law. http://thestar.com.my/news/story.asp?file=/2009/5/3/focus/3820302&sec=focus. Accessed 10 May 2012

Warren S, Brandeis L (1890) The right to privacy. Harv Law Rev IV(5):193

Westin A (1970) Privacy and freedom. Atheneum, New York, p 7

List of Materials

European Community Directive on the Protection of Individuals with regard to the Processing of Personal Data and on the Free Movement of Such Data ('EU Data Protection Directive') http://ec.europa.eu/justice_home/fsj/privacy/law/index_en.htm. Accessed 3 Mar 2012

The Council of Europe's Convention for the Protection of Individuals with regard to Automatic Processing of Personal Data ('Council of Europe's Convention'). http://conventions.coe.int/Treaty/EN/Treaties/Html/108.htm. Accessed 2 May 2012

The Draft General Data Protection Regulation. http://ec.europa.eu/justice/newsroom/data-protection/news/120125_en.htm. Accessed 13 May 2012

The Organisation for Economic Cooperation and Development Guidelines Governing the Protection of Privacy and Transborder Flows of Personal Data ('OECD Guidelines'). http://www.oecd.org/document/18/0,3343,en_2649_34255_1815186_1_1_1_1,00.html. Accessed 2 May 2012

Personal Data Protection Act 2010: An Overview Analysis

Edwin Lee Yong Cieh

> *Observations more than books and experience more than persons, are the prime educators*
> (Amos Bronson Alcott, 29th November 1799 – 4th March 1888,
> Educator, Reformer, Writer & Philosopher)

Abstract
Essentially, the Personal Data Protection Act 2010 ('PDPA') protects data privacy (as opposed to general privacy). The PDPA basically applies to any form of processing of personal data in respect of commercial transactions. The PDPA governs the way personal data is collected, used, transferred or even deleted. Any person who processes personal data ('data user') of an individual ('data subject') is required to comply with the seven personal data protection principles ('PDP Principles') under the PDPA. The PDPA also grants several rights to data subjects. In this chapter, the author starts off by explaining the various definitions and terminologies under the PDPA, the application and non-application of the PDPA, followed by the detailed elaboration on the application of the PDP Principles. The author also sets out the various exemptions, the rights of data subjects as well as criminal offences in easy-to-read table formats.

3.1 Personal Data Protection Terminology

The Personal Data Protection Act 2010 ('PDPA') is influenced by and modeled upon the EU Data Protection Directive rather than the OECD Guidelines or the APEC Privacy Framework.[1] Some of the provisions in the PDPA also mirror those in the UK Data Protection Act 1998 ['DPA 1998 (UK)']. Since the PDPA is a new

---

[1] Greenleaf (2012).

E.L. Yong Cieh (✉)
Christopher Lee & Co, 25-2, Block B, Jaya One Section 13, Petaling Jaya 46200, Malaysia
e-mail: edwin@christopherleeco.com

piece of law in Malaysia, reference has to be made to the laws, cases, guidelines, and guidance notes relating to data protection in the European Union ('EU') (including the UK) and some other jurisdictions having the similar data protection laws. It is a common practice that data protection regulators/commissioners regularly publish guidelines or guidance notes to further explain the application of the data protection legislation, and therefore it is likely that the Personal Data Protection Commissioner in Malaysia ('PDP Commissioner') will also follow this trend and publish guidelines or guidance notes in the near future. In the absence of any guidelines or guidance notes having been published by the PDP Commissioner thus far, the author has made references to two main instruments published by the Information Commissioner's Office of the UK ('ICO'), namely the Legal Guidance to Data Protection Act 1998 ('Legal Guidance') and the Guide to Data Protection ('the Guide'). Reference is also made to the EU's Article 29 Working Party's Opinion 4/2007 on the Concept of Personal Data.

The PDPA applies to (a) any person who processes and (b) any person who has control over or authorises the processing of any personal data in respect of commercial transactions.[2] The PDPA regulates the processing of 'personal data', which does not cover 'company data'.

3.1.1 Definition of 'Data' and 'Personal Data'

According to Section 4, 'personal data' is defined as 'any information in respect of commercial transactions, which:
1) Is being processed wholly or partly by means of equipment operating automatically in response to instructions given for that purpose,
2) Is recorded with the intention that it should wholly or partly be processed by means of such equipment, or
3) Is recorded as part of a relevant filing system or with the intention that it should form part of a relevant filing system that relates directly or indirectly to a data subject, who is identified or identifiable from that information or from that and other information in the possession of a data user, including any sensitive personal data or expression of opinion about the data subject, but does not include any information that is processed for the purpose of a credit reporting business carried on by a credit reporting agency under the Credit Reporting Agencies Act 2010'.[3]

This section has two limbs: The first limb covers paragraphs (1) to (3) which seeks to explain the meaning of 'data', and the second limb covers the paragraph after the first limb which seeks to explain the meaning of 'personal data'.

---

[2] Section 2(1) of the PDPA.
[3] Section 4 of the PDPA.

3.1.1.1 What is Data?[4]

It can be deduced from the definition in Section 4 that the PDPA applies to electronic and manual data:

Electronic Data

Personal data within paragraphs (1) and (2) include those data being processed or recorded with the intention that they should wholly or partly be processed by means of equipment operating automatically in response to instructions given for that purpose.

A computer program is a set of instructions or commands that gives directions to the computer as to the sequence in which its operations should be conducted in order to carry out specific functions. The extent of automatic processing means that paragraphs (1) and (2) will apply to all forms of electronic data. For example, all data stored on a computer is considered electronic data. It is also said that the above definition is not technology-specific, and therefore, the use of any form of equipment that is operating automatically in response to instructions will be covered.[5]

The terms 'recorded with the intention' refers to data that is intended to be stored on a computer. Therefore, data recorded on paper with the intention that it will subsequently be stored on the computer is also considered to be an electronic data.[6] Such an intention to process must exist at the time of recording.[7]

Manual Data

Personal data within paragraph (3) includes those data recorded or intended to be recorded as part of a relevant filing system.

'Relevant Filing System'

The definition of data as presented within paragraph (3) is designed to cover the relevant filing systems, such as manual filing and record keeping systems. 'Relevant filing system' is defined in Section 4 to mean 'any set of information relating to individuals to the extent that, although the information is not processed by means of equipment operating automatically in response to instructions given for that purpose, the set of information is structured, either by reference to individuals or by reference to criteria relating to individuals, in such a way that specific information relating to a particular individual is readily accessible.' As such, in determining what manual data will be covered, the question of when data should be considered 'readily accessible' is of critical importance.

The meaning of 'relevant filing system' was considered in the UK Court of Appeal in *Durant v Financial Services Authority*.[8] Mr. Durant had lost certain

---

[4] See the 'Technical Guidance Note – Determining What is Data?', Information Commissioner's Office.

[5] Jay and Hamilton (1999), p. 32.

[6] Jay and Hamilton (1999), p. 32.

[7] Jay and Hamilton (1999), p. 32.

[8] [2003] EWCA Civ 1746; [2004] FSR 573.

litigation against Barclay's Bank. The Financial Services Authority ('FSA') held certain information about the case that concerned Mr. Durant and others in paper files. Mr. Durant then sought the disclosure of certain information, both electronically and in manual files, which he claimed was personal data relating to him held by the FSA. Mr. Durant thought that obtaining those files might help him in filing another suit against Barclay's Bank. The FSA had provided Mr. Durant with some information in response to his requests, but he sought further disclosure.

The court was of the view that although manual files 'are not processed by means of equipment operating automatically in response to instructions given for that purpose', the Parliament intended the DPA 1998 (UK) to apply to manual files 'only if they are of sufficient sophistication to provide the same or similar ready accessibility as a computerised filing system.'

In other words, to qualify as a relevant filing system, the system should be structured or indexed in such a way as to enable the data user or his employee to easily access and extract the relevant data, without having to perform a manual search for them. It is not sufficient if the manual filing system requires the data user or his employee to leaf through files in a time-consuming and costly manner to discover whether they contain data relating to the person who has made the request for access to his personal data.[9]

Accordingly, the court held that a 'relevant filing system' is limited to a system:
1) In which the files forming part of it are structured or referenced in such a way as to clearly indicate at the outset of the search whether specific data capable of amounting to the personal data of an individual requesting it is held within the system and, if so, in which file or files it is held; and
2) Which has, as part of its own structure or referencing mechanism, a sufficiently sophisticated and detailed means of readily indicating whether and where in an individual file or files specific criteria or data about the applicant can be readily located.

On the facts of that case, the FSA's filing systems did not satisfy those requirements at the time. The manual files were not indexed with particular reference to Mr. Durant, but were arranged according to the subject matter. Substantial time and effort was needed in order to locate and extract the data sought by Mr Durant. The files were not structured or indexed so as to provide ready access to the data. This case was subsequently followed by Laddie J in *Smith v Lloyds TSB Bank plc*,[10] in which the judge held that data kept in a non-computerised manual

---

[9] The court quoted with approval the following passage from Jay and Hamilton (1999):

'Files or systems which do not have any clear systematic internal indexing mechanism should not fall under the definition. So a file with the name on the front arranged in date order may not fall within the term relevant filing system, whereas a file with the name on but arranged in sections to cover health, education, earnings or family connections is more likely to be; the more readily accessible the particular information, the clearer it is that it will be covered ... the nature of the file, for example whether it is a personnel file or a customer file, is completely irrelevant'.

[10] [2005] EWHC 246.

system was to be treated as data if the filing system was sufficiently structured so as to allow easy access to data specific to the data subject. The data controller (data user) should not to be put to a great deal of effort in extracting the relevant data.

As a response to the *Durant* case, the ICO issued a guidance note to address the impact of the decision. For example, when the files are structured in pure chronological order, it will not be a relevant filing system, because a data user has to leaf through the files in order to retrieve the data. However, if the files use individuals' names as the file names and are indexed in such as way as to enable the easy retrieval of data without a manual search, such as is the case with sicknesses, absences, contact details, etc., it will likely be construed as a relevant filing system.[11] The ICO acknowledged that the impact of the *Durant* case is that it is likely that only a very few manual files will be covered by the DPA 1998 (UK) because most of the personal data held in manual form does not fall within the restrictive interpretation held in Durant.[12] Nevertheless, as more and more data are being stored electronically, most of the personal data will be covered by the definition of 'personal data' under paragraphs (1) and (2) of Section 4.

The definition of 'relevant filing system' is in *pari materia* with Section 1 of the DPA 1998 (UK) and hence the above decision would be helpful, though it remains to be seen if the PDP Commissioner or the Malaysian courts would adopt such a restrictive interpretation.

3.1.1.2 What Is 'Personal Data'?[13]

The definition of personal data is one of the most fundamental aspects of the data protection law. However, it is nearly impossible to set out the definition conclusively since the definition and scope of personal data are very wide and remain open to many interpretations. The courts and the data protection regulators in both the EU and the UK have taken different views in approaching the definition of personal data. As the definition of personal data constitutes the threshold requirement of the application of data protection law, it is very important to understand what exactly the PDPA is attempting to regulate.

Name, home address, race, national ID number, occupation, gender and even an expression of opinion about an individual are considered personal data. With the advancement of technology, almost any form of recorded information, such as photograph,[14] video images recorded on CCTV could be deemed as personal data

---

[11] 'The Durant Case and Its Impact on the Interpretation of the Data Protection Act', Information Commissioner's Office, p. 6.

[12] 'The Durant Case and Its Impact on the Interpretation of the Data Protection Act', Information Commissioner's Office, p. 6.

[13] See the 'Quick Reference Guide – What is Personal Data?', and 'Technical Guidance Note – What is Data?', Information Commissioner's Office.

[14] Wong JA in the Hong Kong case of Eastweek Publisher Ltd v Privacy Commissioner for Personal Data [2000] 1 HKC 692 said, 'a photograph can tell many things. It tells the race, sex, approximate age, weight and height of the person shown in the photograph. On the other hand, the

within the ambit of the PDPA if a specific individual is identified or identifiable from that information. Ian Lloyd is of the view that biometric data, such as fingerprint, face, and iris recognition, which forms the cornerstone of modern passports and national identity cards, is also a form of personal data.[15]

The European Commission has set up the Article 29 Working Party to act as an independent European advisory body on data protection and privacy. The Article 29 Working Party plays an important role in shaping the fundamental definitions and concepts of data protection. In this regard, the Article 29 Working Party has issued Opinion 4/2007 on the Concept of Personal Data ('Opinion 4/2007'), which seeks to provide a common understanding of the definition of personal data.

'Any Information'

According to Opinion 4/2007, this phrase can be examined from three aspects, namely:

Nature
The definition of personal data includes any type of statement about a person. It includes 'objective' information, such as the presence of a certain substance in one's blood, and 'subjective' information, such as the opinions or assessments of an individual. The information does not need to be true or proven for it to be considered personal data.[16]

Content
The definition of personal data includes any type of information. It includes general information, sensitive information, information touching on the individual's private and family life, and information regarding the types of activities undertaken by the individual.[17]

Format
The definition of personal data includes any information available in any format, be it alphabetical, numerical, graphical, photographical, or acoustic. For example, it includes information stored on paper, in a computer memory by means of binary code, or on a videotape recorded on CCTV.[18]

---

written description of a person ... does not tell very much about the person ... the person in the photograph can only be the person himself or herself and no one else.'

[15] Lloyd (2008), p. 41.

[16] Opinion 4/2007 on the Concept of Personal Data (2007), p. 6.

[17] Opinion 4/2007 on the Concept of Personal Data (2007), p. 6.

[18] Opinion 4/2007 on the Concept of Personal Data (2007), p. 7.

'Relates Directly or Indirectly to a Data Subject'

The scope of 'relates to' in terms of an individual is very wide. Information can be considered to 'relate' to an individual when it is *about* that individual. The Article 29 Working Party noted that 'data relates to an individual if it refers to the identity, characteristics, or behavior of an individual or if such information is used to determine or influence the way in which that person is treated or evaluated.'[19]

The Article 29 Working Party took a wide interpretation of the terms 'relates to'. It will be sufficient if one of the following elements is present in the personal data:
1) Content element: Data 'relates to' an individual when it is 'about' that individual;
2) Purpose element: Data 'relates to' an individual when the data is used with the 'purpose' of evaluating, treating in a certain way, or influencing the status or behaviour of an individual; or
3) Result element: Data 'relates to' an individual when the use of such data is likely to have an 'impact' on an individual's rights and interests. It is not necessary that the potential result be a major impact. It is sufficient if the individual may be treated differently from others as a result of the processing of such data.

These three elements do not need to apply cumulatively. The same piece of data may relate to different individuals at the same time, depending on what element is present with regard to the others. It is not necessary that the data 'focuses' on an individual in order for it to be considered that it relates to him.

In *Durant v Financial Services Authority*, the Financial Services Authority ('FSA') refused to disclose some other records as they were related to third parties and did not constitute personal data related to Mr. Durant. Counsel for Mr. Durant argued that the term 'relates to' ought to be interpreted broadly in order to cover any data that may be obtained from a search of a database made by reference to an individual's name. On the other hand, counsel for the FSA argued that the term should be interpreted restrictively, i.e., that 'there should be reference to or concern with a subject, implying a more-or-less direct connection with an individual.'

The Court of Appeal preferred the restrictive interpretation and held that the intention of the DPA 1998 (UK) was not to give an automatic right of access to information just because Mr. Durant's name was mentioned in a record or because he has some interest in the matter. The mere fact of searching the database that made reference to a data subject's name did not mean that the documents retrieved constituted personal data relating to him. In the context of this case, the issue was whether any information relating to the FSA's investigation of Mr. Durant's complaint about Barclay's Bank fell within the definition of 'personal data' belonged to Mr. Durant. The court held that data will relate to an individual if it is information that affects [a person's] privacy, whether in his personal or family life or in his business or professional capacity. It may amount to personal data if it affects the individual's privacy or if the name appeared together with other information relating to the individual, such as his or her address, telephone number, or hobbies.

---

[19] Working Party document No WP 105: 'Working document on data protection issues related to RFID Technology' (2005), p. 7.

On the facts, just because the FSA's investigation of the matter was related to the complaint from Mr. Durant, it did not render the information generated by that investigation personal data that belongs to Mr. Durant. A mere mention of the individual in a document does not necessarily mean that the document contains personal data of that individual. The court held that the information being sought by Mr. Durant did not 'relate to' him. The court noted that Mr. Durant's claim was a misguided attempt to use the machinery of the DPA 1998 (UK) as a back-door approach to discover evidence that he could not obtain through the usual means of discovery.

According to the ICO, the impact of this decision is that mere reference to an individual's name alone is not sufficient to amount to personal data. It will amount to personal data when the name appears together with other information that can be linked to the data subject or affect the data subject's privacy, such as the data subject's medical history; salary details, tax liabilities, bank statement, and spending habits.[20] Therefore, the current position in the UK is that in order to amount to personal data, the information must affect a person's privacy, whether in a personal or family capacity or in a business or professional capacity.

Hence, it remains to be seen which approaches the Malaysian courts will take. One must take note that as the notion of a general right to privacy is not yet explicitly recognised in Malaysia, it is doubtful that our courts will have too much regard for whether the data affects the data subject's privacy. The wide interpretation taken by the Article 29 Working Party will be a better guidance to follow.

'Identified or Identifiable from that Information'

Under the PDPA, information about both identified and identifiable persons is considered personal data. An identified person appears to be an individual who is known in person and, based on the information, can be contacted or recognised by others. The most common way to identify an individual is by name. An identifiable person is an individual whose identity is ascertainable, but who is not necessarily known in person. His identity can be ascertained based on the information held and by making some further enquiries. However, name alone may not be enough to identify an individual if he or she is on a name list, because there could be a few individuals with the same name. Nevertheless, if there is further information, such as addresses, identification numbers, places of work, phone numbers, etc. that are sufficient to distinguish one such person from another, an individual can be identified when his name is checked against the other information.[21]

In the Hong Kong case of *Eastweek Publisher Ltd v Privacy Commissioner for Personal Data*,[22] a young lady was photographed without her knowledge and consent whilst walking in a public place. The photograph was then published in a

---

[20] 'The Durant Case and Its Impact on the Interpretation of the Data Protection Act', Information Commissioner's Office, p. 3.

[21] Jay and Hamilton (1999), p. 80.

[22] [2000] 1 HKC 692.

magazine that commented about the dress sense of women in Hong Kong. The majority in the Court of Appeal held that the complaint could not be upheld. Although the court agreed that a photograph constituted personal data, the mere taking of photograph and using it as an anonymous photographic subject did not amount to the collection of personal data. Her identity was not known or not needed for the article, and hence, she was not identified from the photograph. Wong JA dissented and opined that the complainant was identifiable and had indeed been identified by her work colleagues.[23]

'From that and Other Information in the Possession of the Data User'

This phrase intends to cover personal data that by itself, does not identify an individual or make an individual identifiable, but that when combined or cross-checked with other information in the possession of the data user, allows the individual to be identified from the information.[24]

For example, according to David Bainbridge, a computer database may not include names, but might, instead, operate on individuals' national insurance numbers. If the person processing the data also has a card index that contains national insurance numbers and the names of the individuals to whom they belong, that is sufficient for the data being processing by computer to be classified as personal data because the individual can be identified by linking the two sources. Another example is when a data user has a set of numbered photographs of individuals and a card index which relate the photographs to named persons.[25]

'Expression of Opinion About the Data Subject'

Personal data includes expressions of opinion about a data subject. This more often occurs in employment or medical records. For example, an employer may provide some comments in a job appraisal regarding an employee or a doctor may give his professional opinion about the health conditions of a patient.

'Sensitive Personal Data'

The requirements for processing sensitive personal data are much stricter than the general personal data mentioned above.

Under Section 4, 'sensitive personal data' means any personal data consisting of information as to the:
1) Physical or mental health or condition of a data subject;
2) His political opinions;
3) His religious beliefs or other beliefs of a similar nature;
4) The commission or alleged commission by him of any offence; and
5) Or any other personal data as the Minister may determine by order published in the *Gazette*.

---

[23] Berthold and Wacks (2003).

[24] Munir and Yasin (2010a), MLJ cxix, p. 4.

[25] Bainbridge (2008) p. 506.

While the DPA 1998 (UK) includes the racial or ethnic origin of the data subject and his or her sexual life as one of the types of sensitive personal data, the PDPA seems to have omitted these two types of personal data. Given that race and gender are always considered sensitive issues in Malaysia, it was a missed opportunity for the PDPA to have omitted these personal data from the definition of sensitive personal data. According to the Guide, the reason for this special category of personal data is that these types of data could be used in a discriminatory way and are likely to be of a private nature. Therefore, they need to be treated with greater care than other general personal data.[26]

'Processing'

According to Section 4, processing in relation to personal data means the 'collecting, recording, holding, or storing the personal data, including:
1) The organisation, adaptation, or alteration of personal data;
2) The retrieval, consultation, or use of personal data;
3) The disclosure of personal data via transmission, transfer, dissemination or otherwise making it available; or
4) The alignment, combination, correction, erasure, or destruction of personal data.

The definition uses the term 'holding or storing' (the EU Data Protection Directive uses the term 'storage' only).[27] The definition under the PDPA is wider in the sense that merely being in possession of personal data will be considered as processing it for the purposes of the PDPA. Additionally, by using the term 'including', it is submitted that the definition of processing is not intended to be exhaustive and that it shall be construed widely in order to cover every conceivable use of data.

This can be seen in *Bodil Lindqvist*[28] where the European Court of Justice ('ECJ') ruled that placing personal data about individuals on a webpage amounted to the processing of personal data by making them available on the Internet.

Mrs. Lindqvist worked as a catechist in the parish of Alseda. She set up a website in order to allow parishioners to obtain information from the website. The website contained information about herself and 18 colleagues in the parish, including their full names, occupations, hobbies, and telephone numbers. Mrs. Lindqvist had not informed her colleagues about the existence of these webpages nor obtained prior consent from them. She was convicted by the Swedish court for a breach of the data protection law. She appealed and the Swedish court referred the case to the ECJ for a preliminary ruling (See **Chap.** 11 for detailed case analysis).

---

[26] The Guide to Data Protection, Information Commissioner's Office, item 13 A3, p. 24.

[27] Art 2(b) of the EU Data Protection Directive defines 'processing' to mean any operation or set of operations which is performed upon personal data, whether or not by automatic means, such as collection, recording, organization, storage, adaptation or alteration, retrieval, consultation, use, disclosure by transmission, dissemination or otherwise making available, alignment or combination, blocking, erasure or destruction'.

[28] [2003] ECR I-12971; [2004] QB 1014, Case 101/01.

One of the questions at hand was whether the mere mention of a person by name, occupation, and telephone number on a webpage constituted 'the processing of personal data' within the meaning of the EU Data Protection Directive. The Swedish Government argued that as soon as personal data are processed by computer, whether by using a word-processing programme or in order to put them on an Internet page, they have been the subject of processing. The ECJ agreed with this argument and said that as the term 'processing' is defined as meaning 'any operation or set of operations that are performed upon personal data, whether by automatic means or not, such as disclosure by transmission, dissemination, or otherwise making data available',[29] It followed that the operation of loading personal data on a webpage was considered to constitute such processing. It also ruled that placing information on a webpage entailed the operation of loading that page onto a server and operations necessary to make the data accessible to people connected to the Internet. Therefore, the processing was, at least in part, performed by automatic means. The court rejected Mrs. Lindqvist's defence of use for domestic purposes, i.e., her stating that what she did was in the course of leisure activities. The court thought that such an activity was not for domestic purposes because the data were communicated to 'an indefinite number of people' on the Internet.

3.1.2 The Main Actors Under the PDPA

The person who processes any personal data or has control over or authorises the processing of any personal data is referred to as 'data user', and the person whose personal data is processed by the data user is known as 'data subject'.

3.1.2.1 'Data User'

A data user is defined as 'a person who either alone or jointly or in common with other persons processes any personal data or has control over or authorises the processing of any personal data, but does not include a data processor'.[30] Data user under the PDPA is equivalent to 'data controller' under the DPA 1998 (UK).

It is important to establish whether or not someone is a data user because Section 5(1) provides that it is the data user who must comply with the PDP principles and other related provisions under the PDPA. Section 14 provides that if the data user falls within a class of data users specified in the order made by the Minister, such a data user is required to register with the PDP Commissioner in accordance with the registration provisions laid down in Division 2 of the PDPA. However, one should take note that all other data users, who are not required to register with the Commissioner, will still have to comply with all the provisions of

---

[29] Opinion 4/2007 (2007), p. 100.
[30] Section 4 of the PDPA.

the PDPA, including the PDP Principles, except the registration provisions stated in Division 2.[31] In other words, as long as the person is involved in processing personal data, he or she is subject to the PDPA.

According to the Legal Guidance, the term 'person' means that the data controller (data user) must be a legal person and that this shall include human beings, such as individuals, and artificial legal persons, such as companies and other corporate and unincorporated entities.[32]

The phrase 'who either alone or jointly or in common with other persons' seems to indicate that there can be more than one data user who share a central database of personal data. For example, a number of subsidiary companies within a group of companies may share a central database of all their employee records and customer lists.[33] According to the Legal Guidance, the term 'jointly' refers to a situation in which the data controllers (data users) agree between themselves as to the purpose and manner of any data processing of the personal data, whereas 'common' refers to a situation in which, although the data controllers (data users) share a central database of personal data, each of them has their own individual purposes and manner of processing and they process the data independently from one another.[34]

Under the DPA 1998 (UK), the data controller must decide the purposes for which personal data is to be processed and the way in which personal data is to be processed. This element is not expressly provided for under our definition of 'data user'. It can be said that our definition is wider in the sense that even the mere holding of personal data without any intention of processing it further will make the person a data user because the concept of 'processing' under the PDPA is so wide that it can be used to encompass all types of activities/operations that a particular data user may want to use on the personal data in question.[35]

What about a holding/group company that has several subsidiaries within the group? Abu Bakar Munir is of the view that it is likely that each company within a holding/group company will be considered separately as a data user due to the concept of separate legal entity and the fact that each company within the group may be involved in different kinds of businesses and processing various kinds of personal data of data subjects.[36]

3.1.2.2 'Data Subject'

'Data subject' is defined as 'an individual who is the subject of the personal data'.[37] David Bainbridge argues that the use of the term 'individual' suggests that the data subject must be a human being/living individual and that an artificial legal person,

---

[31] Section 13(2) of the PDPA.
[32] Legal Guidance to Data Protection Act 1998, Information Commissioner's Office, p. 16, see also Bainbridge (2008), p. 508.
[33] Munir and Yasin (2010b), p. 74.
[34] Legal Guidance to Data Protection Act 1998, Information Commissioner's Office, p. 16.
[35] Munir and Yasin (2010b), p. 74.
[36] Munir and Yasin (2010b), p. 75.
[37] Section 4 of the PDPA.

such as a company or corporate or unincorporated entity, is not a data subject.[38] However, unlike the DPA 1998 (UK), in which the definition of personal data expressly refers to data related to a living individual, the PDPA is silent as to whether the term 'data subject' relates only to living individuals or also covers deceased individuals.

3.1.2.3 'Data Processor'[39]

Apart from the data user, there is another category of person who also processes personal data. Such a person is known as a 'data processor', which is defined as 'any person, other than an employee of the data user, who processes the personal data solely on behalf of the data user, and does not process the personal data for any of his own purposes'.[40] As Section 5(1) provides that only a data user has to comply with the PDP Principles and Section 4 expressly excludes the data processor from the definition of the data user,[41] this means that a data processor does not have to comply with the PDP Principles. However, if the data processor processes personal data for his or her own purposes, then he or she will become a data user and must then comply with all of the PDP Principles. As a data user is still liable for the actions perform by the data processor,[42] it is therefore important for the data user to ensure that the data processor complies with the PDPA. If the data processor sub-contracts its processing operations, the data user should ensure that every sub-contractor must still comply with the PDPA and abide by the instructions given by the data user.[43]

Having said this, the data processor may still have to comply with one particular principle, i.e., the security principle. Section 9(2) states that when the processing of personal data is carried out by a data processor on behalf of the data user, the onus is on the data user to take steps to ensure that the data processor shall comply with the security principle by requiring the data processor to provide sufficient guarantees with respect to the technical and organisational security measures and take reasonable steps to ensure compliance with those measures. This can be done by entering into a written contract with the data processor, requiring the data processor to act only on instructions from the data user and to comply with the security principle.[44] The data user should also choose the data processor carefully and have in place effective means of allowing the data user to monitor, review, and audit the data

---

[38] Bainbridge (2008), p. 508.

[39] See the 'Outsourcing: A Guide for Small and Medium-Sized Businesses', Information Commissioner's Office.

[40] Section 4 of the PDPA.

[41] Section 4 of the PDPA defines data user is to mean a person who either alone or jointly or in common with other persons processes any personal data or has control over or authorizes the processing of any personal data, but does not include a data processor.

[42] Legal Guidance to Data Protection Act 1998, Information Commissioner's Office, para 2.5, p. 17.

[43] Pastor (2012), p. 62.

[44] Lloyd (2008), p. 55.

processor's processing system.[45] Examples of data processors are Internet Service Providers, web-hosting companies, call centres, companies that provide servers and database back-up facilities, companies engaged to carry out database quality control or to conduct market surveys, companies engaged to use clients' databases to prepare report for clients, etc.[46]

3.2 Application of the Personal Data Protection Act 2010

3.2.1 Application of the PDPA

Section 2(1) states that the PDPA applies to:
- Any person who processes; and
- Any person who has control over or authorises the processing of, any personal data in respect of commercial transactions.

'Person' in the context of Section 2(1) refers to the 'data user', as the 'data user' is defined as 'a person who either alone or jointly or in common with other persons processes any personal data or has control over or authorises the processing of any personal data, but does not include a data processor'.[47]

3.3 Applicability Criteria under the PDPA

According to Section 2(2), the PDPA shall apply to data users in the following two circumstances:
- Where the data user is established in Malaysia and the personal data is processed, whether or not in the context of that establishment, by that person or any person employed or engaged by that establishment; or
- Where the data user is not established in Malaysia but uses equipment in Malaysia for processing the personal data otherwise than for the purposes of transit through Malaysia. For the second circumstance, the data user must nominate a representative established in Malaysia,[48] but such nomination does not absolve the data user from any legal action.[49]

3.3.1 Establishment in Malaysia

A Malaysian company processing personal data is subject to the PDPA by virtue of Section 2(2)(a). However, the effect of the second limb of Section 2(2)(a), which covers any person employed or engaged by that establishment, is not clear. There is

---

[45] The Guide to Data Protection, Information Commissioner's Office, item 27, A3, p. 28.
[46] Stephenson and Kwan (2007), pp. 330–331.
[47] Section 4 of the PDPA.
[48] Section 2(3) of the PDPA.
[49] Munir and Yasin (2010b), p. 78.

no similar provision found in the DPA 1998 (UK).[50] The provision is susceptible to two interpretations: (1) if a Malaysian company engages a third party company to process personal data on its behalf, the third party company is also subject to the PDPA because the company is 'engaged' by the Malaysian company to perform the act of processing of personal data, and hence, they should be considered as joint data users, or (2) the third party company may be considered as a data processor on the basis that it is engaged by the Malaysian company to process data solely on behalf of the Malaysian company. If the second view is taken, then the third party company is not subject to the PDPA.

The term 'establishment' is further defined in Section 2(4) to include:
- An individual whose physical presence in Malaysia shall not be less than 180 days in one calendar year,
- A body incorporated under the Companies Act 1965,
- A partnership or other unincorporated association formed under any written laws in Malaysia, and
- Any person who maintains an office, branch, or agency or a regular practice in Malaysia but does not fall within sub-sections (a)–(c).

A data user who is an individual does not have to be a Malaysian citizen, as evidenced from sub-section (a). A data user who resides in Malaysia for more than 180 days will be regarded as an individual for the purposes of the PDPA. Regarding those multinational companies that have offices or operate businesses in Malaysia, they will be regarded as having an establishment in Malaysia under sub-section (d). It is, however, not clear whether the term 'agency' here refers to one who has the power to enter into a legally binding contract on behalf of his principal or has the broader sense of one who acts on behalf of another.

3.3.2 Establishment Outside Malaysia

Section 2(2)(b) applies to situations in which a non-Malaysian company uses equipment, e.g., computers, computer networks, servers, application systems, situated in Malaysia to process personal data. The non-Malaysian company will be subject to the PDPA, and it must nominate a representative in Malaysia.

---

[50] Section 5 DPA 1998 (UK) provides:

Except as otherwise provided by or under section 54, this Act applies to a data controller in respect of any data only if —

(a) the data controller is established in the United Kingdom and the data are processed in the context of that establishment, or

(b) the data controller is established neither in the United Kingdom nor in any other EEA State but uses equipment in the United Kingdom for processing the data otherwise than for the purposes of transit through the United Kingdom.

(2) A data controller falling within subsection (1)(b) must nominate for the purposes of this Act a representative established in the United Kingdom.

However, if the non-Malaysian company merely transfers personal data to another company located in another country via equipment situated in Malaysia, the PDPA will not apply, because the law allows the processing of personal data for the purposes of transit through Malaysia to other countries.[51] A typical example of this would be the use of telecommunications equipment to transmit and receive data packets solely as a conduit from one server to another, without involving any storing or processing activities.[52]

3.4 Non-application of the Act

Interestingly, the PDPA sets out the organisations and broad categories of processing activities that fall outside the application of the PDPA.

The PDPA shall not apply at all in the following circumstances:
- Personal data processed by the Federal Government and State Governments,[53]
- Personal data processed outside Malaysia (unless that personal data is intended to be further processed in Malaysia),[54]
- Personal data processed in non-commercial transactions,[55]
- Personal data processed under the Credit Reporting Agencies Act 2010,[56]
- Personal data processed for the purposes of transit through Malaysia,[57] and
- Personal data processed by an individual only for the purposes of that individual's personal, family, or household affairs, including recreational purposes.[58]

3.5 The Seven Personal Data Protection Principles

The personal data protection principles ('PDP Principles') form the fundamental backbone of the PDPA. Section 5(1) states that a data user must comply with all the seven PDP Principles as set out in Sections 6–12. Section 5(2) states that a data user who contravenes any one of the PDP Principles shall be liable for a maximum fine of three hundred thousand ringgit (RM300,000) or subject to imprisonment for a maximum term of 2 years or both, unless his processing activity is exempted under Sections 45 or 46. The objective of these principles is to protect the interests of the

---

[51] 2nd limb of Section 2(2)(b) of the PDPA.
[52] Patrikios (2012), p. 75.
[53] Section 3(1) of the PDPA.
[54] Section 3(2) of the PDPA.
[55] Section 2(1) read together with Section 4 of the PDPA.
[56] Section 4 of the PDPA.
[57] Section 2(2)(b) of the PDPA.
[58] Section 45(1) of the PDPA.

Table 3.1 Summary of the PDP principles

Principle	Summary
General	This principle prohibits a data user from processing personal data without the consent of a data subject, and requires personal data to be processed for a lawful purpose directly related to or necessary to conduct an activity of the data user. Additionally, the personal data collected or processed should not be excessive or beyond that required for the purpose it was collected
Notice and choice	This principle requires a data user to inform a data subject of various matters relating to the information of that data subject which is being processed by or on behalf of that data user and provide means of choice to the data subject
Disclosure	This principle prohibits a data user from disclosing personal data of a data subject: (a) for any purpose other than the purpose for which the personal data was disclosed at the time of collection or for a purpose directly related to it; or (b) to any party other than the class of third parties disclosed to the data subject
Security	This principle imposes an obligation on a data user to take measures to protect personal data from loss, misuse, modification, unauthorized or accidental access or disclosure, and alteration or destruction during its processing
Retention	This principle provides that personal data shall not be retained longer than it is necessary to fulfil the purpose for which it was collected, and requires the data user to destroy or permanently delete all personal data which is no longer required
Data integrity	This principle requires a data user to take steps to ensure that all personal data is accurate, complete, not misleading and kept up-to-date
Access	This principle confers on a data subject a right of access to his own personal data and to correct it if it is inaccurate, incomplete, misleading or outdated

individuals whose personal data is being processed. Hence, the key to complying with the PDPA is to follow the seven PDP Principles religiously, unless a relevant exemption applies.

An overview of the PDP Principles is set out as follows (Table 3.1):

3.5.1 General Principle

General rule: According to Section 6(1), a data user shall not process personal data about a data subject, unless the data subject has given his consent to the processing of the personal data, and shall not process sensitive personal data about a data subject, except in accordance with the conditions laid down in Section 40.

Exceptions: Notwithstanding the above, Section 6(2) provides that the data subject's consent is not required to be obtained if the processing is necessary:
- For the performance of a contract to which the data subject is a party,
- For the taking of steps at the request of the data subject with a view to entering into a contract,
- For compliance with any legal obligation to which the data user is the subject, other than an obligation imposed by a contract,
- In order to protect the vital interests of the data subject,
- For the administration of justice, or
- For the exercise of any functions conferred on any person by or under any law.

3.5.1.1 The Meaning of 'Consent'

'Consent' is the key element under the PDPA. Generally, personal data should not be processed unless consent has been given by the data subject, although certain exceptions may apply. However, 'consent' is not defined in the PDPA. The existence and validity of consent are questions of fact in each case. It is not certain whether the consent must be expressed or explicit or whether it is acceptable if such consent is implied from the data subject's conduct.[59] The EU Data Protection Directive defines 'consent' as 'any freely given, specific, and informed indication of his wishes by which the data subject signifies his agreement to personal data relating to him being processed'.[60] This definition suggests that consent comprises the following elements:
- It involved a positive and definite act;
- The data subject must be given a genuine choice to decide whether to give consent;
- Consent must be given specifically for the particular processing activity; and
- The data subject must be given all the necessary details of the processing activity in order for him to make an informed decision.

The phrase 'the data subject must signify his agreement' is interpreted to mean that there must be some active communication between the parties.[61] No consent shall be inferred from a non-response to a communication, for instance, from a customer's failure to return or respond to a leaflet.[62] Also, consent obtained under duress or on the basis of misleading information is not valid consent.[63]

This issue is very important because marketing companies usually incorporate their processing intentions in a mail-order form or a similar document. For instance, a notice such as 'tick here if you do not wish us to share your personal data with other companies who may wish to provide you with information about goods or services that may be of interest to you' is commonly found on mail-order forms. Such an approach is called an 'opt-out,' i.e., unless the data subject indicates his wishes not to have his personal data processed, he is deemed to have given his consent to such a processing act. In reality, many data subjects do not read or even become aware of such a notice being placed on the form, especially when such a notice is placed at the bottom of the form in small print that hardly can be read by anyone. Some may not even understand the implications of their data being processed by these companies.

---

[59] Levi Strauss & Co. v Tesco plc [2002] Ch 109. The court held that whilst consent cannot be inferred from silence, it could be inferred from conduct.

[60] Art 2(h) of the EU Data Protection Directive.

[61] Legal Guidance to Data Protection Act 1998, Information Commissioner's Office, para 3.1.5, p. 29.

[62] Legal Guidance to Data Protection Act 1998, Information Commissioner's Office, para 3.1.5, p. 29.

[63] Legal Guidance to Data Protection Act 1998, Information Commissioner's Office, para 3.1.5, p. 29.

An alternative approach is called an 'opt-in,' i.e., the notice is given to the data subject, and he is given a choice to indicate his intentions regarding whether he wishes to have his personal data processed by the data user. Under this approach, in the absence of expressed consent being given in the form of a positive indication, companies cannot assume that the data subject has given his consent to the processing of any personal data for any purposes.

The Oxford English Dictionary defines 'consent' as meaning voluntary agreement, permission, or compliance.[64] Black's Law Dictionary also defines 'consent' as 'an act of reason, accompanied with deliberation, the mind weighing as in a balance the good or evil on each side'.[65] This seems to suggest that there must at least be some knowledge before consent is given. Abu Bakar Munir argues that consent here refers to a positive act. The learned author cited *Bell v Alfred Franks & Bartlett Co*,[66] in which Shaw LJ stated that 'if acquiescence can arise out of the passive failure to do anything, consent must involve a positive demonstration act, something of an affirmative kind. It is not to be implied.'[67]

As Section 6(1) provides that 'a data user shall not process personal data about a data subject, unless the data subject has given his consent to the processing of the personal data ...' one may argue that the PDPA adopts the 'opt-in' approach, i.e., a data subject has to positively indicate his intention to have his personal data be processed by the data user. This is because more often than not, a data subject has no knowledge regarding the 'opt-out' mechanism.

However, Ian Lloyd argues that at least pending any court decision either in the UK or before the ECJ, it appears that an 'opt-out' or 'opt-in' approach might still be acceptable in the UK, provided the data subject is readily able to give an indication of his wishes.[68] The learned author did suggest that the key to determining the acceptability of the approach depends on the clarity of the notice given to the data subjects. One example can be seen in *Innovations (Mail Order) Ltd v Data Protection Registrar*.[69] In that case, Innovations was in the mail-order business and also in the business of selling its customer lists to other retailers and service providers. Customers who ordered goods from Innovations were not aware of the fact that Innovations was selling their personal data. Innovations only informed the customers by way of notice when acknowledgment forms were sent to the customers. The notice informed the customers that they could have their names removed from the lists if they applied formally to Innovations. The Data Protection Tribunal (now the Information Tribunal) opined that the data were not collected fairly, because customers ought to have been informed at the time the data were collected, not later. The Tribunal held that if the purpose for which the data were

---

[64] The Oxford English Dictionary (1991) p. 310.

[65] Black's Law Dictionary (1990) p. 305.

[66] [1980] 1 All ER 356 which was subsequently applied in Trustees of the Methodist Secondary School Trust Deed v O'Leary (1993) 25 H.L.R. 364.

[67] Munir and Yasin (2002), p. 184.

[68] Lloyd (2008), pp. 98–99.

[69] Case DA/92 31/49/1.

intended to be used was not obvious at the time of collection of data, the data subject must be informed of that non-obvious purpose at that time. If the data subject was not so informed, the data subject's expressed consent must be sought before any processing can be commenced.

The above decision was followed in *British Gas Trading Ltd v Data Protection Registrar*,[70] in which British Gas Trading only inserted a note informing customers that they could opt-out of receiving any marketing materials by writing in. The Tribunal ruled against British Gas Trading, saying that customers should be given an opportunity to object, for example, by ticking an 'opt-out' box at the time data were collected from them, without having to perform a positive act like writing in.

Hence, it appears that as long as the data subject is given a reasonable opportunity to express his intentions (whether to 'opt-in' or 'opt-out') at the time of collection of data, this may be sufficient to amount to consent. The law is still unclear at this point. In this regard, guidelines or guidance notes should be issued by the PDP Commissioner in order to spell out how consent ought to be given, whether it should be performed by way of a positive indication of wishes or a mere opportunity to object to such processing.

However, it is noted that consent once given is not a permanent condition. Under Section 38, even if the data subject has previously consented to such processing, he can at any time by notice in writing request the data user to cease processing his personal data. The data user shall cease the processing of personal data upon receiving such a notice, failing which he shall be liable to a fine not exceeding one hundred thousand ringgit (RM100,000) or subject to imprisonment not exceeding 1 year or both. Although such a withdrawal of consent cannot have a retrospective effect, it would render any future processing of personal data unlawful.

In respect to sensitive personal data, Section 40(1)(a) provides that a data user shall not process any sensitive personal data, except when the data subject has given his explicit consent to such processing, unless the processing falls under one of the exceptions laid down in Section 40(1)(b) or when the information contained in the personal data has been made public as a result of steps deliberately taken by the data subject under Section 40(1)(c).

Unlike the general personal data mentioned above, the requirement for sensitive personal data is more stringent, i.e., it requires 'explicit consent'. Again, such terms are not defined in the PDPA. However, the Legal Guidance suggests that:

> The use of the word 'explicit' suggests that the consent of the data subject should be absolutely clear. In appropriate cases, it should cover the specific detail of the processing, the particular type of data to be processed (or even the specific information), the purpose of the processing and any special aspects of the processing that may affect the individual, for example, any disclosure that may be made of the data.[71]

The PDPA also does not expressly state that a data user must keep written evidence in order to prove that he has obtained consent from data subjects. However, since the onus is on the data user to prove that proper consent has been

---

[70] Case DA98 3/49/2.

[71] Legal Guidance to Data Protection Act 1998, Information Commissioner's Office, para.3.1.5.

obtained, it may be prudent for the data user to keep a record of the consents given by data subjects. The Electronic Commerce Act 2006 recognises electronic consent as amounting to a form of written consent. If consent is obtained electronically, the law requires that the record be retained in the format in which it was generated, sent, or received and that it be accessible, intelligible, and identify the origin and destination of the record and the date and time it is sent or received.[72]

3.5.1.2 How Should Personal Data Be Processed?

Section 6(3) provides that personal data shall not be processed, unless:

- The personal data is processed for a lawful purpose directly related to an activity of the data user,
- The processing of the personal data is necessary for or directly related to that purpose, and
- The personal data is adequate but not excessive in relation to that purpose.

It is noted that the above three conditions are to be read conjunctively and that all the conditions must be satisfied before any personal data can be processed. This principle imposes limits on how a data user may process the personal data.

There is no definition of what constitutes 'lawful purpose', though the meaning of 'unlawful' has been described as 'something that is contrary to some law or enactment or is one without lawful justification or excuse'.[73] The Guide states that a processing activity may be unlawful if it involves committing a criminal offence or it results in[74]:

- A breach of duty of confidence,
- A data user exceeding its legal powers or exercising those power improperly,
- An infringement of copyright,
- A breach of an enforceable contractual agreement,
- A breach of industry-specific legislation or regulations, and
- A breach of statute or common law, whether criminal or civil.

If the personal data was obtained for one purpose that the data subject has given his consent for, and subsequently, the data user wishes to use the personal data for some other purposes that are not directly related to the activity the data user consented to or are not necessary for or directly related to the original purpose, the data user must obtain fresh consent from the data subject for the subsequent use of the personal data. The Guide states that in practice, the data user must often obtain consent to use or disclose personal data for a purpose that is additional to or different from the purpose he originally obtained it for or originally envisaged.[75] For example, the purpose of conventional telephone directories is the disclosure of subscribers' telephone numbers. If one were to use the directories to find out the personal data of an unknown subscriber from a certain telephone number or to find

---

[72] Section 13 of the Electronic Commerce Act 2006.

[73] R v R [1991] 4 All ER 481.

[74] The Guide to Data Protection, Information Commissioner's Office, item 32, B1, p. 51.

[75] The Guide to Data Protection, Information Commissioner's Office, item 15, B2, p. 56.

out the names and telephone numbers of the persons living in a particular area, this would be another use that is completely different from what a subscriber would expect when agreeing to be included in the directories.[76] Another example is when employees' personal data collected for payroll purposes cannot be further used for direct marketing purposes without obtaining fresh consent from the employees.[77]

In respect to the adequacy and non-excessiveness of the personal data, this depends on the purpose of the processing activity. According to the Guide, in complying with this principle, data controller (data user) should identify the minimum amount of personal data that is required in order to fulfill this purpose, which is a question of fact in each case.[78] The general rule is that a data controller (data user) should not collect excessive data that is not needed or irrelevant for the purposes of processing the personal data. Where sensitive personal data is involved, it is even more important to ensure that only a minimum amount of data should be collected.[79] If a data controller (data user) needs to collect particular data about only certain data subjects, he should collect it from those particular data subjects only and not all data subjects, because it is likely to be excessive in relation to the rest of the data subjects.[80] A data controller (data user) should not collect personal data on the basis that it might be useful in the future, without a view of how it will be used. However, it is permissible to collect data for a foreseeable event that may never occur, such as when an employer collects details regarding the blood types of employees engaged in hazardous occupations.[81]

For example, employers may need to know (for certain posts) if the potential job applicants have a car and a driver's license, so it would be acceptable for the employers to ask for such information. However, it would not be acceptable for the employers to ask for the model or the color of the job applicants' cars.[82]

3.5.2 Notice and Choice Principle

Section 7(1) states that a data user has a duty to inform a data subject by way of written notice:
- That the personal data of the data subject is being processed by or on behalf of the data user, and a description of the personal data shall be provided to the data subject,

---

[76] Article 29 Working Party, Opinion 5/2000 on the Use of Public Directories for Reverse or Multi-criteria Searching Services.

[77] Article 29 Working Party, Opinion 8/2001 on the Processing of Personal Data in the Employment Context.

[78] The Guide to Data Protection, Information Commissioner's Office, item 8, B3, p. 59.

[79] The Guide to Data Protection, Information Commissioner's Office, item 13, B3, p. 60.

[80] The Guide to Data Protection, Information Commissioner's Office, item 14, B3, p. 60.

[81] The Guide to Data Protection, Information Commissioner's Office, item 14, B3, p. 60.

[82] The Guide to Data Protection, Information Commissioner's Office, item 14, B3, p. 60.

- Of the purposes for which the personal data is being or will be collected and further processed,
- Of any information available to the data user as to the source of that personal data,
- That the data subject has the right to request access to and the right to request for the correction of the personal data, including how to contact the data user with any inquiries or complaints in respect to the personal data,
- Of the class of third parties to whom the data user discloses or may disclose the personal data,
- Of the choices and means the data user offers the data subject for limiting the processing of personal data, including personal data relating to other persons who may be identified from that personal data,
- Whether it is obligatory or voluntary for the data subject to supply the personal data, and
- When it is obligatory for the data subject to supply the personal data, the consequences for the data subject if he or she should fail to supply the personal data.

The requirements under Section 7(1) are to be read conjunctively, i.e., a data user must comply with all of the above requirements (if applicable).[83] The simplest way to comply with this principle is by way of a 'privacy notice' incorporating all of the above requirements.[84] The intention of this principle is to require data users to be open and transparent about their processing activities so as to empower data subjects by making them aware of what personal data is being collected and processed.[85]

Pursuant to Section 7(2), the written notice under Section 7(1) shall be given as soon as practicable by the data user:
- When the data subject is first asked by the data user to provide his personal data,
- When the data user first collects the personal data of the data subject, or
- Before the data user uses the personal data of the data subject for a purpose other than the purpose for which the personal data was collected or discloses the personal data to a third party.

Section 7(3) further provides that such notice shall be in the National and English languages and that the data subject shall be provided with a clear and readily accessible means of exercising his choice.

It is submitted that Section 7(2) is giving effect to the decisions in *Innovations* and *British Gas Trading* mentioned above, in which the Tribunal ruled that the data controller (data user) ought to give notice to the data subject about the purpose of such collection of data at the time of collection.

---

[83] Munir and Yasin (2010a), MLJ cxix, p. 8.

[84] See the 'Privacy Notices Code of Practice', Information Commissioner's Office.

[85] Jay and Hamilton (1999), p. 222.

3.5.3 Disclosure Principle

Section 8 states that subject to the exceptions laid down in Section 39,[86] in the absence of the consent of the data subject, personal data shall not be disclosed:
1) For any purpose other than
   - The purpose for which the personal data was to be disclosed at the time of collection of the personal data or
   - A purpose directly related to the purpose referred to in the above paragraph or
2) To any party other than a third party of the class of third parties specified in Section 7(1)(e).

In short, this principle says that a data user shall not disclose personal data:
- For purposes other than those that were already disclosed at the time of collection,
- For purposes that are not directly related to the purpose for which the personal data were to be disclosed at the time of collection, or
- To any third party other than those that were already disclosed in the written notice to the data subject.

3.5.4 Security Principle

Section 9(1) requires that a data user shall take practical steps to protect the personal data from any loss, misuse, modification, unauthorized or accidental access or disclosure, alteration or destruction by having regard to:
- The nature of the personal data and the harm that would result from such loss, misuse, modification, unauthorized or accidental access or disclosure, alteration, or destruction,
- The place or location where the personal data is stored,
- Any security measures incorporated into any equipment in which the personal data is stored,
- The measures taken for ensuring the reliability integrity and competence of personnel having access to the personal data, and
- The measures taken for ensuring the secure transfer of the personal data.

---

[86] Section 39 of the PDPA provides that notwithstanding Section 8, personal data of a data subject may be disclosed by a data user for any other purposes only if the data subject has given his consent to such disclosure; the disclosure is necessary for the purpose of preventing or detecting a crime, or for investigations, or was required or authorised by or under any law or by the order of a court; or the disclosure was justified as being in the public interest in circumstances as determined by the Minister.

According to the Guide, in order to comply with this principle, a data controller (data user) should[87]:

- Design and organise the security measures to fit the nature of the personal data he holds and the harm that may result from a data security breach;
- Be clear about who in the organisation is responsible for ensuring data security;
- Make sure he has the right physical and technical security, backed up by robust policies and procedures and reliable, well-trained staff; and
- Be ready to respond to any data security breach swiftly and effectively.

In taking security measures, one could take into account the physical security of the premises; the security measures incorporated into the computer systems, such as firewalls, passwords, and encryption controls; the level of training and supervision of employees; and the manner in which data and equipment is disposed of.[88] For example, in disposing of the computers, the data users should make sure that all data in the computer's memory are permanently destroyed and cannot be retrieved in any manner. Data users should also install secure and highly reliable systems in order to prevent any unauthorised access, such as hacking or cracking.[89] Any unauthorised access to computer data is an offence under the Computer Crimes Act 1997. Some companies and organisations adopt technical standards such as the Information Security Management System (ISMS) and other technical audit approaches based on specific industry sector requirements. Adopting these standards and approaches may help companies and organisations in complying with the security principle.[90]

Section 9(2) states that when the processing of personal data is carried out by a data processor on behalf of the data user, the data user shall ensure that the data processor also complies with the security principle, such as requiring the data processor to provide sufficient guarantees in respect to the technical and organizational security measures governing the processing to be carried out and to take reasonable steps[91] to ensure compliance with those measures.

3.5.5 Retention Principle

According to Section 10, the personal data processed for any purpose shall not be kept longer than is necessary for the fulfillment of that purpose. The data user has a duty to take all reasonable steps to ensure that all personal data is destroyed or

---

[87] The Guide to Data Protection, Information Commissioner's Office, item 4 B5, p. 73.

[88] Lloyd (2008), p. 115.

[89] Jawahitha et al. (2007), p. 736.

[90] A leading international best practice known as ISO 27001 is available via http://www.itgovernance.co.uk/iso27001.aspx.

[91] Some of the suggested reasonable steps are such as obtain references; consider how long the proposed data processor has been in business; obtain technical information as to how the security system is to be operated and have it evaluated by a processing expert; ask for reports as to compliance or any breaches of security on a timely manner; ensure the guarantees offered by the processing company are worth the paper it is written on. See Paul Stephenson and Alisa Kwan, (n 53, p 332).

permanently deleted if it is no longer required for the purpose for which it was to be processed. A data user's obligations under the PDPA begin from the moment he collects the personal data until the time when the personal data has been returned, deleted, or destroyed.[92]

According to the Guide, in order to comply with this principle, a controller (data user) should[93]:
- Review the length of time he keeps personal data;
- Consider the purpose or purposes he holds the personal data for in deciding whether (and for how long) to retain it;
- Securely delete personal data that is no longer needed for this purpose or these purposes; and
- Update, archive, or securely delete personal data if it goes out of date.

This principle requires the data user to regularly review the personal data he holds and to delete personal data that is no longer of value or relevance to the data user's activities.[94] Personal data that the data user no longer needs to access regularly, but which still needs to be retained should be securely archived. It is a good practice to maintain a data retention policy that clearly sets out the retention periods for different categories of personal data, how data should be retained, archived, or deleted after a certain period of time, and audit and review mechanisms.[95]

The retention period depends on the purposes for which the personal data is retained. If it is necessary to retain the personal data for one of the reasons set out in Section 6(2) of the PDPA, such as for the performance of a contract or for compliance with any legal obligation, then the personal data should continue to be retained for as long as the reason applies. Where personal data is retained for more than one purpose, the personal data should continue to be retained until it is no longer needed for all purposes. When personal data is shared between organisations, the shared personal data should be returned to the organisation that supplied it, without keeping a copy for themselves.[96] However, personal data should not be retained indefinitely just because there is a small possibility that it may be needed in the future.

Personal data may be retained so that data user may defend any future legal claims. Certain laws and regulations (such as those related to tax or employment laws) may also require personal data be retained for a certain prescribed period of time. Some of these laws and regulations are as shown in the table below (Table 3.2):

---

[92] The Guide to Data Protection, Information Commissioner's Office, item 35 A3, p. 31.
[93] The Guide to Data Protection, Information Commissioner's Office, item 4 B5, p. 73.
[94] Lloyd (2008), p. 114.
[95] The Guide to Data Protection, Information Commissioner's Office, items 7-9 B5, p. 74.
[96] Section 13 of the Electronic Commerce Act 2006.

Table 3.2 Laws and regulations that stipulate retention period

Law/regulation	Subject matter of retention provision	Retention period
Section 6(1)(a) Limitation Act 1953	Any records which may be relevant in relation to any potential claim/dispute/litigation arising out of contract or tort	Six years from the date on which the cause of action accrued
Section 6(1)(d) Limitation Act 1953	Any records which may be relevant in relation to any potential claim/dispute/litigation arising out of an action for any sum recoverable by virtue of any written law other than a penalty or forfeiture or of a sum by way of penalty or forfeiture	Six years from the date on which the cause of action accrued
Section 9 Limitation Act 1953	Any records which may be relevant in relation to any potential claim/dispute/litigation arising out of an action to recover land	Twelve years from the date on which the cause of action accrued
Section 6(3) Limitation Act 1953	Any records which may be relevant to an action to recover on a judgment	Twelve years from the date the judgment becomes enforceable
Section 7 Civil Law Act 1956 (Revised 1972)	Any records relevant to the wrongful act, neglect or default which resulted in the death of the person	The Civil Law Act 1956 states that actions in relation to wrongful act, neglect or default, causing death shall be brought within 3 years after the death of the person deceased
Section 61 Employment Act 1955	A register containing information regarding each employee	Not less than 6 years after the recording thereof
Section 42(2) Employees Provident Fund Act 1991	A register containing particulars of each employee	Not less than 6 years after the recording thereof
Section 11(3) Employees' Social Security Act 1969/ Regulation 71 Employees' Social Security (General) Regulations 1971	A report setting out particulars of injured employee and accident	Not less than 5 years from the date of its completion
Section 82 and 82A Income Tax Act 1967	Records includes: (a) Books of account recording receipts and payments of income or expenditure; (b) Invoices, vouchers, receipts and such other documents as in the opinion of the Director General of Inland Revenue ('DGIR') are necessary to verify the entries in any books of account; and	Seven years from the end of the year to which any income from that business relates

(continued)

Table 3.2 (continued)

Law/regulation	Subject matter of retention provision	Retention period
	(c) Any other records as may be specified by the DGIR under Section 82(3)	
Section 18 Sales Tax Act 1972	Records written up to date of all transactions which affect or may affect the taxable person's liability to sales tax	Six years from the latest date to which such records relate
Section 11 Service Tax Act 1975	Records written up to date of all transactions which affect or may affect the taxable person's liability to service tax	Six years from the latest date to which the books of account, records and invoices relate
Chapter 20, Bar Council Ruling 2008	Retention of clients' files by solicitors	Conveyancing files: 12 years General litigation files: 6 years Unenforced judgment: 12 years from the date of judgment Probate and administration: 12 years Family matters: 6 years General matters: 6 years

3.5.6 Data Integrity Principle

Section 11 requires a data user to take reasonable steps to ensure that the personal data is accurate, complete, not misleading and kept up-to-date by considering the purpose, including any directly related purposes, for which the personal data were collected and further processed. The word 'accurate' is not defined. The DPA 1998 (UK) states that data is inaccurate if it is incorrect or misleading as to any matter of fact. According to the Guide, in order to comply with this principle, a data controller (data user) should[97]:

- Take reasonable steps to ensure the accuracy of any personal data he obtains;
- Ensure that the source of any personal data is clear;
- Carefully consider any challenges to the accuracy of information; and
- Consider whether it is necessary to update the information.

The PDPA does not prescribe the methods to ensure that the personal data is accurate. It merely requires the data user to take reasonable steps to ensure that the personal data is accurate. The Guide states that what amounts to 'reasonable steps' will depend on the circumstances and the nature of the personal data and what it will be used for. It says that if a data controller (data user) will be using the personal data in making decisions that may significantly affect a data subject or others, the data controller (data user) will have to put more effort into ensuring accuracy. If the

---

[97] The Guide to Data Protection, Information Commissioner's Office, item 5 B4, p. 64.

personal data is given by the data subject himself or by a reliable source, it will be reasonable to assume that the personal data is accurate.[98]

As to the question of whether updating is required, this would depend on the nature of the data and the purpose for which the data is processed. If the data is merely to be used as an historical record of a transaction between the data user and the data subject, no updating is required. However, when the personal data has a material impact on making certain decisions or taking certain actions, such as when the personal data is used to decide whether to grant credit or confer or withhold some other benefit, regular updating may be required.[99] This data integrity principle is linked to the data subject's right to correct his personal data in order to ensure that it is accurate, complete, not misleading, and up-to-date under Section 34 of the PDPA.

3.5.7 Access Principle

Section 12 also provides that a data subject shall be given access to his personal data held by a data user and be able to correct that personal data when the personal data is inaccurate, incomplete, misleading, or not up-to-date, except when compliance with a request for such access or correction is refused under the PDPA.

3.6 Exemptions

The PDPA provides for two types of exemptions—total and partial. Total exemption means the PDPA shall not apply at all. Partial exemption means certain PDP Principles and other related provisions of the PDPA shall not apply to some processing activities.[100] The Minister also has the power to exempt the application of any of the PDP Principles to any data user or impose any terms or conditions as he thinks fit (Table 3.3).[101]

3.7 Rights of Data Subject

The PDPA confers a number of rights to the data subject (Table 3.4):

---

[98] The Guide to Data Protection, Information Commissioner's Office, item 5 B4, p. 68.
[99] Legal Guidance to Data Protection Act 1998, Information Commissioner's Office, para 3.4, p. 38.
[100] Section 45 of the PDPA.
[101] Section 46 of the PDPA.

Table 3.3 Exemptions

Section	Processing activity	Exemption
45(1)	**Personal, family or household affairs** Personal data processed only for the purposes of an individual's personal, family or household affairs, which include recreational purposes	Total exemption
45(2)(a)	**Crime and taxation** Personal data processed for: (i) The prevention of detection of crime; (ii) The apprehension or prosecution of offenders; or (iii) The assessment or collection of any tax or duty or any other imposition of a similar nature.	General Principle; Notice and Choice Principle; Disclosure Principle; and Access Principle.
45(2)(b)	**Physical and mental health** Personal data processed in relation to information of the physical or mental health of a data subject	Access Principle
45(2)(c)	**Research and statistics** Personal data processed for preparing statistics or carrying out research, provided such personal data is not processed for any other purpose and that the resulting statistics or the result of the research are not made available in a form which identifies the data subject	General Principle; Notice and Choice Principle; Disclosure Principle; and Access Principle.
45(2)(d)	**Order or judgment of a court** Personal data processed for the purpose of or in connection with any order or judgment of a court	General Principle; Notice and Choice Principle; Disclosure Principle; and Access Principle.
45(2)(e)	**Discharge of regulatory functions** Personal data processed for the purpose of discharging regulatory functions	General principle; Notice and Choice principle; Disclosure principle; Access principle.
45(2)(f)	**Journalism, literature and art** Personal data processed only for journalistic, literary or artistic purposes provided the following three conditions are satisfied: (i) The processing is undertaken with a view to the publication by any person of the journalistic, literary or artistic material; (ii) The data user reasonably believes that, the publication would be in the public interest; (iii) The data user reasonably believes that in all the circumstances, compliance with the provisions in respect of which the exemption is claimed is incompatible with the journalistic, literary or artistic purposes.	General Principle; Notice and Choice Principle; Disclosure Principle; Retention Principle; Data Integrity Principle; and Access Principle.

3.8 Criminal Offences

The PDPA creates a number of new criminal offences for the failure to comply with the provisions under the PDPA (Table 3.5):

Table 3.4 Rights of data subject

Section	Right	Explanatory statement
30	Right of access to personal data	A data subject is entitled to be informed by a data user whether his personal data is being processed by or on behalf of the data user. A requestor (the data subject or the relevant person on behalf of the data subject) may, upon payment of a prescribed fee, make a data access request in writing to the data user for information of the data subject's personal data that is being processed and to have communicated to him a copy of the personal data in intelligible form
34	Right to correct personal data	Where a copy of the personal data has been supplied by the data user in compliance with the data access request and the requestor considers or the data subject knows that the personal data is inaccurate, incomplete, misleading or not up-to-date, the requestor or the data subject may make a data correction request in writing to the data user that the data user make the necessary correction to the personal data
38	Right to withdraw consent	A data subject may by notice in writing withdraw his consent to the processing of personal data in respect of which he is the data subject. The data user shall, upon receiving the notice, cease the processing of the personal data
42	Right to prevent processing likely to cause damage or distress	A data subject may, at anytime by notice in writing to a data user, require the data user to cease or not begin the processing of or processing for a specified purpose or in a specified manner, of any personal data based on the reasons that the processing of that personal data is causing or likely to cause substantial damage or substantial distress to him or to another; and the damage or distress is or would be unwarranted
43	Right to prevent processing for purposes of direct marketing	A data subject may, at anytime by notice in writing to a data user, require the data user to cease or not to begin processing his personal data for purposes of direct marketing. 'Direct marketing' is defined as the communication by whatever means of any advertising or marketing material which is directed to a particular individuals. The phrase 'communication by whatever means' is wide enough to cover any means of communications, whether electronic or non-electronic

Table 3.5 Criminal offences

Section	Criminal offence	Penalty
5(2)	Failure to comply with any one of the PDP principles	Fine not more than RM300,000 or imprisonment for a term not more than 2 years; or both
16(4)	Failure to register as data user for specified class of data users and processing personal data without a certificate of registration issued by the Commissioner	Fine not more than RM500,000 or imprisonment for a term not more than 3 years; or both
18(4)	Continue to process personal data after the registration is revoked.	Fine not more than RM500,000 or imprisonment for a term not more than 3 years; or both
19(2)	Failure to surrender the certificate of registration to the Commissioner after it is revoked	Fine not more than RM200,000 or imprisonment for a term not more than 2 years; or both
29	Failure to comply with any provision of the code of practice that is applicable to the data user	Fine not more than RM100,000 or imprisonment for a term not more than 1 year; or both
38(4)	Continue to process personal data after withdrawal of consent by the data subject	Fine not more than RM100,000 or imprisonment for a term not more than 1 year; or both
40(3)	Processing sensitive personal data without complying with the conditions stated under Section 40(1)	Fine not more than RM200,000 or imprisonment for a term not more than 2 years; or both
42(6)	Failure to comply with the Commissioner's requirements to cease processing personal data that is likely to cause damage or distress	Fine not more than RM200,000 or imprisonment for a term not more than 2 years; or both
43(4)	Failure to comply with the Commissioner's requirements to cease processing personal data for purposes of direct marketing	Fine not more than RM200,000 or imprisonment for a term not more than 2 years; or both
108(8)	Failure to comply with an enforcement notice	Fine not more than RM200,000 or imprisonment for a term not more than 2 years; or both
129(5)	Transfer any personal data to a place outside Malaysia which has not been specified by the Minister and published in the *Gazette*	Fine not more than RM300,000 or imprisonment for a term not more than 2 years; or both
130(1) and (7)	Unlawfully collect or disclose of personal data or procure the disclosure of personal data that is held by the data user without the consent of the data user	Fine not more than RM500,000 or imprisonment for a term not more than 3 years; or both
130(4)(5) and (7)	Sale or offer to sell personal data	Fine not more than RM500,000 or imprisonment for a term not more than 3 years; or both
131	Abet the commission of, or attempts to commit, or does any act preparatory to in furtherance of the commission of any offence under the PDPA	Imprisonment for a term not more than one-half of the maximum term provided for the offence

(continued)

Table 3.5 (continued)

Section	Criminal offence	Penalty
133(1)	If a body corporate commits an offence under the PDPA, the director, CEO, COO, manager, secretary or other similar officer may be liable severally or jointly in the same proceedings with the body corporate, unless he can prove that: (a) the offence was committed without his knowledge, consent or connivance; and (b) he had taken all reasonable precautions and exercised due diligence to prevent the commission of the offence.	Joint and several liability
133(2)	A person would be similarly liable for act, omission, neglect or default committed by his employee, agent, or employee of the agent	Vicarious liability

References

Article 29 Working Party, Opinion 5/2000 on the Use of Public Directories for Reverse or Multi-criteria Searching Services. http://ec.europa.eu/justice/policies/privacy/docs/wpdocs/2000/wp33en.pdf. Accessed 18 May 2012

Article 29 Working Party, Opinion 8/2001 on the Processing of Personal Data in the Employment Context. http://ec.europa.eu/justice/policies/privacy/docs/wpdocs/2001/wp48en.pdf. Accessed 18 May 2012

Quick Reference Guide – What is Personal Data?. Information Commissioner's Office. http://www.ico.gov.uk/upload/documents/library/data_protection/detailed_specialist_guides/160408_v1.0_determining_what_is_personal_data_-_quick_reference_guide.pdf> and a detailed 'Technical Guidance Note – What is Data?', available via http://www.ico.gov.uk/upload/documents/determining_what_is_personal_data/whatispersonaldata2.htm. Accessed 13 Jun 2012

Bainbridge D (2008) Introduction to Information Technology Law, 6th edn. Pearson, Essex

Berthold M, Wacks R (2003) Hong Kong Data Privacy Law: territorial regulation in a borderless world, 2nd edn. Sweet & Maxwell Asia, Hong Kong

Black's Law Dictionary (1990) 6th edn. St. Paul., West Publishing Co. This was cited by Stirling J in Re Smith (59 LJ Ch 284), p. 305

Legal Guidance to Data Protection Act 1998. Information Commissioner's Office. http://www.ico.gov.uk/upload/documents/library/data_protection/detailed_specialist_guides/data_protection_act_legal_guidance.pdf. Accessed 1 Jun 2012

Greenleaf G (2012) ASEAN 'New' Data Privacy Laws: Malaysia, the Philippines and Singapore, Privacy Laws & Business International Report, Issue 116, UNSW Law Research Paper No. 2012–14. http://papers.ssrn.com/sol3/papers.cfm?abstract_id=2049234&http://www.google.com.my/url?sa=t&rct=j&q=&esrc=s&source=web&cd=1&sqi=2&ved=0CE4QFjAA&url=http%3A%2F%2Fpapers.ssrn.com%2Fsol3%2FDelivery.cfm%2FSSRN_ID2049234_code722134.pdf%3Fabstractid%3D2049234%26mirid%3D1&ei=aBDxT9LbJM3JrAf8w8G9DQ&usg=AFQjCNHfJpPF4IPqeIH6UQIleNn1NmdVnw&sig2=mHYmPdDMlI_wS8mjMDusAQ. Accessed 24 May 2012

Hawkins JM, Allen R (eds) (1991) The Oxford English Dictionary. Clarendon, Oxford, p. 310

Jawahitha S, Ishak M, Mazahir M (2007) E-Data Privacy and the Personal Data Protection Bill of Malaysia. J Appl Sci 7(5):732–742, http://scialert.net/qredirect.php?doi=jas.2007.732.742&linkid=pdf. Accessed 26 May 2012

Jay R, Hamilton A (1999) Data protection law and practice, 1st edn. London, Sweet & Maxwell

Lloyd I (2008) Information Technology Law, 5th edn. Oxford University Press, Oxford

Munir AB, Yasin SH (2002) Privacy and data protection. Sweet and Maxwell Asia, Kuala Lumpur

Munir AB, Yasin SH (2010a) The Personal Data Protection Bill 2009, [2010] MLJ cxix

Munir AB, Yasin SH (2010b) Personal data protection in Malaysia. Law and practice. Sweet and Maxwell Asia, Kuala Lumpur

Opinion 4/2007 on the Concept of Personal Data (2007) http://ec.europa.eu/justice/policies/privacy/docs/wpdocs/2007/wp136_en.pdf. Accessed 5 Jun 2012

Outsourcing: A Guide for Small and Medium-Sized Businesses, Information Commissioner's Office, which gives more advice about using data processors. http://www.ico.gov.uk/upload/documents/library/data_protection/detailed_specialist_guides/outsourcing_gpn_version_2.1_080409.pdf. Accessed 13 Jun 2012

Pastor N (2012) Chapter Four, Data protection concept. In: European Privacy, Law and Practice for Data Protection Professionals. IAPP Publication, p. 62

Patrikios A (2012) Chapter Five, Application of the law. In: European Privacy, Law and Practice for Data Protection Professionals. IAPP Publication, p. 75

Privacy Notices Code of Practice, Information Commissioner's Office. http://www.ico.gov.uk/upload/documents/library/data_protection/detailed_specialist_guides/privacy_notices_cop_final.pdf. Accessed 13 Jun 2012

Stephenson P, Kwan A (2007) Cyberlaw in Hong Kong, 2nd edn. LexisNexis, Hong Kong, pp. 330–331

Technical Guidance Note – Determining What is Data?. Information Commissioner's Office. http://www.ico.gov.uk/upload/documents/determining_what_is_personal_data/whatispersonaldata2.htm. Accessed 6 Jun 2012

The Durant Case and Its Impact on the Interpretation of the Data Protection Act. Information Commissioner's Office. http://www.ico.gov.uk/upload/documents/library/data_protection/detailed_specialist_guides/the_durant_case_and_its_impact_on_the_interpretation_of_the_data_protection_act.pdf. Accessed 5 Jun 2012

The Guide to Data Protection. Information Commissioner's Office. http://www.ico.gov.uk/for_organisations/data_protection/the_guide.aspx. Accessed 1 Jun 2012

Working Party document No WP 105: Working document on data protection issues related to RFID Technology (2005) http://www.iot-visitthefuture.eu/fileadmin/documents/dataprotection/190105_Working_Document_on_Data_Protection_Issues_29_wp105_en.pdf. Accessed 10 Jun 2012

Limitations of the Personal Data Protection Act 2010 and Personal Data Protection in Selected Sectors

Edwin Lee Yong Cieh

> *There are three methods to gaining wisdom. The first is reflection, which is the highest. The second is limitation, which is the easiest. The third is experience, which is the bitterest*
> (Confucius, 551-479 BC, Teacher, Editor, Politician and Philosopher)

Abstract
While it is commendable that the Personal Data Protection Act 2010 ('PDPA') was finally passed by the Malaysian parliament after a long wait of a decade, the PDPA has received several criticisms due to its peculiar limitations. This chapter addresses many of these limitations and draws comparative analysis with data protection law in other jurisdictions. In addition to the PDPA, there are also several sectoral rules and regulations which specifically govern processing of personal data in certain sectors such as the banking and financial institutions sectors, healthcare sector, insurance sector, telecommunications and multimedia sectors. The Malaysian Parliament also passed the Credit Reporting Agencies Act 2010 to govern the processing of credit information by credit reporting agency in Malaysia. The author examines the relevant rules and regulations in these respective sectors.

E.L. Yong Cieh (✉)
Christopher Lee & Co, 25-2, Block B, Jaya One Section 13, Petaling Jaya 46200, Malaysia
e-mail: edwin@christopherleeco.com

4.1 Limitations of the Personal Data Protection Act 2010

4.1.1 The PDPA Does Not Apply to the Federal and State Governments

Clause 3(1) of the earlier draft of the Personal Data Protection Bill ('PDP Bill') specifically stated that 'this Act shall bind the Government'. However, this position had been totally changed. Section 3(1) of the Personal Data Protection Act ('PDPA') states that 'this Act shall not apply to the Federal Government and State Governments'. No reason has been proffered as to why there was such a drastic change.

Federal and State Governments[1] are not defined in the PDPA. Section 3 of the Interpretation Acts 1948 and 1967 (Consolidated and Revised 1989) defines 'Federal Government' as the Government of Malaysia, and 'State Government' as the Government of a State. Logically, the definition would include the Cabinet, which is assisted by the respective Ministries (for Federal Government), and the Chief Minister who is assisted by the respective State departments (for State Government). What is not clear is about those Government departments that are established to carry out public and administration duties for the respective Ministries and State departments. For example, the Royal Malaysian Police Force, the Immigration Department of Malaysia, the National Registration Department, and the Prison Department of Malaysia under the Ministry of Home Affairs; the Inland Revenue Department under the Ministry of Finance, hold and process large amount of individuals' personal and financial data. Are they considered to form part of the Government?

What about local authority, which is established under the Local Government Act 1976?[2]

In *Ganad Media Sdn Bhd v Dato' Bandar Kuala Lumpur (No.2)*,[3] the High Court held that as local authority is not free from governmental control and is subservient to the Minister responsible for the local authority, it is therefore considered to be a Government department.[4] However, another High Court in *Muniandy a/l*

---

[1] Malaysia is a federation of 13 states. There is a federal government that functions under the Federal Constitution and 13 states governments that functions under the Federal Constitution and their own state constitution.

[2] Section 2 of the Local Government Act 1976 (Act 171) defines 'local authority' to include any City Council, Municipal Council or District Council, as the case may be, and in relation to the Federal Territory, it means the Commissioner of the City of Kuala Lumpur. Local authority is also similarly defined in Section 3 of the Interpretation Acts 1948 and 1967 (Act 388) to include any municipal council, town council, town board, local council, rural board, sanitary board or similar local authority established by a written law.

[3] [2002] 1 MLJ 508. The court followed the decision of another High Court in Yap Ea Teck v Yang DiPertua Majlis Daerah, Kota Tinggi, Johor [1995] 2 BLJ 157, [1995] MLJ 55.

[4] The courts said that as the State Government may from time to time give the local government directions of a general character on the policy to be followed in the exercise of the powers conferred and the duties imposed on the local government, therefore, local government is part of the government.

Subramanian v Majlis Perbandaran Langkawi Bandaraya Pelancongan[5] refused to follow that case, and held that local authority is not a Government department. According to the court, where the meaning of the words in the statute is plain, clear, and unambiguous, judges should not invent fancy ambiguities, or rewrite the statute and give it another meaning. The Interpretation Acts 1948 and 1967 clearly defined the meaning of Federal and State Government. The Government Proceedings Act 1956 which governs all proceedings by and against the Federal and the State Government also defines "Government" in the same fashion as the Interpretation Acts 1948 and 1967. The element of governmental control and supervision are not mentioned in these two pieces of legislation as a requirement for any agency to be a Government department. Had the Parliament intended to include local authority in the legislation, it would have done so. This view was echoed by another High Court in the case of *Abdul Aziz bin Mohamed Ginan v Datuk Bandar Kuala Lumpur*,[6] where the court held that unlike Government departments such as the Road Transport Department, the Immigration Department, the Police Department or the Department of Customs and Excise, a local authority is not a Government department.

Applying the same reasoning in *Muniandy a/l Subramaniam* and *Abdul Aziz*, it is submitted that had the Parliament intended to exclude the local authority from the application of the PDPA, it would have expressly stated under the PDPA. For example, in Section 3 Occupational Safety and Health Act 1994, Section 3 Development Financial Institutions Act 2002, Section 3 Stamp Duty (Exemption) (No.12) Order 1997, the term 'Government' is expressly defined to include Federal Government, State Government, and local authority. By omitting the terms 'local authority' from the definition of 'Federal and State Governments' in the PDPA, it could be inferred that the local authority is not exempted from the application of the PDPA.

In respect of those agencies and statutory bodies established under the Acts of Parliament or State Enactments to perform specific public functions, such as Bank Negara Malaysia,[7] Employees Provident Fund,[8] Securities Commission,[9] Companies Commission of Malaysia,[10] it is submitted that as these bodies are established under their respective Acts of Parliament, and may sue and be sued in their own name, they are unlikely to be considered part of the Federal and State Governments.

Furthermore, many economic activities in the provision of electricity, telecommunications, and postal services in Malaysia have been corporatised or privatised. Examples of these entities are Tenaga Nasional Berhad, Telekom

---

[5] [2003] 6 MLJ 177.

[6] [2007] 3 MLJ 12.

[7] Central Bank of Malaysia Act 2009 (Act 701).

[8] Employees Provident Fund Act 1991 (Act 452).

[9] Securities Commission Act 1993 (Act 498).

[10] Companies Commission of Malaysia Act 2001 (Act 614).

Malaysia, and Pos Malaysia. The Federal Government, through the Ministry of Finance, has also invested in various business sectors by way of institutional shareholdings in several government-linked companies.[11] It is submitted that as these entities are incorporated bodies under the Companies Act 1965, they would not fall under the purview of the Federal and State Governments, despite their close link with the Government.

According to the Minister, the reason the PDPA does not apply to the Federal and State Governments, is because the Government already possesses sufficient legal mechanisms, such as the Official Secrets Act 1972 ('OSA 1972') to protect and safeguard the personal data held by the Government.[12] It is humbly submitted that this view may not be entirely correct.

First of all, the OSA 1972 was enacted to protect official secrets. An 'official secret' is defined as any document specified in the Schedule, and any information and material relating thereto, and includes any other official document, information, and material which may be classified as 'top secret', 'secret', 'confidential', or 'restricted', as the case may be, by a Minister, the Chief Minister of a State, or other such public officers.[13] According to the Schedule to the OSA 1972, documents such as Cabinet documents, State Executive Council documents, any documents concerning national security, defence, and international relations, are classified as official secrets. It is therefore clear that not all data processed by the Government would automatically fall under the OSA 1972; therefore, to say that the OSA 1972 is sufficient to protect and safeguard data held by the Government is misleading. Furthermore, assuming all data are automatically protected under the OSA 1972, the Act does not have clear provisions to regulate the way data ought to be collected, kept, processed, or even transmitted between Government departments. There is no other legislation that regulates how personal data is processed and stored by Government departments.

During the parliamentary debate, several Members of Parliament ('MPs') questioned the rationale for excluding the Government from the application of the PDPA.[14] The Minister, in his reply, acknowledged that while the Government has always processed personal data of its people, processing is carried out for the purposes of administering public duties and handling claims and so on. Hence, the rationale behind such exclusion is to avoid hampering the administration of the Government in carry out its public duty.[15] Besides, as the Government is not

---

[11] Examples are such as Khazanah Nasional Berhad and Permodalan Nasional Berhad.

[12] Yeng (2009).

[13] Section 2 of the Official Secrets Act 1972 (Act 88).

[14] Parliamentary Debates, (House of Representatives), Twelfth Parliament, Third Session, First Meeting, 5 April 2010, Tuan Lim Lip Eng (Segambut), p. 117; Prof Dr. P Ramasamy (Batu Kawan), p. 128; Tuan Sim Tong Him (Kota Melaka), p. 144.

[15] Parliamentary Debates, (House of Representatives), Twelfth Parliament, Third Session, First Meeting, 5 April 2010, Dato' Seri Utama Dr Rais Yatim, p. 147.

involved in the processing of any personal data in respect of commercial transactions, it does not therefore fall within the context of the PDPA.[16]

However, it is not necessary to exclude the Government from the application of the PDPA, as the PDPA provides certain exemptions that could be relied upon by data users (in this case, it would be the Government) who process personal data for the purposes of administering public duties, such as for the prevention or detection of crime, the apprehension or prosecution of offenders, the assessment or collection of any tax or duty,[17] or discharging regulatory functions.[18] Under these exemptions, data users are exempt from complying with certain Personal Data Protection Principles ('PDP Principles'). These exemptions are meant to facilitate Government departments and regulatory bodies in performing and discharging their public duties. Now, assuming Government departments and regulatory bodies are considered as forming part of the Government, these exemptions will be redundant.

It is noted that massive amounts of personal data are processed and stored by Government departments, regulatory bodies and agencies for various reasons and purposes, making the Government one of the biggest data users in the country. One of the objectives behind the PDPA is to safeguard personal data by requiring data users to comply with certain obligations, and conferring certain rights to the data subject in respect of his personal data. To exclude the Government from the application of the PDPA will have far-reaching legal implications. It would be contrary to the underlying objective of the PDPA,[19] and inconsistent with the practice in other jurisdictions where governments are bound by their respective data protection or privacy legislation.

4.1.2 The PDPA Only Applies to Processing of Personal Data in Commercial Transactions

Section 2(1) of the PDPA asserts that the PDPA applies to any person who processes, has control over, or authorises the processing of any personal data in respect of commercial transactions. 'Commercial transaction' is further defined in Section 4 as 'any transaction of a commercial nature, whether contractual or not, which includes any matters relating to the supply or exchange of goods or services, agency, investments, financing, banking, and insurance, but does not include a credit reporting business carried out by a credit reporting agency under the Credit Reporting Agencies Act 2010.'

---

[16] Parliamentary Debates, (House of Representatives), Twelfth Parliament, Third Session, First Meeting, 5 April 2010, Dato' Seri Utama Dr Rais Yatim, p. 156.

[17] Section 45(2)(a) of the PDPA.

[18] Section 45(2)(e) of the PDPA.

[19] Khaw (2002), p. 12.

The term 'commercial' has various meanings. According to the Oxford English Dictionary,[20] it is defined as being 'engaged in, or concerned with, commerce and having profit as a primary aim rather than artistic etc. value'.[21] The word 'commercial purpose' is defined as 'used for a purpose relating to trade and the buying, selling and exchange of commodities for profit'.[22] Black's Law Dictionary also defines 'commercial activity' as 'any type of business or activity which is carried on for a profit'.[23] It appears that there must be an element of 'profit making', or at least some form of monetary value attached to a transaction for it to be deemed 'commercial transaction'.

In respect of the term "transaction", there is no need to have a valid contract to constitute a transaction. Any dealing or negotiation between the parties may be considered a transaction.[24] As the phrase "whether contractual or not" is used in Section 4, there is no need to prove the existence of a contract.

It is submitted that it is rather restrictive and undesirable to limit the scope of the PDPA to only 'commercial transactions'. By virtue of this definition, any processing of personal data in non-commercial transactions is thereby excluded from the application of the PDPA. Under the earlier draft of the PDP Bill,[25] the definition of personal data was substantially in *pari materia* to Section 1 of the Data Protection Act 1998 of the UK ['DPA 1998 (UK)'], and the terms 'commercial transactions' were not mentioned in the draft. The terms were only inserted in the PDPA, and it appears that such limitation is very peculiar to the PDPA.

The mindset of the Government in enacting the PDPA seems to place more emphasis on the protection of personal data in commercial transactions. The Government has repeatedly stressed that the PDPA will regulate the processing of the personal data involved in commercial transactions, which is critical in this age of e-commerce. The Government hoped that the PDPA will solve problems such as

---

[20] The Oxford English Dictionary (1991), p. 293.

[21] Dena Bank, Ahmednagar v Prakash Birbhan Katariya, AIR 1994 Bom 343, 345. The court held that loan advanced for construction of a hospital can be said to be service-oriented, and it is difficult to see how it is profit oriented.

[22] Words and Phrases legally defined (1988), p. 283, Re Ashley Colter (1961) Ltd and Minister of Municipal Affairs (1970) 10 DLR (3d) 502, 505, NBCA, Hughes JA.

[23] Black's Law Dictionary (1990), p. 270. Lanski v Montealegre, 361 Mich. 44, N.W. 2d pp. 772–774.

[24] Baldeo Kumar v Managing Director AIR 1997 MP 147. The High Court held: 'on a fair construction of the word "business transaction", the word cannot be construed to mean a business contract or deal. The word "transaction" is from the verb "transact" which according to dictionary meaning means "to carry through, accomplish, execute, do or to carry on". Transaction may comprehend a series of many occurrences. It cannot be read narrowly to mean as synonymous to the word "contract". In fact, in one contract there may be many business transactions'.

[25] Munir and Yasin (2002), p. 174.

credit card fraud, identity theft, and selling of personal data without customers' consent.[26]

The Government, in redrafting the PDPA, had probably taken into consideration the approach adopted in the Asia-Pacific Economic Cooperation ('APEC') Privacy Framework, which aims at promoting e-commerce throughout the Asia-Pacific region. According to the Preamble of the APEC Privacy Framework:

> the APEC recognises the importance of protecting information privacy and maintaining information flows among economies in the Asia Pacific regions and among their trading partners. As APEC Ministers acknowledged in endorsing the 1998 Blueprint for Action on Electronic Commerce, the potential of electronic commerce cannot be realized without government and business cooperation to develop and implement technologies and policies, which build trust and confidence in safe, secure and reliable communication, information and delivery systems, and which address issues including privacy.

Be that as it may, the nine information privacy principles set out in APEC Privacy Framework do not have provisions limiting its application to 'commercial transactions' only, despite its focus on encouraging the growth of electronic commerce through strengthening data protection law.

It appears that the definition of commercial transactions may have been derived from that of the Electronic Commerce Act 2006.[27] The definition works well in this Act, as its objective is to govern any commercial transactions conducted by electronic means.[28] However, personal data protection is not just about safeguarding data in the commercial world. It should be noted that not all activities that involve processing of personal data are conducted in commercial transactions. Personal data may be processed in non-commercial transactions, such as collection of personal data through surveys, contest forms or application forms that do not involve monetary transactions.

---

[26] Patrick (2009). The Deputy Minister II of the Ministry of the Information, Communications and Culture, Senator Heng Seai Kie, was quoted as saying that: 'the drafting and enactment of a law that regulates the collection, processing and storage of people's personal data is critical in this age of e-commerce. We have read horrifying stories about people losing their money due to credit card fraud, customer-privacy infringements and data theft. Such incidents threaten the integrity of Malaysia as an emerging market economy. Without clear rights and obligations on the collection and storing of personal data, individuals (inside and outside the country) will be reluctant to carry out (electronic) transactions'.

[27] Section 2 of the Electronic Commerce Act 2006 (Act 658) defines 'commercial transactions' as 'a single communication or multiple communications of a commercial nature, whether contractual or not, which includes any matters relating to the supply or exchange of goods or services, agency, investments, financing, banking and insurance.'

[28] Munir and Yasin argue that that the prudent and sensible approach would be to allow the Electronic Commerce Act 2006 to apply to any electronic communication, rather than commercial transaction. The term 'communication' ought to be defined to include any statement, declaration, demand, notice, including an offer and acceptance. This would give legal recognition to all and any electronic communications and at the same time, provides legal recognition to electronic transactions. See Munir and Yasin (2006), p. 2.

Personal data such as medical and health records, employee records, financial records, property records, and even criminal records may be used for social, employment, education, professional, taxation, social security, and welfare reasons, among others. The use of personal data in these situations may not necessarily involve a 'profit making' element, and is hardly able to be considered for 'use in respect of commercial transactions'. The effect of this restrictive limitation is that any processing of personal data in non-commercial situations would not be subject to the application of the PDPA, and it would become a lacuna in the law.

Consider this scenario: Mr. James is looking for job vacancies on a job employment website. He uploads his personal data, ranging from his name, address, marital status, gender, education qualification, employment history, and current and past salary to the website. All these data are stored in the database of the said website. The website owner is considered a data user, since the website processes personal data. However, as the website does not charge Mr. James any fee, there is no commercial transaction involved. Therefore, there is nothing to prevent the website owner from processing Mr. James' personal data for any purpose, and disregarding the obligations imposed by the PDPA.

Some MPs[29] have argued that the application of the PDPA should not be restricted to only 'commercial transactions'. However, the Minister in his reply said that the aim of the PDPA is to protect the personal data of individuals in respect of commercial transactions, and it does not cover any other aims or purposes.[30] Unfortunately, the Minister did not clarify the rationale behind such a limitation.

It is interesting to note that the data protection law in Canada also restricts the application of its law to 'commercial activities'. Section 4(1)(a) of the Personal Information Protection and Electronic Documents Act 2000 ('PIPEDA') provides that 'this Part [referring to the PIPEDA] applies to every organization in respect of personal information that the organization collects, uses or discloses in the course of commercial activities…'[31]

An Ontario Superior Court in *Rodgers v Calvert*[32] has dealt with the meaning of 'commercial activity' under the PIPEDA. The counsels argued that the 'preponderant purpose' test established under the Canadian Assessment Act for purposes of taxation ought to be applied in interpreting the terms of 'commercial activity'. According to the test, if the activity makes a profit, then the activity is considered a business. However, if there is another preponderant purpose to which any profit

---

[29] Parliamentary Debates, (House of Representatives), Twelfth Parliament, Third Session, First Meeting, 5 April 2010, Tuan Lim Lip Eng (Segambut), p. 117; Tuan Saifuddin Nasution bin Ismail (Machang), p. 141; Tuan Sim Tong Him (Kota Melaka), p. 144.

[30] Parliamentary Debates, (House of Representatives), Twelfth Parliament, Third Session, First Meeting, 5 April 2010, Dato' Seri Utama Dr Rais Yatim, p. 146.

[31] Section 2(1) of the PIPEDA defines 'commercial activity' as 'any particular transaction, act or conduct or any regular course of conduct that is of a commercial character, including the selling, bartering or leasing of donor, membership or other fundraising lists.'

[32] [2004] O.J. No. 3653, 244 DLR (4th) 479 (SCJ).

earned is merely incidental, then it will not be considered a business. This test was rejected by the court, as the objectives of the PIPEDA and the Assessment Act were different. The test for 'commercial activity' under the PIPEDA required more than a mere 'exchange of consideration' under the concept of contract law.

The court found that although the association collected membership fees in exchange for the services and benefits of membership in the association, this exchange of consideration did not constitute commercial activity. The test is whether the specific activities are commercial in nature. The court noted that although dictionary definitions assist in interpreting the term 'commercial activity', it relied more heavily on the interpretation from the Canadian Privacy Commissioner's statement on its website, which stated that, 'collecting membership fees, organizing club activities, compiling a list of members' names and addresses and mailing out newsletters should not be considered considered commercial activities'.

In *State Farm Mutual Automobile Insurance Company v Privacy Commissioner of Canada*,[33] the Federal Court of Canada accepted the view that if the primary activity is commercial, then it will be caught by the PIPEDA. However, if the activity is merely incidental, it will fall outside the PIPEDA. The primary characterisation of the activity is the dominant factor in assessing the commercial character of the activity under the PIPEDA.[34] Furthermore, just because the processing of personal data is performed by a non-profit organisation, this does not automatically mean the organisation is exempt from the application of the PIPEDA, or even our PDPA.

A non-profit organisation that administers university entrance exams was found to be engaged in commercial activity.[35] On the other hand, a private school was found not to be engaged in a commercial activity when it collected personal data for admissions purposes.[36] In this case, the Canadian Assistant Commissioner applied the following test to determine whether the organisation was covered by the PIPEDA:

- What is the organisation's core activity? If the organisation's core activity is providing educational services, then the activity should not be considered to have a commercial character;
- However, if one of the organisation's objectives is to earn profits from its services, then the presumption that the activity of an educational organisation does not have a commercial character will be rebutted.

---

[33] 2010 FC 736.

[34] In this case, the insurer's act of hiring private investigator to conduct investigation and surveillance was simply incidental to the primary activity at hand, namely the collection of evidence by the defendant in order to defend herself in the civil action brought against her by the plaintiff.

[35] PIPEDA Case Summary #389 – Report of Findings – Law School Admission Council Investigation.

[36] PIPEDA Case Summary #345 – Private school not covered by the PIPEDA.

It would be interesting to see how the Malaysian courts would approach the interpretation of 'commercial transactions'. Since the definition of 'commercial transactions' under the PDPA is defined as any transaction of a commercial nature, arguably the test propounded by the Canadian courts and the Canadian Privacy Commissioner[37] would be applicable or at least should be considered by the Malaysian courts.

Having discussed these two main limitations, one can reach the conclusion that the PDPA only applies to the private sector. Within the private sector, it is further narrowed down to companies and organisations which process personal data in commercial transactions. The narrow application of the PDPA is undesirable and bound to create many legal complications and uncertainties in the future.

4.1.3 No Civil Remedies Available

Clause 88 of the earlier draft of the PDP Bill stated that an individual who suffers any damage (which includes injury to feelings) or distress by reason of a contravention of a requirement under this Bill by the data user shall be entitled to compensation for such damage or distress. The sub-section provided that damage includes injury to feelings. Clause 88 mirrored the provision under the Hong Kong Personal Data (Privacy) Ordinance.[38]

However, this provision has been entirely omitted in the PDPA. This is ironic, because while Section 42 of the PDPA provides the right for a data subject to prevent processing that is likely to cause damage or distress, the data subject has no right to claim compensation from the data user who causes such damage or distress. Furthermore, as any prosecution for an offence under the PDPA can only be instituted by or with the written consent of the Public Prosecutors,[39] should the Public Prosecutor decide not to prosecute the data user, the data subject is left with no remedy whatsoever. Denial of civil remedy is unfair to the aggrieved data subject.

In many other jurisdictions, any breach of the data protection law is punishable under both criminal and civil law. For instance, under the DPA 1998 (UK), a data subject who suffers damage or distress by reason of any contravention of the Act by a data controller can claim for compensation from the data controller.[40] However, to claim compensation for distress, the data subject must also suffer damage, or the contravention is related to the processing of personal data for special purposes.

---

[37] Interpretation of 'Commercial Activity' under the PIPEDA.

[38] Section 66 of the Hong Kong Personal Data (Privacy) Ordinance provides that an individual who suffers damage by reason of a contravention of a provision under this Ordinance shall be entitled to compensation from that data user for that damage. For the avoidance of doubt, it is hereby declared that damage may be or include injury to feelings.

[39] Section 134 of the PDPA.

[40] Section 13 DPA 1998 (UK).

During the parliamentary debate, the Minister said that any aggrieved data subject can take civil action against the data user who has misused the data subject's personal data. If banks and financial institutions have misused personal data, action can also be taken under the relevant banking laws which have provisions to deal with protection of bank customers' personal data.[41] However, the Minister did not explain why no provision was expressly provided under the PDPA. The question of whether one can institute a civil action against the data user is therefore unclear. If the intention of the Parliament was to allow for civil remedy, this should have been stated clearly in the PDPA.

4.1.4 Non-independence of the PDP Commissioner

Another criticism towards the PDPA is that the Personal Data Protection Commissioner ('PDP Commissioner') is not independent. The PDP Commissioner will be appointed by the Minister to carry out the functions and powers assigned to him or her under the PDPA.[42] The PDP Commissioner can hold the office for up to 3 years, and may be reappointed,[43] but he or she may also be dismissed by the Minister who only needs to state the reason for such dismissal.[44] The PDP Commissioner will be responsible to the Minister who may give him or her directions in relation to the discharge of functions and powers. The PDP Commissioner's remuneration and allowances are determined by the Minister.[45]

These provisions may severely curtail the powers of the PDP Commissioner in carrying out his or her functions under the PDPA, as the public may perceive that the PDP Commissioner is acting under the directions and orders of the Government. The non-independence of the PDP Commissioner is not in line with the international standards, which require data protection commissioners to be independent from the government and operate free from political or government interference.[46] Commissioners in the UK, Australia, New Zealand, and Hong Kong play their role independently of their governments. Recently, the European Court of Justice also ruled that the data protection authorities must be completely independent as 'they are the guardians of fundamental rights and freedoms, and their existence is an essential component of the protection of individuals' personal data.'[47]

---

[41] Parliamentary Debates, (House of Representatives), Twelfth Parliament, Third Session, First Meeting, 5 April 2010, Dato' Seri Utama Dr Rais Yatim, p. 151.

[42] Section 47 of the PDPA.

[43] Section 53 of the PDPA.

[44] Section 54 of the PDPA.

[45] Section 57 of the PDPA.

[46] Article 28 of the EU Data Protection Directive, Article 23 of the Madrid Resolution 2009.

[47] Commission of the European Communities v Federal Republic of Germany (Case Number C-112/05), November 2010.

Several MPs criticised the non-independence of the PDP Commissioner, arguing that he or she should be answerable directly to the Parliament, not the Minister.[48] However, the Government was of the view that to place the PDP Commissioner under the control of the Parliament would violate the doctrine of separation of powers, as the Parliament's duty is to make law, and the administration and enforcement of the law should be placed under the Government.[49] The non-independence of the PDP Commissioner is not unusual in Malaysia, as most Commissioners are answerable to the Minister or the Government in some capacity.

Personal data protection is a matter of public interest as it affects almost everyone in the country. Non-independence of the PDP Commissioner will only undermine public confidence towards the purpose of the PDPA and the credibility of the PDP Commissioner. One may argue that the issue of non-independence is not so grave since the Government is excluded from the application of the PDPA. However, in order to prevent any form of allegation that the Government may have a vested interest in protecting certain parties from investigation and prosecution (especially when the government-linked companies and statutory bodies are subject to the PDPA), it is submitted that an independent PDP Commissioner would be the most ideal way for the Government to show its commitment in protecting its people's rights.

4.1.5 Adequacy Level of the Personal Data Protection Act 2010

Article 25 of the EU Data Protection Directive requires the European Economic Area ('EEA') countries[50] to ensure that transfer of personal data to a country outside the EEA may only take place if the third country has an adequate level of data protection, unless one of the exceptions apply.[51] The reasoning behind this provision is to ensure that personal data transferred to non-EEA countries is not then processed in such a way that is contrary to the data protection law in the EU. Hence, to facilitate the transborder flow of personal data from any EEA countries to Malaysia, it is necessary for Malaysia to have an adequate data protection regime.

---

[48] Parliamentary Debates, (House of Representatives), Twelfth Parliament, Third Session, First Meeting, 5 April 2010, Tuan Lim Lip Eng (Segambut), p. 118; Tuan Saifuddin Nasution bin Ismail (Machang), p. 143; Tuan Sim Tong Him (Kota Melaka), p. 145.

[49] Parliamentary Debates, (House of Representatives), Twelfth Parliament, Third Session, First Meeting, 5 April 2010, Dato' Seri Utama Dr Rais Yatim, p. 148.

[50] For example, in the UK, The DPA 1998 (UK) has given effect to this provision by inserting a data protection principle into the Act. This principle provides that personal data shall not be transferred to a country or territory outside the European Economic Area (EEA) unless that country or territory ensures an adequate level of protection for the rights and freedoms of data subjects in relation to the processing of personal data. The principle is further supplemented by interpretation provision in Schedule 1 Part II and Schedule 4.

[51] Art 25 of the EU Data Protection Directive.

However, one criticism towards the PDPA is that it may not be able to satisfy the EU adequacy test. In practice, the adequacy issue is generally made at the community level, although the member states are required to inform each other of any cases where they feel that a third country does not provide an adequate level of protection.[52]

The Article 29 Data Protection Working Party ('Article 29 Working Party') has been tasked to examine the adequacy level of data protection in any third countries the member states may deal with. If the Article 29 Working Party determines that the third country does not provide an adequate level of protection, it will give a report to the European Commission ('EC') which has the power to declare any third countries as failing to provide an adequate level of data protection.

The Article 29 Working Party has adopted the Working Paper 12 entitled 'Transfer of Personal Data to Third Countries: Applying Article 25 and 26 of the EU Data Protection Directive' ('Working Paper 12'),[53] which laid down certain criteria to analyse the adequacy issue. The Working Paper 12 suggests that for a data protection law to be considered as adequate, the law in the third country should at least comprise two basic elements: (1) the content of the rules applicable ('content principles'); and (2) the means to ensure effective application of these rules ('procedural/enforcement requirements').

The 'content principles' sets out six minimum principles that any data protection law should contain, namely: the purpose limitation principle; data quality and proportionality principle; transparency principle; security principle; right of access, rectification and opposition; and restrictions on onwards transfers. The PDPA contains all these principles. The additional principles to be applied to specific types of processing are handling of sensitive data; possibility to 'opt-out' from direct marketing; and rules for automated individual decision-making.

The Article 29 Working Party will also consider the scope of the protection and has suggested that the data protection law of a third country must apply to all individuals and entities. However, as mentioned earlier, the Federal and State Governments are exempt from the application of the PDPA. It also suggested that a data protection law that is adequate shall apply to all forms of processing. Under the PDPA, only processing of personal data in commercial transactions will trigger the application of the PDPA. It is submitted that the PDPA may face the risk of being declared as failing to provide an adequate level of data protection.

In respect of the 'procedural/enforcement requirements', for a data protection law to be considered as adequate, it should possess the following three requirements: to deliver a good level of compliance with the rules; to provide support and help to individual data subjects; and to provide appropriate redress to the injured party. The Article 29 Working Party opines that a system of external supervision in the form of an independent authority is a necessary feature of a data

---

[52] Art 25(3) of the EU Data Protection Directive.

[53] Working Paper 12 entitled 'Transfer of Personal Data to Third Countries: Applying Article 25 and 26 of the EU Data Protection Directive'.

protection law so as to ensure impartiality in the decision-making process.[54] However, as discussed earlier, the PDP Commissioner under the PDPA is not an independent authority. In respect of appropriate redress, such remedy includes allowing compensation to be paid and sanctions to be imposed where appropriate. Although criminal offences have been created, the PDPA may be seen as inadequate as it fails to provide a civil remedy to the aggrieved data subject. Malaysia remains one of the largest trading partners of the EU, with bilateral trade in goods reaching 31.9 billion euro in 2010. Abu Bakar Munir argues that the enactment of the PDPA would be the best opportunity for Malaysia to encourage free flow of personal data from the EU countries, so as to facilitate and further stimulate the growth of trade and investment. However, failure to comply with the EU adequacy requirement would be much regretted.[55]

To date, only a small number of countries have been declared as providing an adequate level of data protection law.[56] It is generally recognised that cross-border flows of personal data are necessary in today's international trade. The adequacy element imposed under the EU Data Protection Directive has been seen as a serious barrier to international trade.[57] Some organisations have tried to rely on the exemptions provided under their respective data protection law which permits transfer of personal data to another country in specified circumstances, such as where the data subject has given his or her consent, where the transfer is necessary for the performance of a contract, or where the data user has taken all reasonable precautions and exercised all due diligence to ensure that the personal data will not be processed in any manner which would contravenes the data protection law in its country.[58]

Alternatively, some have adopted the EU-approved Model Contract, which requires the parties sending and receiving personal data to incorporate certain approved contractual clauses into the commercial agreement between the parties, which have been regarded by the EC as offering sufficient safeguards with respect to data protection.[59] The effect of incorporating such clauses is that personal data

---

[54] Although the Working Party also recognised that this feature may not always present in every countries. It is thus necessary to identify the underlying objectives of a data protection procedural system, and on this basis, judge the different judicial and non-judicial procedural mechanisms used in third countries.

[55] Munir (2010).

[56] As at June 2012, the countries are the US, Andorra, Argentina, Australia, Canada, Switzerland, Faeroe Islands, Guernsey, State of Israel, Isle of Man, Jersey.

[57] Ustaran (2012), p. 174.

[58] Such exemptions are similarly provided under Section 129(3) of the PDPA.

[59] Grant (2009), p. 48. The author criticised that these Model Contract has a number of problems. First, it would cause complexity where there are multiple transfers within a group of companies, resulting in the need for a contract for each transfer. Secondly, some jurisdictions require local registration and/or notification and approval of the contract while other jurisdictions may not require as such. Thirdly, the contract requires both parties to accept joint and several liability for any breaches of contract. The impact of this is that, the data subject may choose to sue both parties jointly or either one. Given the difficulties of taking legal action in foreign jurisdiction, data subject may choose to sue the party who sends the data, even though the main person who causes the problem may be the party who receives and processes the data.

can flow from any of the EEA countries to non- EEA countries which may not have an adequate level of data protection.[60] It has been suggested that the contractual clauses must be incorporated on a verbatim basis i.e. no amendments to the clauses are allowed.[61] In respect of data transfers within a multinational corporations or international organisations, the Article 29 Working party has also developed the 'Binding Corporate Rules' that allows multinational corporations, international organisations and group of companies to make data transfers within the organisations across border in compliance with the EU Directive.[62] Corporations or organisations may implement internal privacy rules to ensure data transfers within the corporations or organisations are properly conducted. It should also be noted that the 21 Asia Pacific Economic Cooperation ('APEC') members also plan to implement the APEC Cross Border Privacy Rules Systems ('CBPRs') to facilitate information flows within the APEC member states.[63]

4.2 Data Protection and Privacy Law in Selected Sectors

4.2.1 Introduction

Prior to the enactment of the PDPA, Malaysia adopted the sectoral approach in data protection. Legislation, rules, regulations, guidelines, and codes of practice have been developed to regulate the collection, use, and dissemination of personal data in specific sectors, such as the banking and financial institutions sectors,[64] healthcare sector,[65] insurance sectors,[66] as well as the telecommunication and multimedia sectors.[67] However, these laws and regulations do not comprehensively cover all aspects of data protection. As such, parties had resorted to protecting their personal

---

[60] For an analysis of the Model Contract, see Ustaran (2012), pp. 180–183.

[61] Munir and Yasin (2010), p. 224.

[62] For an analysis of the Binding Corporate Rules, see Ustaran (2012), pp. 184–186.

[63] The Honolulu Declaration—Toward a Seamless Regional Economy, the 19th APEC Economic Leaders' Meeting, 12–13 November 2011.

[64] See Banking and Financial Institutions Act 1989 (Act 372); Guidelines on the Provision of Electronic Banking (e-banking) Services by Financial Institutions (BNM); Guidelines on Data Management and Management Information System (MIS) Framework (BNM).

[65] See Code of Medical Ethics adopted by the Malaysian Medical Association, Guidelines on the Medical Records and Medical Reports issued by the Malaysian Medical Council and Confidentiality Guidelines issued by the Malaysian Medical Council.

[66] See Insurance Act 1996 (Act 553); Code of Ethics and Conduct (Second Edition, February 1999) issued by the Life Insurance Association of Malaysia.

[67] See General Consumer Code 2003 drawn up by the Communications and Multimedia Commission; Computer Crimes Act 1997 (Act 563); the Malaysian Communications and Multimedia Content Code ('Content Code') developed by the Communications and Multimedia Content Forum of Malaysia.

data by invoking the common law duty of confidentiality, or by entering into data protection or processing agreements with the other party.

With the enactment of the PDPA, Malaysia finally has a comprehensive law that governs data protection. As the PDPA is the primary legislation that specifically governs data protection, the PDPA is therefore applicable to all sectors mentioned above. The existing laws and regulations shall continue to be applicable to the relevant sectors, although there might be a need to revisit and amend these laws and regulations, if necessary, to ensure that they are in line with the PDPA.[68] In relation to the credit reporting sector, the Credit Reporting Agencies Act 2010 has also been enacted to govern the processing of credit information by credit reporting agencies.

4.2.2 Banking and Financial Institutions Sectors

It is of paramount importance for banks and financial institutions to maintain strict confidentiality in dealings with customers, and respect the privacy of their personal and financial data in order to earn their trust and confidence in the banking system. The Government has devised the legislative and regulatory framework to ensure the rights and interests of banks and customers are adequately protected.

Under the common law, a bank owes a contractual duty to maintain confidentiality of affairs, transactions, or any other information relating to the accounts of its customers, unless the bank is compelled to do so by a court, or the circumstances give rise to a public duty of disclosure, or the protection of the bank's own interests requires it.[69] This banking secrecy duty has been codified into legislation under the Banking and Financial Institutions Act 1989 ('BAFIA').[70] According to Section 97 of the BAFIA, a director or officer of any bank (whether during or after his employment with the bank), or a person who has access to any record relating to the affairs of any customer of the bank, shall not give, produce, divulge, reveal, publish, or otherwise disclose any information or document relating to the affairs or account of the customer of the bank to any other person unless the disclosure falls under one of the exceptions. Anyone found to have breached Section 97 of the BAFIA is liable to a maximum of 3 years imprisonment, and/or a maximum fine of Ringgit Malaysia three million.[71] Directors, CEOs, COOs, and bank managers may also be severally and jointly liable for hefty fines and imprisonment unless they can prove that the offence was committed without their consent or connivance, and that

---

[68] Munir and Yasin (2010), p. 240.

[69] Tournier v National Provincial and Union Bank of England [1924] 1 KB 461; recently affirmed by Ng Lee Kiau v Malayan Banking Berhad [2011] 1 LNS 605 and Wong Yeng Mun v CIMB Bank Berhad [2011] 1 CLJ 785.

[70] Sections 96–102 of the BAFIA. Banking secrecy provisions are also similarly found under Section 34 of the Islamic Banking Act 1983 and Section 178 of the Labuan Financial Services and Securities Act 2010.

[71] Section 103(1)(a) and Fourth Schedule of the BAFIA.

they have exercised all such due diligence to prevent the commission of the offence.[72]

In *Tan Eng Soon v Malayan Banking Berhad*,[73] the High Court held that banks have an implied duty under contract to maintain the confidentiality of its customers' affairs, accounts, or any other details. However, this duty of confidentiality is not absolute. In *The Attorney General of Hong Kong v Zauyah Wan Chik*,[74] it was held that if the banks are required under the law or an order of the court to divulge confidential information about its customers, the banks are duty-bound to divulge the information to the courts, and will be protected from any criminal liability under Section 132 of the Evidence Act 1950.[75] The court also held that even if the information is divulged in a court of law in the country which issued the request, the banks will still be protected as though the divulgence was taken in this country. However, Section 132 only expressly protects the banks from criminal liability but not civil liability. Arguably, a civil proceeding can be brought against the banks for breach of confidence for the divulgence of information made to the courts. However, the banks can rely on the defence that there is a just cause or a legitimate excuse for the breach of confidence as it is bound by law to make the divulgence.[76] In the words of NH Chan JCA, 'The duty of confidence is outweighed by the requirements of Section 132 of the Evidence Act 1950'.

As can be seen from the above, the duty of confidentiality is not absolute. In the following limited circumstances, a bank may disclose information relating to its customers:

1) Where disclosure is to necessitate the exercise of powers, performance of functions, or discharge of duties of the bank[77] or the Malaysia Deposit Insurance Corporation[78];
2) Where disclosure is made to any person rendering professional services to the Central Bank of Malaysia ('Central Bank'), where he is authorised by the Central Bank to obtain the information from the bank for the purpose of his services to the Central Bank[79];
3) Where the customer has given his consent in writing to allow disclosure[80];

---

[72] Section 106 of the BAFIA.
[73] [1997] 2 CLJ Supp 552.
[74] [1995] 3 CLJ 35.
[75] Section 132 of the Evidence Act 1950 provides that a witness is bound to answer any relevant question put to him, whether in examination-in-chief, cross-examination or re-examination and that he cannot refuse to answer on the ground of self-incrimination. The Parliament has taken away the common law privilege of not answering on the ground of self-incrimination.
[76] Fraser v. Evans [1969] 1 QB 349.
[77] Section 98(1)(a) of the BAFIA.
[78] Section 98A of the BAFIA.
[79] Section 98(1)(b) of the BAFIA.
[80] Section 99(1)(a) of the BAFIA.

4) Where the customer is declared bankrupt, or if the customer is a corporation, the corporation is being or has been wound up in Malaysia or in any country outside Malaysia[81];
5) Where the information is required by a party to a *bona fide* commercial transaction, to which the customer is also a party, to assess the creditworthiness of the customer relating to such a transaction, provided the information required is of a general nature and does not enable the details of the customer's account or affairs to be ascertained[82];
6) Where disclosure is made for the purposes of any criminal or civil proceedings between the bank and its customer, or between the bank making adverse claims to money in a customer's account[83];
7) Where the bank has been served with a garnishee order attaching monies in the customer's account[84];
8) Where disclosure is made to an external bureau established, or an agent appointed by the bank with the prior written consent of the Central Bank[85]; and
9) Where disclosure is required or authorised under any other provisions of the BAFIA,[86] under any Federal law to be made to a police officer,[87] or authorised in writing by the Central Bank,[88] or under a court order issued pursuant to the Banker's Books (Evidence) Act 1949.[89]

In addition to the BAFIA, the Central Bank has also issued specific guidelines, circulars, directives, orders, best practices, and guidance notes in respect of the conduct of the financial institutions. There is a penalty for non-compliance.[90] Of particular relevance to the discussion in this chapter is the Guidelines on the Provision of Electronic Banking (e-banking) Services by Financial Institutions ('E-Banking Guidelines') which outline the broad principles that should be adopted by all financial institutions in Malaysia that offer e-banking services. These guidelines stipulate the minimum standards that should be observed by financial institutions in accordance with the risk levels. Examples of best practices are also included in some of the broad principles.[91] E-banking is defined as the provision of banking products and services through electronic channels, which includes the Internet, telephone, automated teller machines (ATMs), and any other electronic channel.

---

[81] Section 99(1)(b) of the BAFIA.
[82] Section 99(1)(c) of the BAFIA.
[83] Section 99(1)(d) of the BAFIA.
[84] Section 99(1)(e) of the BAFIA.
[85] Section 99(1)(f) of the BAFIA.
[86] Section 99(1)(g) of the BAFIA.
[87] Section 99(1)(h) of the BAFIA.
[88] Section 99(1)(i) of the BAFIA.
[89] Section 100 of the BAFIA.
[90] Sections 103 and 104 of the BAFIA.
[91] The E-Banking Guidelines which was issued in 2010, replaced the Minimum Guidelines on the Provision of Internet Banking Services by Licensed Banking Institutions that was issued in 2000.

Principle 10 of the E-Banking Guidelines requires all financial institutions to take appropriate measures to preserve the confidentiality of key e-banking information. These measures should be commensurate with the sensitivity of the information being transmitted and/or stored in databases. Paragraphs 20.2 and 20.3 of the E-Banking Guidelines state that all financial institutions should ensure that:

- Confidential data and records are accessible by duly authorised and authenticated individuals or systems only;
- Confidential data are maintained in a secure manner and protected from unauthorised viewing or modification during transmission over public, private, or internal networks e.g. the cryptographic technologies;
- Standards and controls for data use and protection must be maintained by all parties involved in an outsourcing relationship;
- Access to restricted data is logged and access logs are resistant to tampering; and
- Access to key e-banking information should be permitted strictly according to the 'need to know' principle (e.g. application developers should have no need to access live customer data).

Principle 12 of the E-Banking Guidelines requires all financial institutions take appropriate measures to ensure customer privacy is protected. It recognises that misuse or unauthorised disclosure of confidential customer data may expose a financial institution to both legal and reputation risk. Paragraphs 22.2–22.4 provide that:

- Customers should be made aware of the financial institution's privacy policies and relevant privacy issues concerning the use of e-banking products and services;
- Financial institutions should not share customer data with third parties for cross-marketing purposes without prior explicit consent of customers. In addition, customer data should not be disclosed beyond what customers have authorised; and
- Customers should be given the option to disallow financial institutions from disclosing their information to third parties, including the financial institutions' partners, without affecting their access to the e-banking services rendered.

If a financial institution processes any personal data, has control over, or authorises the processing of any personal data of its customers, it shall be considered a data user under PDPA,[92] and therefore required to comply with the seven PDP Principles under the PDPA. As the PDP Principles are drafted in a very general form, the E-Banking Guidelines shall complement the interpretation and application of the PDP Principles in the banking and financial institutions sectors. For example, the Security Principle requires a data user to take practical steps to protect personal data from any loss, misuse, modification, or unauthorised or accidental access. The E-Banking Guidelines have set out the best practices on security control measures. The data integrity principle requires a data user to take reasonable

---

[92] Section 4 of the PDPA.

steps to ensure that the personal data is accurate, complete, and not misleading. The E-Banking Guidelines have also set out recommendations on protecting the data integrity of e-banking transactions, records, and information.

Other than the E-Banking Guidelines, the Guidelines on Data Management and Management Information System (MIS) Framework also sets out high level guiding principles on sound data management and MIS practices that should be followed by financial institutions. There are also many other guidelines and guidance notes on the specific scope of the conduct of the financial institutions which are beyond the scope of discussion of this chapter. It is therefore imperative for the financial institutions to ensure all their conduct and operations are in compliance with the guidelines and guidance notes issued by the Central Bank and other regulatory authorities from time to time.

4.2.3 Healthcare Sector

In the healthcare sector, hospitals, clinics, and their employees, such as doctors, dentists, pharmacists, and nurses (collectively referred to as 'healthcare professionals'), often process large amount of patients' personal data, and are therefore required to comply with the PDPA. In addition to their obligations under the PDPA, they must also comply with their existing common law and statutory duty of confidentiality.

4.2.3.1 Duty of Confidentiality

Under the common law, a doctor owes a duty of confidentiality to patients to maintain information obtained from any dealings with them, and not to disclose the same to any third party without patients' consent.[93] This duty is important as it gives patients the confidence to be uninhibited in disclosing their medical conditions to the doctors. This duty has been practiced since time immemorial as far back as the Roman Hippocratic Oath taken by each doctor on entry into the medical profession. It reads as follows:

> ... whatever, in connection with my professional practice, or not in connection with it, I see or hear, in the life of men, which ought not to be spoken of abroad, I will not divulge, as reckoning that all such should be kept secret.

The International Code of Medical Ethics also states that doctors have a duty to preserve, in absolute secrecy, all he or she knows about a patient due of the confidence entrusted to him or her. The Medical Act 1971 is silent on the duty of confidentiality.[94] Reference is therefore made to the Code of Medical Ethics

---

[93] W v Egdell & Ors [1989] 2 WLR 689, [1990] 1 All ER 835 (CA).

[94] There are certain provisions on patients' privacy under the Private Healthcare Facilities and Services Regulations 2006.

adopted by the Malaysian Medical Association in May 2001 ('Code of Medical Ethics'); Guidelines on the Medical Records and Medical Reports issued by the Malaysian Medical Council in 2006 ('Medical Records Guidelines') and Confidentiality Guidelines issued by the Malaysian Medical Council in October 2011 ('Confidentiality Guidelines').

4.2.3.2 Code of Medical Ethics

The Code of Medical Ethics recognises that the basis of the relationship between doctor and patient is one of absolute confidence and mutual respect, and states that a doctor has a duty to respect a patient's dignity and privacy. The doctor shall not voluntarily disclose information obtained in the course of his or her professional relationship with the patient without the patient's consent. If a patient does not wish the doctor to share certain information with his team members, the doctor must respect those wishes.[95] An injunction may be granted to prevent doctors from disclosing a patient's data to a third party without the patient's consent.[96]

However, this duty is not absolute and there are certain exceptions. Information about the medical conditions of patients may be disclosed to other doctors, provided such disclosure is related to the treatment of that patient and serves the patient's best interests. Disclosure may also be permitted if the patient has given consent to the same. In addition, the statutory duty of disclosure overrides the common law duty of confidentiality. For example, the Prevention and Control of Infectious Diseases Act 1988 requires a doctor who becomes aware of the existence of any infectious disease (such as the Ebola virus, dengue fever, malaria, or HIV) to disclose the information to the relevant health authorities.[97]

The Drug Dependents (Treatment and Rehabilitation) Act 1983 requires a doctor to notify the relevant health authorities of patients they are treating or rehabilitating for drug dependency.[98] Disclosure is justified as public interest requires doctors to disclose this information to prevent potential harm to the general public. Disclosure may also be made under a court order. If a court orders a doctor to produce the medical information or testify as a medical witness, the doctor has no alternative but to comply with the order, as failure to do so may amount to a contempt of court and the doctor may be liable for imprisonment.[99]

Medical Records

Today, many hospitals and clinics store patients' data and medical records on computer databases for speedy retrieval, ease of transmission of information from one doctor to another, and for secure storage purposes. This also assists healthcare

---

[95] Paragraph 3 of Section II of the Code of Medical Ethics.

[96] Specific Relief Act 1950 (Revised 1974), Section 52 illustration (i) and Section 53 illustration (f).

[97] Section 10 of the Prevention and Control of Infectious Diseases Act 1988.

[98] Section 18 of the Drug Dependents (Treatment and Rehabilitation) Act 1983.

[99] Paragraph 4 of Section II of the Code of Medical Ethics.

professionals to provide better services as they can view patients' histories instantly, detect adverse drug reactions easily, and reduce the need to conduct the same tests repeatedly. Medical records usually Contain the personal particulars of the patient, history of allergy or chronic illness, last menstrual period (for female patients), blood pressure, temperature, laboratory/x-ray results, and doctors' opinions based on patient examination or assessment. All these information are considered as 'personal data' within the realm of the PDPA.

The Code of Medical Ethics encourages healthcare professionals to record all relevant details of their management of a patient in an accurate, legible, and comprehensive manner. Healthcare professionals should ensure all medical records are treated as private and confidential, and will not be divulged to any third party without the patient's consent.

In an Australian High Court case,[100] it was held that medical records remain the property of the healthcare professionals,[101] and patients have no right of access to their medical records. As such, the healthcare professionals have the discretion to decide whether to keep the records, allow the patients access, or even destroy the records. However, the healthcare professionals cannot disclose those medical records for profit, or disclose to unauthorised third parties.[102] In some jurisdictions, legislations have been enacted to allow patients the right of access to their medical records under certain conditions.[103]

In Malaysia, the Code of Medical Ethics asserts that patients are entitled to receive a copy of their medical records, and doctors are obliged to provide this report without unreasonable delay. The withholding of medical records is unethical. However, where medical records are sought by third parties such as employers, insurance companies, or solicitors, doctors cannot disclose these in the absence of patients' consent.[104]

4.2.3.3 Guidelines on the Medical Records and Medical Reports

The Guidelines on the Medical Records and Medical Reports issued by the Malaysian Medical Council in 2006 ('Medical Records Guidelines') also contains detailed guidelines on the manner in handling medical records and medical reports.

Some relevant provisions taken from the Medical Records Guidelines:
Paragraph 1.7: Right of access to medical records
It is generally accepted that patient should:
- Have access to records containing information about his/her medical condition for legitimate purpose and in good faith;
- Know what personal information is recorded;

---

[100] Breen v Williams [1996] CLR 186.

[101] McInerney v MacDonald [1992] 2 SCR 138.

[102] Reid (2003), p. 61.

[103] For example, the Access to Health Records Act 1990 (UK); Health Information Privacy Code 1994 (New Zealand); and Health Insurance Portability and Accountability Act 1996 (US).

[104] Paragraph 7 of Section II of the Code of Medical Ethics.

- Expect the records are accurate; and
- Know who has access to his/her personal information.

A patient's medical record is the property of the doctor and the healthcare facility and services. However, patients can also inform the doctors of any factual errors in the patients' personal data.

Paragraphs 1.9 and 1.10: Confidentiality of the medical records

Medical records are to be classified 'Confidential' for administrative purposes within a healthcare facility. All medical staffs must be aware of and respect the confidentiality nature of the medical records.

Paragraph 1.11: Security of medical records

Medical records must be stored in safe and secure rooms at all times when not in use. They must be easily accessible and retrievable when required and returned in a complete form after use.

Paragraph 1.12: Ownership of medical records

Consent from the patient or next of kin before the medical records can be released to any third person. The personal information that the doctor has recorded belongs to the patient. The result of investigations (blood tests, tests on secretions, imaging and scans) belongs to the patient and may be released to him/her upon request.

Information obtained by the doctor from a third party (such as relatives) about the patient is not part of the patient's information, as such information may have been revealed on strict instructions of confidentiality.

4.2.3.4 Confidentiality Guidelines

The Confidentiality Guidelines was approved and adopted by the Malaysian Medical Council on 11 October 2011. It is the first guidelines issued by the Council that comprehensively set out the confidentiality duty owed by doctors to patients and the need to respect patients' privacy rights. The Confidentiality Guidelines have been developed as a result of the enactment of the PDPA.

Salient features of the Confidentiality Guidelines:

1) *Principles*
    - No disclosure of patient's personal information unless patient gives consent to such disclosure.
    - Duty of confidentiality is not absolute. Doctors may disclose personal information if it is required by law; with the patient's consent; or it is justified in the public interest.
    - It sets out rules to be adhered to in disclosing information about a patient.
    - Doctors shall respect and help patients to exercise their rights to be informed about how their information will be used and have access to, or copies of, their health records.
2) *Protecting information*
    - Doctors shall take steps to ensure that patients' confidentiality is maintained regardless of the technology used to communicate health information.
    - Doctors shall avoid unintentional disclosures.

- Doctors shall ensure the information and any documentation are protected against improper disclosure at all times.
- There should be an information governance policy with protocols and procedures to ensure that patient information is documented, maintained and disclosed in accordance with the principles of confidentiality.

3) *Disclosure required by law*
   - Disclosure may be justified if it is required by law, such as notification of a known or suspected case of certain infectious diseases.
   - Disclosure may also sometimes be required to be made to regulatory bodies for investigation purposes.
   - Doctors shall disclose information if ordered to do so by a judge or presiding officer of a court but may object to the order if the information appears to be irrelevant to the proceedings.
   - Doctors shall not disclose personal information to a third party such as lawyers, police officers or officers of a court without the patient's express consent, unless it is required by law or can be justified in the public interest.

4) *Disclosure with consent*
   - Disclosure can be made with patient's consent. Seeking patient's consent to disclosure of information is part of good medical practice.
   - Where the disclosure of information between a doctor and his team members is required for treatment to which a patient has agreed, the patient's express consent may not be required.
   - If a patient does not wish a particular information to be shared within the team members, the doctor must respect those wishes, unless to do so would put others at risk of death or serious harm.
   - All team members should understand and observe confidentiality duty.
   - Where a doctor or hospital has contractual obligations to third parties such as companies or insurance companies, the doctor or hospital must obtain patient's consent before undertaking any examination or writing a report for the third party.

5) *The patient's interest*
   - Disclosure without patient's consent may be justified where failure to do so may expose the patient to risk of death or serious harm.
   - If a doctor believes a patient to be a victim of neglect or physical, sexual or emotional abuse and the patient cannot give or withhold consent to disclosure, the doctor shall disclose the information to a relevant person or statutory agency provided it is in the patient's best interests.

6) *The public interest*
   - Disclosure may be made in the public interest without the patient's consent where the benefits to an individual or to a society outweigh the public and the patient's interest in keeping the information confidential.
   - The doctor shall inform the patient that a disclosure will be made wherever it is practicable to do so and he shall document in the patient's record any steps

taken to seek or obtain consent and the reasons for disclosing information without consent.
- For secondary uses such as medical teaching, research and clinical audit, doctors should only disclose anonymised or coded information. Where identifiable information is needed, doctors should obtain the patient's express consent.

7) *Disclosures about patients who lack capacity to consent*
- Disclosure may be made in certain exceptional circumstances where the patient lacks the capacity to give consent. The doctor must take into consideration of the factors listed under this category.

8) *Sharing information with a patient's spouse, partner, carers, relatives or friends*
- Doctors should communicate with the patients what information they want to share, to whom and in what circumstances can the information be shared.
- Doctors can listen and discuss with anyone who close to the patient about the patient's health, but they cannot guarantee that the doctors will not tell the patient about the conversation. Doctors may need to share with the patient of information they received from others if it has influenced the doctors' assessment and treatment of the patient.

9) *Disclosure after a patient's death*
- Doctors may still have obligation to keep a patient's personal information confidential after his or her death, although this obligation is subject to certain exceptions.

4.2.4 Insurance Sector

Insurance companies often process large amount of individuals' personal data, which may include general personal data such as names and addresses, and sensitive personal data such as physical, mental, and health conditions. An insurance company usually requires its clients to make full disclosure of all material facts as these information would influence the setting of the premium, and have a bearing on whether the company will take the risk. As such, all information received by the company, including material facts relating to the physical, mental, or health conditions of the clients, should be treated with utmost care and in strict confidence. This duty of confidentiality is very much needed to give clients the confidence to disclose all material facts to the company.

There is no specific legislation that governs the processing of personal data by life insurance companies. The only provision that deals with secrecy of information is found in Section 195 of the Insurance Act 1996, which prohibits any person exercising any power under this Act to disclose information relating to the affairs of its customers obtained in the course of carrying out his functions under this Act, unless the information has already been made lawfully available to the public. Disclosure to the Central Bank, the director, or employee of the insurance company is permissible provided the disclosure is in the course of performance of functions, or to a person rendering service to the Central Bank in relation to a matter requiring professional knowledge.[105]

The Code of Ethics and Conduct (Second Edition, February 1999) issued by the Life Insurance Association of Malaysia ('Insurance Code')[106] provides some useful guidance on protecting policy owners' personal data. The Insurance Code recognises that life insurance[107] is a business essentially built on trust and honesty, and that the confidence of policy owners and members of the public in the integrity and honesty of insurers must be safeguarded and enhanced.[108]

The Insurance Code sets out the minimum standards of conduct expected to be practiced and adhered to by all employees[109] of Malaysian life insurance companies.[110] It serves as a guide for the promotion of proper standards of conduct, and sound and prudent business practices among the life insurance companies. The life insurance companies are encouraged to formulate more comprehensive sets of rules for maintaining ethical standards among their employees.[111]

There are seven principles underlying the Insurance Code.[112] The principles that are of relevance to personal data protection are as follows:

1) *To avoid misuse of information*
   Employees must not utilise any information gained through their company's operation, either for personal gain, or for any purpose other than that intended by the life insurance company.
2) *To ensure completeness and accuracy of relevant records*
   Employees must ensure that any entries made to the account, record, or document of the company must be complete and accurate. All records and computer files or programs of the company (including personnel files, financial statements, and policy owner information), must be accessed and used only for management-approved purposes.
3) *To ensure confidentiality of communication and transactions between the life insurance company and its policy owners and clients*
   Employees must take every precaution to protect the confidentiality of policy owners' and other clients' information and transactions. No employee shall,

---

[105] Section 196 of the Insurance Act 1996.

[106] The Insurance Code comprised three parts—Guidelines on the Code of Conduct, Code of Ethics and Conduct for Life Insurance Selling, and Statement of Life Insurance Practice.

[107] The term 'life insurance' covers all types of home service and/or ordinary life insurance, all types of annuities, pension contracts, investment-linked insurances, and permanent health insurance.

[108] Statement of Philosophy of the Insurance Code, p. 4.

[109] Employees include directors (executive and non-executive), employees and intermediaries of a life insurance company.

[110] 'Life Insurance Companies' refer to insurers duly registered to conduct life insurance business by Bank Negara Malaysia in accordance with Section 4 of the Insurance Act 1996.

[111] Paragraph 1 of the Insurance Code (Guidelines on the Code of Conduct).

[112] Paragraph 3 of the Insurance Code (Guidelines on the Code of Conduct).

during, or after termination of employment with the company (except in the proper course of his duties or with the company's written consent), divulge or make use of any secrets, copyright material, correspondence, accounts, or dealings of the company or its policy owners or clients. No employee shall use any information obtained for personal financial gain.

Business and financial information about any policy owner or client may only be used or made available to third parties when disclosure is required by law, or in accordance with any agreed information exchange program within the life insurance industry.

4.2.5 Telecommunications and Multimedia Sectors

The General Consumer Code of Practice ('GCC'), developed by the Communications and Multimedia Consumer Forum of Malaysia, sets out a number of principles concerning consumer protection, one of which is the protection of consumers' personal information in the telecommunications and multimedia sectors. The GCC binds all licensed service providers under the Communications and Multimedia Act 1998 and all non-licensed service providers who are members of the Consumer Forum.[113] It shall have effect notwithstanding anything to the contrary in any agreement between a customer and a service provider.[114] In other words, it means service providers must have regard to the GCC in developing the policies and procedures on personal data protection. Paragraph 2 of Part 2 of the GCC sets out the responsibility of a service provider in the protection of its consumers' personal information. Paragraph 2.2 outlines the guiding principles to be adopted by the service provider in processing and handling its consumers' personal information. It basically states that a service provider may collect and maintain necessary data/information of its consumers provided the information must be:
- Fairly and lawfully collected and processed;
- Processed for limited purposes;
- Adequate, relevant and not excessive;
- Accurate;
- Kept not longer than necessary;
- Processed in accordance with the data subject's rights;
- Secure; and
- Transferred only with prior approval from the consumer.

---

[113] Paragraph 6.1 of Part 1 of the GCC.

[114] Paragraph 1 of Part 1 of the GCC.

In addition, the service provider must take appropriate measures to provide adequate security, and respect consumers' preferences regarding unsolicited mail and telephone calls.

Paragraph 2.3 of Part 2 of the GCC sets out the following rules to be observed by the service provider:

- *Implement a 'Protection of Consumer Information Policy'*

  A service provider should implement a policy that protects the privacy of identifiable information. The policy should ideally contain all the guiding principles stated in paragraph 2.2 of Part 2 of the GCC.

- *Notice and disclosure*

  A service provider's policy on the protection of consumer information should be made available in the most accessible, easy to read and understood manner and should be disclosed to the consumer before his or her information is collected or requested. The policy must set out clearly what information is being collected; purpose of the collection; whether the information will be transferred to third party; the choices available to the consumer regarding the collection, use and transfer of his or her information; a statement of the service provider's commitment to data security; the steps taken to ensure data quality and access; and the consequences of consumer's refusal to provide the necessary information.

- *Choice and consent*

  A service provider must provide the consumers with the opportunity to exercise choice regarding how their information may be used.

- *Data security*

  A service provider should take appropriate measures protect the information from loss, misuse or alteration. In the event it transfers the information to a third party, it should ensure that the third party is aware of this data security practice, and that the third party also takes the same precautions to protect any transferred information.

- *Data quality and access*

  A service provider should take reasonable steps to ensure that the data is accurate, complete and timely for the purposes for which they are to be used. It should also establish appropriate processes or mechanisms that allow correction of inaccurate or incomplete information.

Multimedia companies should also bear in mind of the privacy provisions under the Malaysian Communications and Multimedia Content Code ('Content Code') developed by the Communications and Multimedia Content Forum of Malaysia.

Para 4.1(vii) of Part 3 of the Content Code states that advertisements shall not portray or refer to, by whatever means, any living person, unless their express prior permission has been obtained. It further states that this requirement applies to all persons, including public figures and foreign nationals. Advertisers should also take note not to offend the religious or other susceptibilities of those connected in any way with deceased persons depicted or referred to in any advertisement.

Para 3.9(f) of Part 4 the Content Code states that broadcasters should ensure that content of news and current affairs programs are presented with due respect to privacy of an individual. However, an intrusion into an individual's privacy may be justified in the public interest such as for purposes of detecting or exposing crime or a serious misdemeanor, protecting public health or safety and preventing the public from being misled by some statement or action of an individual or organization.

4.2.6 Credit Reporting Sector

Section 76 of the Credit Reporting Agencies Act 2010 ('CRAA') expressly states that the PDPA shall not apply to the processing of credit information by a credit reporting agency ('CRA'). The definition of personal data under the PDPA also explicitly excludes any information that is processed for the purpose of a credit reporting business carried on by a credit reporting agency under the CRAA.[115]

4.2.6.1 What Does Credit Reporting Business Mean?

Credit reporting business under the realm of the CRAA means a business that is involved in the processing of credit information for the purpose of providing a credit report to another person, whether for profit, reward or otherwise. However, it does not include the processing of credit information for the purpose of discharging regulatory functions or that is required or authorised by or under any law or by a credit rating agency.[116] Prior to the introduction of CRAA, credit reporting business was not regulated by any laws or regulations. With the enactment of the CRAA, agency or company that wishes to carry out the credit reporting business must first register itself and obtain a certificate of registration from the Registrar of Credit Reporting Agencies.[117] Once registered, the agency or company is not allowed to carry out any business other than a credit reporting business.[118] It has been reported that five credit reporting companies in Malaysia, namely, CTOS Sdn Bhd, SME Credit Bureau Sdn Bhd, RAM Credit Information Sdn Bhd, Dun & Bradstreet Malaysia Sdn Bhd and Financial Information Services Sdn Bhd will be registered under the CRAA to provide credit reporting business.[119] However, the Central Credit Reference Information System (CCRIS) is exempted as it is an agency under the Central Bank.[120]

The credit report shall contain credit information (whether in a written, oral or other form) which may have a bearing on a customer's eligibility to be provided with credit, history in relation to credit or capacity to repay credit which is used, has been used or is capable of being used as one of the factors in establishing a

---

[115] Section 4 of the PDPA.
[116] Section 2 of the CRAA.
[117] Section 11 of the CRAA.
[118] Section 12 of the CRAA.
[119] Tan (2010).
[120] Section 47 of the Central Bank of Malaysia Act 2009.

customer's eligibility for credit.[121] These credit information are usually collected from records available in the public domain such as government gazettes, bankruptcy notice advertised in newspapers, data from searches conducted at the Registry of Business and the Companies Commission of Malaysia, data supplied by debt collectors, banks and financial institutions. The CRA will then sell these credit information to credit providers such as banks, financial institutions and other legitimate moneylenders who wish to assess the creditworthiness of an individual or organisation.

4.2.6.2 Why Do We Need CRAA When We Already Have PDPA?

The PDPA applies to the processing of individual's personal data whereas the CRAA applies to the processing of credit information which includes individual's personal data, corporate information, and credit facility information (which includes information about application, approval, rejection, repayment and enquiry about credit facility).[122] The PDPA covers only individuals whereas the CRAA includes individuals, companies and businesses. The scope of information processed under the CRAA appears to be wider than that of the PDPA. This might be one of the reasons why Parliament saw the need to enact two different pieces of legislation as they cover different aspects of information, even though some of the information may be overlapping with each other.

4.2.6.3 Recent Cases Involving Credit Reporting Agencies Prior to the CRAA

There have been some interesting developments in the legal arena involving several suits against CTOS Sdn Bhd, one of the largest credit reporting companies in Malaysia.

In *Shafie Abdul Rahman v CTOS Sdn Bhd*,[123] the plaintiff claimed that CTOS had failed to update its database which showed that the plaintiff had been served with a bankruptcy notice when in fact, the plaintiff had already settled the debts. As a result of the outdated information, plaintiff failed to obtain bank loans as the banks had relied on the outdated information. CTOS argued that it had put up a warning notice on its report to inform the recipient of the report that the information on the report was not intended as confirmation of the 'current status' of the case and it urged the recipient of the report to seek confirmation from the relevant parties. However, the court rejected this argument on the basis that the warning notice was only meant to protect CTOS from any liability initiated by its clients but it did not extend to shield CTOS from any liability taken by the individuals whose information were recorded on the report. CTOS was negligent in failing to update its

---

[121] Section 2 of the CRAA.
[122] Section 2 and First Schedule of the CRAA.
[123] [2011] 9 CLJ 439.

database and had defamed the plaintiff by continuing to publish the outdated information.

The High Court in *Mohd Zaid bin Johan v CTOS Sdn Bhd*[124] reached a different conclusion. In this case, the plaintiff claimed that CTOS was negligent in storing the information as to the details of the plaintiff's bankruptcy notice when such notice had been set aside and the plaintiff was no longer a bankrupt. He claimed that as a result of the inaccurate information on the credit report, he failed to obtain bank loans as the banks had relied on the information obtained from CTOS. The court, however, held that CTOS was not responsible to investigate or make enquiries and ensure that the information it kept was true and accurate. The warning notice on the CTOS's credit report showed that the information on the report was not meant to be final and conclusive and it was the bank's duty to verify the information stated on the report. There was also no evidence to show that the banks would rely solely on the information obtained from CTOS. Mere presumption that the banks may rely on the information did not impose any liability against CTOS. The banks should have investigated the current status of the plaintiff before making any decision on whether to approve or reject the plaintiff's loan application.

Similarly, in *Soh Chun Seng v CTOS-EMR Sdn Bhd*,[125] CTOS-EMR failed to update its database and it issued a report which showed that the plaintiff had been served with a creditor's petition when in fact, the said petition had long been struck out as the debts had been fully settled. The Court of Appeal ruled in favour of the plaintiff and held that the inaccurate information on the credit report was capable of bearing a defamatory meaning. The warning notice did not absolve CTOS-EMR from liability for its mistakes.

4.2.6.4 Salient Features of the CRAA

Part V of the CRAA sets out the provisions on how the CRA should collect, give notice to customer, disclose, store and maintain the security and accuracy of credit information. These provisions share some of similar features found in the PDPA, though the provisions are not identical with each other. The CRAA also gives customer the right to access to his or her credit information or credit report and the right to correct any credit information or credit report that is inaccurate, not up to date, incomplete, irrelevant or misleading.

The provisions can be summarised as follows:

- *Collection of credit information (Section 22)*
  It provides that credit information can only be collected for a specific and lawful purpose directly related to an activity of the CRA, directly related to that purpose and is adequate but not excessive. Surprisingly, it allows the CRA to collect and use credit information without the need to first obtain customer's consent.
- *Notice to customer on processing of credit information (Section 23)*

---

[124] [2012] 8 MLJ 51.
[125] [2012] 2 CLJ 886.

It requires a CRA to give written notice to the customer that his credit information is being processed by or on behalf of the CRA.
- *Disclosure of credit information (Section 24)*
  It prohibits a CRA from disclosing the credit information to any third party unless one of the exceptions applies.
- *Prohibited disclosure in credit information (Section 25)*
  It sets out certain information that should and should not be included in a credit report.
- *Storage and security of credit information (Section 26)*
  It requires a CRA to take practical steps to protect the credit information from any loss, misuse, modification, unauthorized or accidental access or disclosure, alteration or destruction.
- *Accuracy of credit information (Section 29)*
  It requires a CRA to take reasonable steps to ensure that the credit information is accurate, up-to-date, complete, relevant and not misleading before it can further process the credit information.
- *Right of access to credit information or credit report (Section 30)*
  It gives customer the right to access to his or her credit information or credit report.
- *Right to correct credit information or credit report (Section 31)*
  It gives customer the right to correct any credit information or credit report that is inaccurate, not up to date, incomplete, irrelevant or misleading.

4.2.6.5 Some Criticisms Towards the CRAA

With the enactment of the PDPA and CRAA, it appears that an individual will enjoy better protection under the law in terms of his or her personal data and credit information. In facts, the duty which requires a CRA to take reasonable steps to ensure that the credit information is accurate and up-to-date will resolve the problems that arose in the few cases discussed above where the information contained in the credit reports provided by the CRAs were not accurate, resulting in the individuals being blacklisted by the banks. However, upon closer examination of the CRAA, the CRAA is by no means a perfect piece of legislation.

One significant criticism towards the CRAA is that a CRA does not need to first obtain customer's consent before it could collect and use the credit information.[126] This is in contradiction with the PDPA which requires a data user to first obtain the data subject's consent before he could process the data subject's personal data.[127] The implication of this is that, on one hand, one cannot process an individual's personal data without the latter's consent while on the other hand, that individual's credit information can be freely collected and used without his consent.

---

[126] Section 22 of the CRAA.
[127] Section 6 of the PDPA.

It is believed that the CRAA is modeled upon the New Zealand Credit Reporting Privacy Code 2004 (which is a code established under the Privacy Act 1993).[128] Rule 2(1) of the New Zealand's Code requires that credit information must be collected from the individual concerned,[129] but it does not have similar provision which allows collection of credit information without individual's consent. Abu Bakar Munir and Siti Hajar Mohd Yasin suggest that the CRAA should differentiate the information collected from the customer and those collected from the public domain. For the former, the information should only be collected with customer's consent as 'consent' is the key principle of data privacy.[130]

Another main criticism is that it appears that anyone, not just the credit provider such as banks, can obtain a copy of the credit report from the CRA.[131] Abu Bakar Munir and Siti Hajar Mohd Yasin suggest that credit information should only be given to a person with 'legitimate business need' (such as in the US); or a person who wishes to offer a customer credit-based products (such as in the UK); or to credit providers (such as in Australia); or to debt collectors, credit providers, prospective landlords or employers (such as in New Zealand).[132]

References

Black's Law Dictionary (1990) 16th edn. St. Paul Minn, West Publishing Co, p 270
Code of Ethics and Conduct (Second Edition, February 1999) issued by the Life Insurance Association of Malaysia. http://www.liam.org.my/index.php?option=com_content&view=article&id=563&Itemid=74. Accessed 24 May 2012
Code of Medical Ethics adopted by the Malaysian Medical Association. http://www.mma.org.my/Portals/0/pdf/MMA_ethicscode.pdf. 20 May 2012
Confidentiality Guidelines issued by the Malaysian Medical Council. http://mmc.gov.my/v1/docs/2011%203%20Confidentiality%20guidelines%20Approved%20on%2011%20October%202011_1.pdf. Accessed 21 May 2012
General Consumer Code 2003 drawn up by the Communications and Multimedia Commission. http://www.kpkk.gov.my/akta_kpkk/GeneralConsumerCode%20Malaysia.pdf. Accessed 15 June 2012
Grant H (2009) Data Protection 1998–2008. Comput Law Secur Rev 25:48
Guidelines on the Medical Records and Medical Reports issued by the Malaysian Medical Council. http://mmc.gov.my/v1/docs/Medical%20Records%20&%20Medical%20Reports.pdf. Accessed 21 May 2012
Hawkins JM, Allen R (eds) (1991) The Oxford English Dictionary. Clarendon, Oxford, p 293
Interpretation of 'Commercial Activity' under the PIPEDA. http://www.priv.gc.ca/leg_c/interpretations_03_ca_e.asp#_ftnref1. Accessed 3 Jun 2012

---

[128] Munir and Yasin (2010), p. 225.

[129] Rule 2(1) New Zealand Credit Reporting Privacy Code 2004.

[130] Munir and Yasin (2010), p. 228.

[131] See Section 2 of the CRAA which says that a credit business reporting business means a business that involves the processing of credit information for the purpose of providing a credit report to another person whether for profit, reward or otherwise.

[132] Munir and Yasin (2010), p. 235.

Khaw LT (2002) Towards a personal data protection regime in Malaysia. J Malays Comp Law 11:12, available via http://www.commonlii.org/my/journals/JMCL/2002/11.html. Accessed 30 May 2012

Malaysian Communications and Multimedia Content Code developed by the Communications and Multimedia Content Forum of Malaysia. http://cmcf.my/download/CONTENT_CODE_%28V6-Final%29.pdf. Accessed 16 Jun 2012

Munir AB (2010) 'Malaysian Data Protection Law is Inadequate', (7 January 2010) a blog post posted on 7 January 2010. http://profabm.blogspot.com/2010/01/malaysian-data-protection-law-is.html. Accessed 28 May 2012

Munir AB, Yasin SH (2002) Privacy and data protection. Sweet & Maxwell Asia, Kuala Lumpur

Munir AB, Yasin SH (2006) Electronic Commerce Bill 2006: an oversight or wanting a different or...? Malayan Law J 4:2

Munir AB, Yasin SH (2010) Personal data protection in Malaysia, Law and Practice. Sweet and Maxwell Asia, Kuala Lumpur

Patrick S (8 October 2009) Bill to Better Protect Your Personal Data, The Star. http://startechcentral.com/tech/story.asp?file=/2009/10/8/technology/20091008134431&sec=technology. Accessed 16 Apr 2012

PIPEDA Case Summary #345 - Private school not covered by the PIPEDA. http://www.priv.gc.ca/cf-dc/2006/345_20060705_e.asp. Accessed 3 Jun 2012

PIPEDA Case Summary #389 - Report of Findings - Law School Admission Council Investigation. http://www.priv.gc.ca/cf-dc/2008/389_rep_080529_e.asp. Accessed 3 Jun 2012

Reid A (2003) Privacy and the health industry. Allied Health Professions 5:61, http://www.austlii.edu.au/au/journals/LegIssBus/2003/7.pdf. Accessed 23 May 2012

Saunders JB (1988) Words and Phrases legally defined, 3rd edn. Butterworths, London, p 283

Tan S (2010) Credit Reporting Agencies Limited to 5. http://www.theedgemalaysia.com/business-news/164357-credit-reporting-agencies-limited-to-5.html. Accessed 5 Jun 2012

Ustaran E (2012) International data transfer, in European Privacy, law and practice for data protection professionals. IAPP Publication

Working Paper 12 entitled 'Transfer of Personal Data to Third Countries: Applying Article 25 and 26 of the EU Data Protection Directive'. http://ec.europa.eu/justice_home/fsj/privacy/docs/wpdocs/1998/wp12_en.pdf. Accessed 9 Jun 2012

Yeng AC (2009) Personal Data Protection: Govt Has Own Mechanisms. http://thestar.com.my/news/story.asp?file=/2009/7/15/nation/20090715212420&sec=nation. Accessed 15 Apr 2012

List of Material

APEC Privacy Framework. http://www.apec.org/Groups/Committee-on-Trade-and-Investment/~/media/Files/Groups/ECSG/05_ecsg_privacyframewk.ashx. Accessed 18 Jun 2012

Technology and 'Actors' in Data Protection

Noriswadi Ismail

> *Computer themselves, and software yet to be developed, will revolutionise the way we learn.*
>
> (Steven Paul Jobs, Co-Founder and Chief Executive of Apple Inc; 24th February 1955-5th October 2011)

Abstract
The approach of this chapter is by way of issues-based. As prelude, it touches on digital economy and its connection with data protection in general. Complementing the previous Chaps. 1–3, it then unveils the trends and the hypes of Malaysian scenarios and cases in dealing with data protection. As a disclaimer, the given scenarios and cases have nothing to do with existing parties, companies and organisations that I consulted and engaged. The final section draws the attention on what I coined as: 'bubble' relationship—government-business-consumer—that is, how to manage and draw the data protection governance within the 'bubble' in view of the PDPA.

5.1 Digital Economy and Data Protection

The first quarter of 2012 is a progressive period for data protection. On 25th January 2012, the European Commission proposed a comprehensive reform of the EU's 1995 data protection rules to strengthen online privacy rights and boost Europe's

N. Ismail (✉)
Quotient Consulting, 29 Duffell House, Loughborough Street, London SE11 5PX, UK
e-mail: noris@qconsultant.com

Digital Economy and beyond.[1] On 9th February 2012, the Department of Personal Data Protection Malaysia under the Ministry of Information Communications and Culture Malaysia was established.[2] On 23rd February 2012, the US unveiled its privacy blueprint, which includes the Consumer Privacy Bill of Rights.[3] On 19th March 2012, a high level EU–US cooperation on data protection to facilitate interoperability of commercial data privacy regimes was reaffirmed.[4] In the words of Viviane Reding[5]:

> Let us build a new gold standard of data protection based on clear and strong laws allowing our businesses and citizens to fully benefit from the digital economy.

These developments have called for the need to balance data protection law, business and technology to being on the same page. But, the task is not easy. In the US and EU, the advancement of technology poses unsettled challenges to data protection laws. As we may have already known, the technology speeds up, whilst the laws are still crawling, walking and catching the technology. This global problem has made data protection lawyers, consultants and experts to device win-win sophisticated ways to achieving their clients and stakeholders' needs. The territorial nature of data protection laws has added to the complexity. There are many principles and approaches which I categorise these in five different camps. First, the comprehensively compliant camp (DPD 95/46/EC), second, the self-regulatory camp (the US Safe Harbor) third, the rest of the regional camp (OECD and APEC) fourth, the technical standardisation camp (International Organization for Standardization) and lastly, the sector-specific legislation (based on industry-based regulations, guidelines and rules). These camps, at times, are unique by its own although it leads to certain foggy application in practice. Each camp has its own set of challenges, issues and uncertainties to date.

On 29th November 2001, the Minister of Information Communications and Culture, (the Minister) Datuk Seri Utama Dr. Rais Yatim remarked in his keynote address that Malaysian legislation at the time, such as Copyright Act 1987, Trade

---

[1] Commission proposes a comprehensive reform of data protection rules to increase users' control of their data and to cut costs for businesses. http://europa.eu/rapid/pressReleasesAction.do?reference=IP/12/46&format=HTML&aged=0&language=EN&guiLanguage=en. Accessed 25 January 2012.

[2] The Star Online, 12th February 2012, Sunday, Datuk Seri Dr Rais Yatim, Protecting your personal data. http://thestar.com.my/news/story.asp?file=/2012/2/12/nation/10716006&sec=nation. Accessed 12 February 2012.

[3] Consumer Data Privacy in a Networked World, A Framework For Protecting Privacy and Promoting Innovation in the Global Digital Economy. http://www.whitehouse.gov/sites/default/files/privacy-final.pdf. Accessed 24 February 2012.

[4] EU–US joint statement on data protection by European Commission Vice-President Viviane Reding and U.S. Secretary of Commerce John Bryson. http://europa.eu/rapid/pressReleasesAction.do?reference=MEMO/12/192&format=HTML&aged=0&language=EN&guiLanguage=en. Accessed 19 March 2012.

[5] See the joint statement.

Marks Act 1976, Computer Crimes Act 1997, Digital Signature Act 1997, the Communications and Multimedia Act 1998 and the Communications and Multimedia Commission Act protects legitimate rights and interests of individuals.[6] These laws, as the Minister rationalised, are the precursors towards the necessary protection although it does not mirror rights of privacy. Since then, PDPA was gazetted on June 2010—which marks the beginning for Malaysia's data protection chapter.

What motivates the laws? Technology. The answer to this question is straightforward. Nonetheless, it opens to open-ended issues that are left to the stakeholders and industry to solve. Taking the technology as the backbone that influences data protection, consider these hypothetical scenarios:

- A Malaysian driver uses a contactless card to pay toll along the highways for the past 10 years;
- A Malaysian airline company uses online archived data to promote future products and services to their previous and existing passengers;
- A Malaysian citizen having five accounts in social networking sites, five online banking and e-commerce based websites' accounts and various personal data archived in government and private hospital, telecommunications service provider and in his/her previous and present employment;
- A Malaysian doctor who manages patients' database for research, linkable and transferable between government hospitals;
- A newly-born baby who wears a tagged Radio Frequency Identification (RFID) wristband, the purpose of which is to avoid theft and mishandling of babies in the private hospital; and
- A Malaysian business traveler who uses her credit card for business transactions and having subscribed online cloud-based banking services and cloud-based loyalty services in New York, London, Paris, Kuala Lumpur, Tokyo, Jakarta and Dubai.

These scenarios, ideally, seem to be convenient due to the technology that resides behind it. It holds one ultimate aim: data processing, backed by various deployable technologies. In a typical data processing activity, these are the basic questions I always ask:

- *Who is the data subject?*
- *Who is the data user?*
- *Who is the data processor?*
- *Is there any personal data involved?*
- *Is there any sensitive personal data involved?*
- *Is there any third party involved?*
- *Is there any relevant filing system involved?*

---

[6] Keynote address of the Minister during the 'Jagat Cyber Law Seminar' on Data Protection at KUB Theatre, Wisma KUB, Jalan Yap Kwan Seng, Kuala Lumpur on 29th November 2001, 12.30pm. At the time he is the Minister in the Prime Minister Department. See Department of Personal Data Protection Malaysia booklet, *'Lindungi Hak Rakyat, Akta Perlindungan Data Peribadi 2010 (Akta 209)'* 20-21.

After determining the preliminary answers to the above, a basic understanding on how technology works is particularly crucial. As a starting point, readers should consider to appreciate the basic operations of a technology that processes data. For example, e-mail and mobile communications are the medium that typically send, receive, forward, transfer, mirror, delete and archive one's data from one point to another point. The ability to understand the mechanics of data processing will further bring one's understanding to link it with the posted questions above (I encourage readers to cross-refer Eva's **Chap. 8** to understanding selected trendy technologies). To further ascertain whether such data processing is lawful or unlawful in Malaysia, the PDPA 7 data protection principles (**must always be collectively**) applied to assess such technology—whether it complies with, or against to, the principles. I have coined it as 'Data Diagnosis Table':

5.1.1 Transacting with the Government

As reiterated by Edwin in **Chap. 3**, PDPA 2010 exempts the federal government, state government and the credit reporting agencies. The essential question is: how should we deal with data protection whilst transacting with the government? Hypothetical scenarios:

- A governmental agency appoints an external (non-Malaysian) consultant to advice on a specific subject matter. When the consultancy appointment is issued, one of the terms of reference includes the involvement of a Malaysian-based consultant. This is to ensure transfer of knowledge and expertise exercise takes place;
- A foreign governmental department based in the EU requests for sensitive personal data details (bank account, address, employment history and previous criminal convictions—if any) of a potential criminal from the Malaysian government. A private investigator's local based firm is appointed to coordinate;
- Three major critical systems of Malaysian governmental database will be merged and consolidated for the purpose of efficiency and convenient. A local leading company and three multinational companies are involved with this pursuit. The database contains personal and sensitive personal data of over 28 million of Malaysian citizens;
- A governmental agency manages e-procurement related transaction between companies in Malaysia. The system links to related ministries. The e-procurement process involves appointed consultants and companies to dealing with the stability of the system; and
- Malaysian public universities and hospitals' database will be integrated for the purpose of research, internship and housemanship. The integration is led by local based company and several multinational companies.

Once the PDPA is enforced, how will the above legal entities (local/global consultants, local and multinational companies) deal with data protection whilst transacting with the government?

I argue and take the position that the responsibility to manage data protection in any of these scenarios remains intact if the legal entity's engagement is considered as 'commercial transaction'. In other words, it is meant for business that exposes to data processing activities. In parallel, the liability is even greater due to its involvement with government and massive data subjects' of Malaysian citizens that links to national interest or national security's sensitivity. If such circumstances take place, two strategic routes should be considered:

- *Strategic route 1*: adopt exemption provision (if applicable); and
- *Strategic route 2*: register code of practice (commendable).

5.1.1.1 Strategic Route 1

The guidance to the exemption route is that one should be able to look into the six exemptions under Section 46 of the PDPA. Probably, or occasionally, certain engagement may fall under one of the exempted requirements. If exemption applies, it's best to clearly indicate this in such contract. In certain instances, the government has its obligation to maintain high level of secrecy under the relevant provisions of the Official Secrets Act 1972, supplemented by certain internal directives issued by its governmental department at the Federal level. In addition, there might also be certain technical security guidelines and requirements to be complied with. If this situation applies, the obligation to comply with data protection is equally footed between the person who transacts with the government, and vice versa.

5.1.1.2 Strategic Route 2

The strategy to register a code of practice representing groups of data subjects is commendable. It is a given privilege that should be explored. For instance, if the group of consultants, companies and multinationals decided collectively that this strategy is viable, they should sit together and propose the relevant provisions that could be incorporated in the code of practice. The code, in particular, should represent the data subjects' interest. Added focus and extra cautious must be made towards incorporating the relevant provisions that offer adequate level of protection. Whichever situation applies, and subject to the formality and process by the Data Protection Commissioner (the Commissioner), if approved, this strategic route will beef up the level of trust by any third parties who might intend to audit the level of adequacy of data protection compliance (see Philipp's **Chap. 10** in greater detail).

Bearing in mind that these two strategic routes may not sail smoothly if certain level of satisfactory is not fulfilled and if the Commissioner decided that the intention and actions are partly half-baked and not within the spirit of the code of practice's obligations. In this respect, interested readers who may want to opt for, either of, this route should be able to carefully invoke the accurate exemption provisions and/or clearly undertake a comprehensive code of practice that reaches the required level of adequacy determined by the Commissioner.

5.2 The Actors in Data Protection

5.2.1 The Case of Mukhsin

Mukhsin is an ambitious young professional working for a multinational based in Kuala Lumpur. He belongs to generation 'X', daily connected with social networking sites (SNS) accounts and web-based emails. He has ten different accounts, which he consistently accessed every day. An avid e-commerce shopper and transacts mostly online. Due to his back-to-back work demands, he rarely backup his data and occasionally deals with sensitive personal data at work. At times, his work deals with global data transfer from Malaysia to London, Boston, Hong Kong, Bangalore, Beijing, Brussels and Buenos Aires. One unfortunate day, his SNS and e-mail accounts were hacked. Bulk of his personal data, business counterparts' personal data and social friends' personal data have been leaked. He is now distress, and seeking your advice.

Mukhsin's case is not unique. It is happening every day and perhaps, some readers might have had experienced this. As a data subject, Mukhsin should be aware of his personal data protection rights and obligations. Prior to opening the SNS and email accounts, it's recommended to understand the privacy terms and setting. This should be equally applied when he is at work too. Although the situation in Malaysia is quite blurry to address privacy in the working environment or in the work place, Mukhsin should be able to consider to have familiarised with the existing Company's privacy policy with regards to e-mail communications, related information communications technology's security policy, data sharing policy (if any) and relevant updated policies issued and shared by the multinational's knowledge management bank pertaining to data protection and privacy. The advantage on this is that the multinational might have had the relevant governance and framework in place, reflected through its policies and practices. In addition, the understanding to differentiate between personal data and sensitive personal data is also crucial.

If you are the counsel, consultant, or data protection advisor to Mukhsin, these are five strategic steps worthy to pursue:

- *Strategic step 1*
  Notify the breach to the employer, the affected parties and voluntarily notify the same to the Commissioner (if the level of breach is critically severe);
- *Strategic step 2*
  Assemble the team that manages the breach (ranging from human resource, legal and compliance, information security, internal audit, business and development and corporate communication), to initiate immediate mitigation plan and disseminate how the plan works to the affected parties—consider the short, immediate and long term impacts of the Company's reputation and brand;
- *Strategic step 3*
  Issue an apology notice to the relevant parties that are affected by the breach incident and undertake the preventive actions that have been made. It's best to

provide pro-active assurance on the need to audit, review, educate and manage the company's data protection governance and management periodically;
- *Strategic step 4*
Develop and execute data protection training and development programme for the company's employees. The programme should be developed across the board; from the board of directors, senior management, middle management, executives and supporting staff. A specially designed programme could also be tailor-made for the company's business partners, associates and clients, which are potentially exposed to substantial data processing activities; and
- *Strategic step 5*
Update the status of the company's data protection management quarterly and work closely with the corporate communications/affairs team to develop short/immediate/long term data protection and privacy campaign at work.

5.2.2 The Case of 1Malaysia Group of Companies

1Malaysia Sdn. Bhd (1MSB) is a private limited company incorporated in Malaysia. 1MSB is a data processor on behalf of a data controller, 1Malaysia Global Ltd (1MGL), based in London. 1MSB processes data based on the authorisation and instructions of 1MGL. At the same time, 1MSB processes data exported from 1Malaysia Global Inc. (1MGI), based in California. At the time of these data processing activities, neither one of these companies has formalised the necessary data transfer agreement, nor, being advised on the priority to comply. 1MSB seeks your advice.

There will be potential review of business plans, processing and activities that involve data when PDPA 2010 is enforced. Business and the marketplace deals with data every seconds, day, month and year non-stop. Data is the 'currency' of the digital economy! And due to this, companies should be able to consider these for their business deliberation and resolution (at the board of directors and executive committee level):
- *Consideration 1*
Upon approving a strategic business plan, determine whether the company is a data user (under the PDPA 2010), data controller (under the DPD 95/46/EC) and data processors in various establishments and locations that they operate. Once determined, consider its roles and obligations in data processing activities to be effectuated in a data transfer agreement;
- *Consideration 2*
A risk mitigation plan strategy should be developed. This is to assess the nature of data processing in different marketplace, jurisdiction as well as the formality that is involved. In order to do this, at the executive committee level, it's best to coordinate the strategy with a group of data protection lawyer, consultant, expert and advisor of the respective marketplace and jurisdictions (I recommend readers to cross refer to Eduardo's **Chap. 7** for further analysis and apprehension); and

Table 5.1 The actors' table

Who's who	Description	Guidance
Data subject and data user	Anyone is, and can be, a data subject. Data user is a person or party who processes data of data subject(s) by way of contractual obligation or commercial transaction	Identify and ascertain whether a data subject is also a data user, and likewise, whether a data user is also a data subject within the contractual obligation or a commercial transaction
Data processor	A party which is authorised by the data user to conduct data processing activities on behalf of the data user by way of contractual obligation and commercial transaction	Identify and ascertain whether the role of data processor may also fall under the role of data user
Third party	Other then data user and data processor, but having some indirect commercial transaction relationship with the data user or data processor's data processing activities	Identify and ascertain whether such third parties could get access or privy to the data processing activities
The regulator	The Commissioner, Deputy Commissioners and Assistant Commissioners	Their terms of reference are to govern and enforce the obligations that are stipulated in PDPA
PDPAC	The members consist a Chairman, 3 members from the public sector and at least 7 but not more than 11 other members	Appointment of members of the PDPAC will be potentially made known once PDPA is enforced. It serves as a sounding board to the Regulator, and when necessary, to the Minister
AT	The members comprise a Chairman, two members or more (subject to the Minister's discretion), a member from the Judicial Legal Service of the Federation and a Secretary that is assisted by officials (determined by the Minister)	Appointment of members of the AT will be potentially made known once PDPA is enforced. It serves as an appeal platform for data subject, data user, data processor and third party who are aggrieved by the Commissioner's decision

- *Consideration 3*
  Careful consideration should be given to determine the deployed technology within the data processing activities. For example, if the company deploys cloud computing as the technology backbone in its data processing activities, members of the board and executive should be able to assess potential risks that may incur from the chosen cloud computing business model and deliberate the viable mitigation steps to be taken in its business plan.

5.2.3 Who's Who in Data Protection

In the world of data protection, there are many actors (see Table 5.1). To identify them, the coined data diagnosis table (see Fig. 5.1) may help the readers towards defining their data protection obligations. In any context (whether business, organisation, institution or government), there should be clear level of accountability

5 Technology and 'Actors' in Data Protection

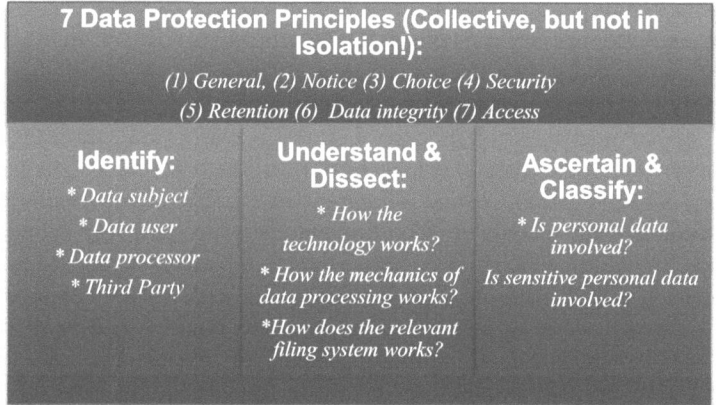

Fig. 5.1 Data diagnosis table

that starts from the top to the bottom of a management hierarchy. There are five classes of actors that I typically encounter in a commercial transaction setting:

5.2.3.1 Class 1
A legal entity, acts as a data user [or a data controller in the European Economic Area (EEA), which has in-house data processing capabilities and activities;

5.2.3.2 Class 2
A legal entity, acts as a data user (or a data controller in the EEA), which outsources its data processing activities to a data processor;

5.2.3.3 Class 3
A legal entity, acts as a data processor on behalf of a data user (or a data controller in the EEA);

5.2.3.4 Class 4
A legal entity acts as a data user (or a data controller in the EEA), which partly manages its data processing activities in-house and partly outsources the same to a data processor;

5.2.3.5 Class 5
A legal entity that acts as a data processor which its data processing roles' capabilities and activities are greater than the data user (or a data controller in the EEA).

The above classification is not definite as it may change subjected to the business plan, model, contractual arrangement as well as the flexibility of operations. It may also change when the legal entity is merged and acquired or subjected to winding up. Irrespective whichever model and situation applies, I take the strand that a higher responsibility, obligation, liability and governance should be bestowed onto the legal entity that manages and processes data, the most. From the micro setting of the legal entity in the abovementioned classes, these are the relevant team that collectively leads data protection management:

- *Start up and medium-sized*: in view of limited resources and capital, it's best to outsource the data protection management function to a credible data processor;
- *Beyond medium-sized (whether a public listed company or a multinational)*: a dedicated team of data protection counsels/leaders by way of pooling or reporting structure which may comprise (counsel, human resource/capital, internal audit, project leader, business development leader, research & development leader, finance and most importantly, information security leader); and
- *Governmental departments*: a dedicated team of officials by way of pooling or reporting structure, which may comprise (representation from the relevant governmental departments and agencies that deal with massive critical data processing activities of Malaysian citizens). Although the government and credit reporting agencies are exempted, it's best for them to consider (see Rani's **Chap. 8** to appreciate her articulated experience and analysis);

5.2.4 Who's Who in PDPA

Besides the data subject, data user, data processor and third party, PDPA has expressly provisioned the relevant actors that form the formality process. The Commissioner is assisted by a team of Deputy Commissioners and Assistant Commissioners, based on the terms of reference of their appointment. The Commissioner is accountable to the Minister. In executing the function, the Personal Data Protection Advisory Committee (PDPAC) plays a leading role to advise the Commissioner on any matters related to the PDPA. The PDPAC is also involved with the relevant governance and enforcement matters together with the Commissioner. At the time of this writing, the Director General of the Personal Data Protection Department oversees the governance of the PDPA. Once the appointment of the Commissioner is formalised, readers will be informed on potential hosts of developments pertaining to future appointments of the members of PDPAC.

If such formality process within the PDPA is in disputable or potentially challengeable or aggrieved by the decision of the Commissioner, data user, data processor and third party may appeal to the Appeal Tribunal (AT). To date, the members of the AT have not been appointed. Nonetheless, it is advisable to keep abreast with future developments on this. Appeals can only be made in relation to:

- Registration of data user;
- Refusal of registration to register the code of practice;
- Failure to comply with such data access request or data correction request;
- Any matters relating to enforcement notice;
- Refusal of the Commissioner to revoke or vary the enforcement notice; and
- The refusal of the Commissioner to carry out or continue such lodged complaints or investigations.

5.3 The 'Bubble' Relationship

I coin the term 'bubble' relationship due to two main stances. Firstly, the relationship between the actors in a data protection management is crucial to achieve a desired commercial objective. It requires close collaboration between the actors in the company, organisation and institution. The first stance mirrors the marketplace. Secondly, the relationship between the actors and the who's who in the PDPA must not be drifted apart. The marketplace autonomously needs the regulator to strike the balance of fairness, rights and obligations in data protection compliance and enforcement. This 'bubble' is not new. As akin to other areas of laws, regulations and governance, it is all about the interaction, engagement and capacity building between the government, the business and the consumer.

In Malaysia, the bubble relationship in data protection is about to take place. PDPA, besides being 'business-friendly, instead of controversially 'human rights friendly' as claimed by some, is a good law. Ultimately however, a good law needs practical application, real life examples and less bureaucracy, which leads to productivity in the marketplace. Readers may wonder, how should we lead this? When is the right time? And what is needed?

> **How Should We Lead This?**
> Technology. Technology. Technology. This emphasis shows that one must be able to ensure the deployed technology is, by all means, data protection and privacy compliant. As Malaysia's e-commerce transactions have increased by leaps and bounds, and towards Malaysia's determination to achieving Vision 2020, it's vital to position one's technology leadership through strong data protection governance. To transform one's company by revisiting its existing business plan, innovative products and services and offerings to being data protection friendly and compliant take time. It requires concerted effort between and amongst the actors. Diffusion and dissemination activities could be done via data protection training programme and awareness. It's always commendable to start this from basic and gradually develop the same to the required expectation of the company, organisation or institution.

> **When Is the Right Time?**
> Now, and forever! There is no timeline and deadline to start. The appropriate mindset, enthusiasm, strong will to lead and consistency to pursue is the key.

And What Is Needed?

Data protection is a 'sexy' subject matter. It requires passion and 360-degree understanding. To continuously lead the 'bubble' relationship, readers should consider going beyond than the legal aspects of data protection. Develop the interest to understand how the technology interacts with, and perhaps, against to, data protection. Relate the understanding by way of viewing data protection in holistic manner. This could be established through multidisciplinary relationship management and engagement with various stakeholders in the marketplace. As this progress develops, one could initiate potential thought leadership representing the data user to the government and the regulator.

It may not be easy as there might be one ongoing argument: *The reality is that, as this subject matter is quite new in Malaysia, one needs to have competent resource to manage the technical and formality aspects of data protection. So, how should I lead?* The answer is that start from zero until you being a hero. To engage data protection leadership within the bubble relationship does not require exceptional hero, nonetheless, everyone can be a hero of data protection from the respective company, organisation and institution. Malaysia, specifically, and ASEAN generally, requires data protection leaders and this is the time readers can strategise to considering this headway.

Selected Technologies' Appraisal from the PDPA's Lens

Noriswadi Ismail

> *Les Mots Juste Et Injustice Sont Entendus Par Touts Les Cosciences*
> *Transliterated: 'Too many Laws, Too Few Examples'*
> (Louis Antoine Léon de Saint-Just, French Revolutionary,
> 25th August 1757-28th July 1794)

Abstract
The difficulty to translate new laws and regulations into practice is uncommon. Typically, there are baggage of predictions, speculations and mosaics of interpretations. Owing to these, the PDPA, is partly trapped, within the latter's landscape. Whilst awaiting a clear direction, this chapter provides strategic guidance to the readers via twofold. Firstly, it attempts to explain how selected technologies could be appraised by collectively adopting the PDPA 2010s 7 data protection principles. It anticipates critical concerns that may be prevalent, the requited strategic approaches and guidance. Secondly, it guides the readers to go beyond than the Malaysia's contour by appreciating the EU and US's experience.

6.1 Expectations

In the previous chapter, I have emphasised the importance to determine and understand the actors' involvement in the PDPA. I have also provided guidance to readers on the significance to collectively apply the 7 Data Protection Principles (7DPP). In this chapter, I outline the expectations how these principles may offer to balance the data protection interest in business, operations and day-to-day life. I approach this by selecting relevant technologies that readers may find quite common or may have experienced.

N. Ismail (✉)
Quotient Consulting, 29 Duffell House, Loughborough Street, London SE11 5PX, UK
e-mail: noris@qconsultant.com

6.1.1 E-Mail Communications

Having had more than one e-mail is not surprising at all. In your daily e-mail communications, you may open your working e-mail (employer's email), personal e-mails and subscribed-based e-mails (for example, web-based membership e-mail or group e-mail based on interests, activities, social life and networking). Throughout the communications, you receive various e-mail messages ranging from work, personal, update and to advertisement of products and services—to name a few. You may reply, delete, forward, save and mark it later (subject to its priority).

6.1.2 Expectations from 7DPP

The principles of general, notice, choice, disclosure, security, retention, data integrity and access have elaborated the conditions. Of these, in any communications, consent plays an important role. This is mentioned generally under the general principle (although it is not defined explicitly in the PDPA). Consent **must always be** equally linked to the purpose:

$$Consent = Purpose$$

If someone intends to forward your e-mail, which has third parties' personal or sensitive personal data (for example, medical informatics), to a third party, consent must always be sought from the third party. This situation only applies if there is no contractual obligation or commercial transaction purpose. Nonetheless, if the latter is formalised, it is generally acceptable to forwarding the e-mail if it complies with the relevant e-mail communications and data protection policy or data sharing policy of the company.

In the PDPA, the period of data retention is not explicitly expressed (silent). Readers should consider to define, redefine and revisit the period of data retention (as in this context, archived e-mails in the database) and consult the PDPA's regulations/guidelines. Some sector specific legislation requires a period of 7 years to 12 years for the purpose of evidence and audit trails (see Edwin's **Chap. 3**). The fundamental question to ask is: *What is the ideal period of retention?* I take the position that sensitive personal data requires longer retention period and such personal data requires reasonable retention period. The formulae:

$$Sensitive\ personal\ data : longer\ retention\ period\ (lrp)$$
$$Personal\ data : reasonable\ retention\ period\ (rrsp)$$
$$lrp \Rightarrow 12\ years$$
$$rrsp \Rightarrow 7\ years$$

The basis in deriving the above formulae is based on the nature and sensitivity of data within the company, organisation and institution. Some data may be retained longer, depending upon the purpose of retention. As a best practice, if this situation applies, the extended period of retention should be notified to the data subject.

One of the 'privilege' rights that everyone has in the PDPA 2010 is the Data Access Request (DAR). For example, if a data subject wants to know about a specific data that is processed by a data user, he or she has the statutory right to exercise the DAR. This privilege, however, should not be abused; rather, it should be strategically applied (see Rani's **Chap. 10**). The circumstances that warrant DAR should be observed so that it will not be refused due to technical formality grounds that are stipulated in Section 32 of the PDPA. Why DAR matters? It matters because:

- Data subject is able to ascertain the volume of personal data or sensitive personal data withheld by the data user;
- Data subject may ascertain whether the data is updated or otherwise;
- Data subject may utilise the status of the DAR as audit trail, potential evidence, litigation exhibits and record retention (whenever necessary); and
- Data subject may be able to pre-empt the data user on certain inaccuracy of his or her outdated personal and sensitive personal data.

The tedious process whilst dealing with DAR requires lengthy manly hours, cost, and at times, requires third party's consent (whom his or her name or personal data was mentioned in the required data that is requested by the data subject). These are the growing concerns:

- Redacting the name of a third party that is contained in the DAR by way of manual or automated means involves lengthy process and approval—*Bureaucracy prevails!*
- The method of redacting takes considerable time, energy and resource for the data user—*It's all about the money!*
- Repeated DAR that does not serve reasonable purpose may waste the time of all parties (data user and potentially the Commissioner, if the subject matter of DAR is contentious) – *Hence, counter-productive!*
- The required formality; between the data subject, data user and the relevant third party (if applicable) takes time, depending upon the turnaround time to responding to the DAR—*It's a snail versus rabbit race!*
- Refusal to grant DAR may be potentially subjected to the Commissioner's involvement (if the refusal is disputable, challengeable and contentious)—*It's the buy-the-time tactic!* and
- The DAR process may take a longer time if the data user does not longer exist due to winding up, death and other unexpected events—*Expect the unexpected!*

What's the recommended way to deal with bad-faith DAR? I have pedantically tabulated the ideal and reasonable way, as follows:

6.2 Emerging Technologies

Technologies such as RFID, the Cloud and to a certain extend, the Closed Circuit Television (CCTV) gives a wake up call to the PDPA. I have dissected how the 7DPP applies to these technologies:

6.2.1 RFID

This technology has been deployed commercially in the marketplace since early 2000 and to date. It comprises a reader, a chip/tag, middleware and a database. The main mission of this technology is to uniquely identify any objects, living identifiable individual and animal for the purpose of aggregation, analysis, retrieval and retention of such data (personal and sensitive personal data). RFID is deployed amongst others in supply chain environment, inventory, parcel tracking, sporting event, cartel, hospital, transportation and the food industry. The basic illustration on how RFID relates to the actors of the PDPA, is illustrated as follows:

How RFID works: RFID wristband system identifies the baby by way of a unique code of identification specially assigned (in a chip/tag format) and transfers the personal data of the baby to a dedicated database. The reader transmits the details of the personal data to the database and subject to the system integration and application; the database may be linked to other systems, such as the patient tracking system or the hospital management system.

Data user: a hospital deploys RFID wristband system to identify newly born baby, which supports the patient tracking management system of the hospital.

Data subject: mother and newly born baby

Data processor: the IT company that processes the personal and the sensitive personal data on behalf of the data user

Third party: any sub-contractor that the IT company transacts with for the purpose of data processing activities

Nature of transmitted, collected, aggregated and retained data: personal data and sensitive personal data of the baby and the mother

In the above scenario, these are the considerations that I tabulated as Data Diagnosis Application Table.

6.2.2 The Cloud

Applying the RFID wristband system setting above, the Cloud technology may save substantial cost of the data user. The cloud may reduce the involvement of resources that rely on technical hardware and at the same time the visualised cloud environment will make the operations and processes, effectively on time. For example, if the data user intends to revisit and transform the existing RFID wristband system to a cloud-based, strategic top 3 priorities must be considered beforehand.

6.2.2.1 Strategic Top Priority 1

Negotiation stage: during the negotiation of a data transfer agreement or a master outsourcing agreement, consider the issues of: applicable jurisdiction; choice of cloud (whether private, public or hybrid); establishment and location of the data processor and any third party (if any); alternative dispute resolution strategy; data protection audit; exit strategy—in the event of dispute or force majeure; cyber insurance (if any, and if applicable); level of status reporting—data protection higher level report (on the Cloud) to the board of directors and the executive committee at the data user and data processor's level; and voluntary disclosure to the Commissioner (if applicable and if any). Most importantly, continuing training on data protection management and compliance at all level (board of directors, executive committee, senior management, executives, supporting staff, vendor, partners and associates) is recommended.

Note that these lists are not exhaustive and it may be depending upon the business plan, model and execution of the proposed cloud-based application.

6.2.2.2 Strategic Top Priority 2

Designing stage: during the designing stage or the systems requirement of the cloud-based system architecture, the solutions architect and programmer should be able to interact closely with the data protection counsel, auditor, consultant and expert for independent opinion. From the context of the PDPA, the 7DPP should be the benchmark and taking into account whilst at this stage. It should be collectively applied. Extra cautious and emphasis should be applied to the principles of data security, access, integrity and retention.

At the user acceptance test level, independent opinions from the data protection auditor, consultant, counsel and expert should be sought so that the cloud-based system is data protection compliant and friendly.

6.2.2.3 Strategic Top Priority 3

Implementation stage: the application of 7DPP must be collectively applied. The data user should develop continuing technical training on cloud-based system and data protection compliance. The similar approach should be applied (as mentioned in *Strategic Top Priority 1* on training). Periodic data protection audit, qualified independent opinion and voluntary disclosure of the state of data protection compliant of the cloud-based system should be considered. As a best practice, initiate a data protection compliance review in the end of the implementation stage (subject to the duration of the project) and propose strategic and practical recommendations for improvement.

Consider the need to disseminate the importance of data protection through public relations' campaigns. This may enhance the value creation of the data user, data processor and such third party's brand, trust and respect.

6.2.3 CCTV

CCTV is deployed for the purposes of surveillance and security. This technology has been massively deployed throughout external and internal private and public buildings that require surveillance. The purpose of deployment differs—subject to the required security level. CCTV is also deployed in an employer's building. This is to ensure safety and control amongst the employees. Depending upon the industry where employee works, CCTV may be deployed and used effectively at working place. This is how readers may dissect the CCTV actors:

Data user: employer

Data subject: employee

Data processor: the company that the data user has authorised for data processing activities (ranging from deployment and to the purposes of data processing activities)

Third party: any third party that the data processor interacts and transacts with by way of contractual obligation and commercial transaction

6.2.3.1 Strategic Top Priority 1

Policy and governance: prior to, and once, the PDPA and the regulations/guidelines are enforced, employer should be able to revisit the existing employment policy that relates to data retention and employment agreement too. A proposed data sharing, retention or a stand-alone data protection policy should be established (this is not limited to CCTV processing only, but also extendable to any technologies that the employer deployed).

6.2.3.2 Strategic Top Priority 2

Pooling the team: depending upon the size of a company, organisation and institution, there should be a team of resources that deal with DAR (see Table 6.1) in the event an employee demands for DAR due to a specific purpose of request. The team should comprise human resource, in-house counsel and the technical team. Subject to the level or seriousness of the request, the DAR strategy should be considered.

6.2.3.3 Strategic Top Priority 3

Contractual obligation: formalise a contractual obligation and data processing agreement with the data processor. The agreement should be able to address the obligation to comply with the 7DPP, periodic audit, governance, reporting and enforcement (if necessary and applicable). Designate key resources to govern and administer the agreement. This is to avoid potential security breach or illegal access of the CCTV images or data retained by the data processor.

During the negotiation, drafting, management and enforcement stages of the contract or agreement, appoint a lead project manager who will be the key person to interact with the data user and any third party. Such issues pertaining to the CCTV management could be channelled to the project manager. In the event of potential dispute that may be contentious, the project manager should be able to work and

Table 6.1 The DAR guiding table

Data subject's expectations	Description of DAR	Guidance
Data subject exercises repeated DAR	The request is repeated without a reasonable interval, justifiable and qualified reasons/grounds	Refuse the DAR with cited reasons and email a carbon copy of DAR refusal notice to the relevant official of the Commissioner's office as an audit trail
Data subject uses DAR to ascertain details of negotiation, forecast and employment reference	The request may not qualified to be regarded as DAR	Assess the purpose, ascertain the reason(s) and if it's trivial or falls within the grounds of refusal in Section 32 of the PDPA, notice of refusal with cited reasons should be appropriately notified sent to the data subject (by e-mail or post). A DAR refusal notice should also be e-mailed by way of carbon copy to the named third parties that may also be the subject of the DAR
Data subject opts DAR as fishing of litigation evidence by himself or through/represented by a litigator/barrister	A 'fishy' DAR or potentially a 'good faith' DAR	The request may be qualified if it fulfills the requirements under Section 32 of the PDPA. Nonetheless, it may fall under the risk of repeated DAR or if it may not be able to fulfill the requirements under Section 32 of the PDPA

consult closely with the data user's pooling team. If the case is severe and may lead to conflict, consider adopting the alternative dispute resolution strategy (see Table 6.2).

6.2.4 Other Technologies

The above briefly described RFID, the Cloud and CCTV are just amongst the many technologies that are in the marketplace. For example, there are many data users, which have deployed biometrics technology, retina identification technology and voice recognition system for various purposes. These technologies are handy and attractive. There are also potential technologies that we have not been exposed to, or awaiting it to be unveiled in anticipation. In view of these technologies and trends, the importance to adopt the data diagnosis and the 7DPP must not be ignored and abandoned. I am of the opinion that the potential guidelines/regulations the PDPA offer may not be able to answer all questions. It is a useful guidance that may help the marketplace to embark on its data protection governance and compliance framework. Admittedly it will be very much interesting to see how it reacts and matures.

Table 6.2 Data diagnosis application table

Data diagnosis application vis-à-vis the PDPA 2010	Description	Guidance
Collectively apply 7DPP and consider whether the overall design and function is data protection compliant and friendly	The 7DPP should be applied throughout the actors who are involved	Avoid burdensome and lengthy technicality process that may hinder the expected deliverables of the RFID system. Consider to highlight anticipating issues that may affect the 7DPP
Apply the 7DPP holistically throughout the RFID chain of actors	The 7DPP should be included in a data processing agreement (or such agreement to that nature, for example, master outsourcing agreement)	In the interest of covering the data user's liability, consistent back-to-back terms and conditions that mirrored the 7DPP's obligations should be extended to the data processor and any third parties involved
Audit significant issues that may arise throughout the RFID system	The basis of audit should take the 7DPP as the key terms of audit's reference	It's best to pursue the data protection audit yearly (depending upon the scale and requirements of the RFID system). In any event, the auditing task may be initiated with the respective actors' auditing team. It's also recommended to appoint an independent data protection auditor to verify and provide an independent opinion in relation to the state of the RFID system
Voluntary disclosure on the state of 7DPP	The voluntary disclosure, although not required by the PDPA is a good exercise. Some actors (company, organisation and institution) require disclosure in relation to the state of their internal control. Disclosing the state of the data user's RFID system control leads to a commendable data protection leadership. It may boost respect, trust and brand value	Potential voluntary disclosure should be agreed by the board of directors and executive committee based on qualified opinions of the data protection auditors. This could also be highlighted through the data user's annual report (if any) or management report
Consider alternative dispute resolution strategy (if such dispute happened)	Litigation process takes time. As alternative, if such RFID system may result to potential security breach throughout the chain of actors, an alternative dispute resolution strategy should be developed	The strategy should contain means of settling such dispute that may arise from the security breach. Typically, such means are pre-agreed during the contractual negotiations between the data user and the

(continued)

Table 6.2 (continued)

Data diagnosis application vis-à-vis the PDPA 2010	Description	Guidance
		data processor. In any event, if the cause of the security breach is not from the data user, but the data processor or the third party, an independent impartial team (consist of agreed data protection auditor, barrister/litigator and the general counsel/in-house counsel) should be able to ascertain and determine whether the cause is inter-related with the data user or other contributing factors If such cause is identified, consider win-win way to settle the dispute and voluntarily notify the relevant official of the Commissioner's office (if the breach is critically severe)

6.3 Learning from the Best, but Not Copying Them

I may be bias to rely heavily on the EU and the US's experience. Nonetheless, putting the conceptual, academic and policy-based argument aside, of the latter, I aim to let the readers know that significant technologies and data protection progress are very much robust at these parts of the world. In Malaysia, the PDPA, the regulations/guidelines and the Commissioner, its team and relevant governmental departments have had taken a leadership role to realise how importance data protection boosts the trust and respect to consumer in digital economy and e-commerce environment. In this section, I am not paraphrasing and importing what the EU and the US have had achieved. I wear the visionary and analyst hat to call for certain structured mechanism and level of engagement for Malaysia and ASEAN as a whole.

6.3.1 For Malaysia

The reality in Malaysia today is that, beside the Department of personal Data Protection (as at the time of this publication), and potentially, the Commissioner, we have also sector specific legislation's regulator, governmental agencies and Ministries that may have interest or obligations in data protection, whether as a sounding board, advisor or having strong interest in the required deliverables of its

key performance indicators (although it may not be partly significant due to certain exemptions under the PDPA or silent provisions that may affected the administered legislation of these regulators and agencies). They are:
- Attorney General's Chambers under the Prime Minister's Department;
- Credit Reporting Agencies (CRA) of the Registrar under the Ministry of Finance;
- Department of Chemistry Malaysia (DCM) under the Ministry of Science, Technology and Innovation (MOSTI);
- Malaysian Communications and Multimedia Commission (MCMC), a regulator under the Ministry of Information Communications and Culture Malaysia;
- Central Bank of Malaysia (Bank Negara Malaysia – BNM);
- CyberSecurity Malaysia (CyberSecurity), an agency under MOSTI;
- Ministry of Health (MOH);
- Ministry of Human Resources (MHR);
- Multimedia Development Corporation (MDC);
- The Malaysian Administrative Modernisation and Management Planning Unit (MAMPU) under the Prime Minister's Office (PMO) of Malaysia; and
- Securities Commission (SC) Malaysia, which reports to the Minister of Finance.

These 12 actors are the closest that may work with the Commissioner on such issues that affect the PDPA. In order to lead the data protection leadership at the national level, I propose the establishment of an oversight body that represents Malaysia's interest, chaired by the Commissioner. The body should have representation from these actors as to relay their concerns that may affect their administered legislation after having heard potential feedbacks and comments from the marketplace (stakeholders). This oversight body is not replacing the Commissioner at all. It should be able to represent Malaysia at the international level. For instance, to be potentially involve in the higher level policy discussions between the members of the Asia-Pacific Economic Cooperation Privacy Framework, European Commission (EC), Article 29 Data Protection Working Party of the EC, members of the OECD under the Directorate for Science, Technology and Industry, the US Federal Trade Commission and the US Department of Commerce (which administers the US Safe Harbor). The oversight body's policy discussions and engagements should be disseminated by way of annual report to the parliament, accessible by the marketplace. The potential funds may be collectively contributed by the respective members (subject to the level of interest and accountability).

If and when necessary, the body should be able to issue clear guidance and direction as to how the PDPA and its regulations/guidelines may affect its existing administered legislation, guidelines/regulations and directives. The rationale is to avoid confusion, misinterpretation and silence in its application.

6.3.2 Challenge for Malaysia

The biggest challenge lies onto having the right resource and expertise to understanding data protection beyond than its legal aspects. The creation of skill sets in data protection should be made in holistic manner, instead of, restricted to laws and regulations. Indeed, the Public Service Department, which is an agency under the PMO may have a herculean task to having the right resources to lead this.

6.3.3 For ASEAN

In ASEAN, Malaysia is the first to lead the data protection initiative. At the time of this writing, the Philippines passed its similar legislation.[1] Singapore has issued two rounds of consultations on its proposed consumer data protection regime.[2] It is expected that Indonesia, Brunei, Vietnam and Thailand will follow suit. By 2015, the ASEAN Economic Community (AEC) shall take place and potential harmonisation of laws, trades and services amongst the ASEAN member states shall also gradually take place.[3] Under B6 on e-commerce, the Strategic Schedule of the blueprint targets by 2010–2015, the member states should be able to initiate and execute these:

- *Update and/or amend relevant legislations in line with regional best practices and regulations in e-commerce activities;*
- *Adopt the best practices/guidelines on other cyber-law issues (i.e. **data privacy**, consumer protection, intellectual property rights, internet service providers' liability, etc) to support the regional e-commerce activities; and*
- *Advancing cross border electronic transactions, through pilot implementation of mutual recognition of foreign digital signatures.*

The members aim that by 2015, a harmonised legal infrastructure for e-commerce should be fully in place in ASEAN. Given this ambitious commitment, ASEAN member states should consider the regional integration of its respective data protection legislation and to what level it main achieve the desired level of regional adequacy amongst them. Although it's quite early to consider, ultimately however, I propose this strategic guidance for consideration:

6.3.3.1 Strategic Consideration 1
Application of data transfer between the ASEAN member states: this needs to take into account the DPD 95/46/EC (the proposed Data Protection Regulation) on data transfer to third countries and APEC Cross-Border Privacy Rules.[4]

---

[1] See http://www.senate.gov.ph/lisdata/1218710275!.pdf. Accessed 1st October 2011.

[2] See Ministry of Information, Communications and the Arts (MICA) http://app.mica.gov.sg/Default.aspx?tabid=481. Accessed 1st June 2012; See also Public Consultation issued by MICA Proposed Personal Data Protection Bill. http://app.mica.gov.sg/Default.aspx?tabid=487. Accessed 1st June 2012.

[3] See ASEAN Economic Community Blueprint. http://www.aseansec.org/5187-10.pdf. Accessed 1st June 2012.

[4] See http://www.apec.org/Groups/Committee-on-Trade-and-Investment/Electronic-Commerce-Steering-Group.aspx. Accessed 1st June 2012.

6.3.3.2 Strategic Consideration 2

Establishment of a proposed ASEAN data protection supervisor: learning from the EU's experience (the European Union Data Protection Supervisor),[5] this establishment is vital to ensure the level of accountability and independence is intact, especially matters pertaining to the harmonised application, governance and enforcement of the respective member states' data protection legislation.

6.3.3.3 Strategic Consideration 3

Establishment of a clear accountability, formality, governance and enforcement regime: although this consideration will need a long time to be executed, nonetheless, it is pertinent to the ASEAN member states to pre-empt on how this may contribute to boost ASEAN's economy as a whole.

6.3.4 Challenge for ASEAN

The biggest challenge for ASEAN is that data protection is a new law. It requires maturity of governance, implementation and enforcement between and amongst the member states. The different cultural demography, its historical legal systems and legislative influences (from the common, civil and mixture of both laws) and political enthusiasm differ. So much so, ASEAN should be together to lead the data protection irrespective of these hybrid differences.

List of Materials

APEC Privacy Framework. http://publications.apec.org/publication-detail.php?pub_id=390. Accessed 30 Apr 2012
ASEAN Economic Community Blueprint. http://www.aseansec.org/5187-10.pdf. Accessed 30 Apr 2012
CCTV – Guide for Organisations – ICO. http://www.ico.gov.uk/for_organisations/data_protection/topic_guides/cctv.aspx. Accessed 30 Apr 2012
Central Bank of Malaysia Official Portal. http://www.bnm.gov.my/. Accessed 1 May 2012
CyberSecurity Malaysia. http://www.cybersecurity.my/en/index.html. Accessed 1 May 2012
Data Protection Technical Guidance Radio Frequency Identification. http://www.ico.gov.uk/upload/documents/library/data_protection/detailed_specialist_guides/radio_frequency_indentification_tech_guidance.pdf. Accessed 2 Feb 2012
Department of Chemistry Malaysia. http://www.kimia.gov.my/. Accessed 1 May 2012
European Data Protection Supervisor. http://www.edps.europa.eu/EDPSWEB/. Accessed 1 May 2012
Export.gov – Main Safe Harbor Homepage. http://export.gov/safeharbor/. Accessed 16 Jun 2012
Ismail N (2007) RFID; the Internet of things that threats data protection and privacy? Dissertation, University of Strathclyde

---

[5] See European Data Protection Supervisor. http://www.edps.europa.eu/EDPSWEB/. Accessed 1st June 2012.

Ismail N (2010) RFID: is legal risk management relevant in consumer privacy? Int J Technol Transfer Commercialisation. doi:10.1504/10.30216

Ismail N (2011) Cursing the Cloud (or) Controlling the Cloud. Comput Law Secur Revew. doi:10.1016/j.clsr.2011.03.005

Ismail N (2012a) Data Transfer in Association Southeast Asian Nations (ASEAN) Economic Community (AEC) – The Malaysian Personal Data Protection Act (PDPA) 2010 approach. In: British and Irish Law Education and Technology Association 2012 Conference, Northumbria University Law School, Centre for Life in Newcastle, 29–30 March 2012

Ismail N (2012b) Personal data protection in Malaysia. Different principles. Different approaches. In: 2nd Annual Research Student Conference, Brunel Law School, Brunel University, London, 14 June 2012

Ismail N (2012c) Selected issues regarding the Malaysian Personal Data Protection Act 2010. Int Data Privacy Law. doi:10.1093/idpl/ips005

MAMPU Official Portal. http://www.mampu.gov.my/web/bi_mampu. Accessed 1 May 2012

Multimedia Development Corporation. http://www.mdec.my/. Accessed 1 May 2012

OECD Guidelines on The Protection of Privacy and Transborder Flows of Personal Data. http://www.oecd.org/document/18/0,3746,en_2649_34223_1815186_1_1_1_1,00.html. Accessed 2 Jun 2012

Official Portal of the Attorney General's Chambers of Malaysia. http://www.agc.gov.my/. Accessed 1 May 2012

Official Portal of the Ministry of Health Malaysia. http://www.moh.gov.my/. 1 May 2012

Official Website of the Ministry of Finance Malaysia. Functions of Creditor Reporting Agencies Office of the Registrar. http://www.treasury.gov.my/index.php?option=com_content&view=article&id=2060&Itemid=152&lang=en. Accessed 1 May 2012

Organisational Structure of the Personal Data Protection Department Malaysia. http://www.kpkk.gov.my/images/stories/m_jabatan/jpdp/co_jpdp2012_2.jpg. Accessed 8 Jul 2012

Securities Commission Malaysia. http://www.sc.com.my/. Accessed 1 May 2012

The Official Website, Ministry of Human Resources Malaysia. http://www.mohr.gov.my/. Accessed 1 May 2012

Acclaiming Accountability. Preaching Best Practices 7

Noriswadi Ismail

> *Management of many is the same as management of few. It is a matter of organisation – The Art of War*
>
> (Sun Wu, known as Sun Tzu, Military General and Tactician, 544 BC-496 BC)

Abstract

This chapter advocates about leadership and strategy that company, organisation and institution should be able to adopt. It brings the readers to consider how crucial accountability plays its role and the need to continuing such best practices. This is neither a secret recipe, nor, exceptional in data protection, as it may also be applicable to other subject matters. Data protection, at times, is slightly understated, but certainly, it is not underrated. It raises the eyebrows of the board of directors, executive committee and senior management if breach happened. Otherwise, it may be regarded as another mundane, routine and monotonous compliance tick-in-the box exercise if it is fully complied with. In order to debunk the latter, I attempt to impress the readers that data protection is not another area of law that adds the burden; rather, it boosts the brand, governance and leadership of your company, organisation and institution.

7.1 From Top to Bottom

In Chaps. 4 and 5, I have, in some occasions, supplicated the involvement of the board, executive committee and senior management to appreciate data protection. This is followed by the executive, supporting employee, business partner and

---

N. Ismail (✉)
Quotient Consulting, 29 Duffell House, Loughborough Street, London SE11 5PX, UK
e-mail: noris@qconsultant.com

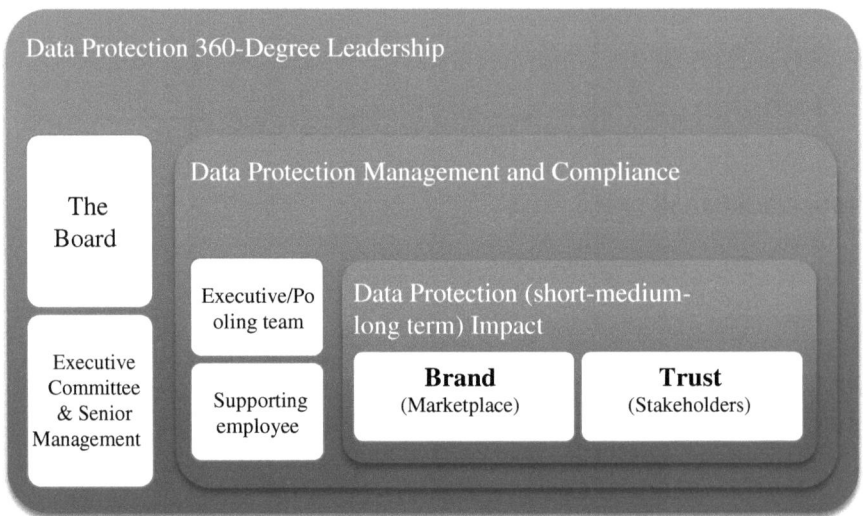

Fig. 7.1 Data protection leadership

associate (who may have the contractual obligation and commercial transaction interest) with a company, organisation or institution—either as a data user, data processor or a third party. In data protection leadership, it is a 360-degree exercise. It is not isolated and a stand-alone leadership that is helmed by a general counsel, data protection advisor, consultant and expert. The leadership flows from top to bottom of a company, organisation and institution's hierarchy, as figured (Fig. 7.1):

Instilling data protection 360-degree leadership culture within the 'DNA' of a company, organisation and institution is the key to accountability. This may also apply to the exempted entities of the PDPA (the Federal and State Governments and credit reporting agencies). Everyone should be able to take the lead and appreciate data protection not within the commercial transaction setting, but also in his or her personal life. To execute the leadership, I have considered useful strategic guidance for potential adoption:

7.1.1 Strategic Guidance: For the Board

Data protection governance should be one of the main agenda to be deliberated and resolved at the board level. The Chairman of the Board may propose an independent non-executive board member to lead the strategic deliberation on matters pertaining to data protection for the board's resolution. For example, a special board committee on data protection could be established to ascertain whether the company's business, deployed technologies, products and services are data protection compliant and friendly. The committee members may be composed of an executive board member, independent board member, independent data protection auditor/

consultant/counsel/expert (by invitation) and the general counsel/data protection advisor of the company. The frequency of the special board committee in data protection may be convened quarterly (for public listed company—Berhad) or mid-yearly (if the company is a private limited company—Sdn. Bhd). Alternatively, the Chairman of the Board's Audit Committee (the Committee) could compulsorily outline data protection governance as a compulsory agenda that requires attention to the Committee. If this alternative may be the preferred route, the company's data protection team shall be accountable to report, present and highlight this, through the Audit Committee. Once the Committee deliberated and resolved the agenda, it will form the company's state of internal control that is required for disclosure to the shareholders (in annual report).

7.1.2 Strategic Guidance: For the Executive Committee/Senior Management

Subject to the size of the company, organisation and institution, data protection leadership may be helmed by a dedicated data protection counsel/advisor, having a pool of diversified executives. They may represent the company's division, department, unit, and projects that are exposed to critical data processing activities. Data protection leadership role may be led by the general counsel, risk management advisor and internal auditor. Typically, start-up and semi-medium sized company may initiate the leadership role to the nearest group/team or unit, which deals with data processing activities, management and compliance on a daily basis. Clear key performance indicators (*kpis*) on data protection leadership must be spelled out so that it may be achievable based on the mission and vision of the company/organisation/institution's business. If cost and resource is the main constraint to execute the leadership role, the owner of the start-up and semi-medium sized company may outsource the required roles and functions by way of terms of reference to data protection consultant/solicitor/expert. Nonetheless, it should be cautiously borne in mind that accountability will never be acclaimed if it is totally outsourced!

7.1.3 Strategic Guidance: For the Executive and Pooling Team

The execution of *kpis* should be updated quarterly. This is to accelerate the reporting process by the Executive Committee and the Senior Management. A template report on data protection governance and compliance should be established and adopted throughout the company/organisation/institution. In order to reduce duplication of reporting, and in the interest of time, cost and resource, an agreed template report should be agreed beforehand and it's best to develop this via online. If and when necessary, a lead executive in the pooling team should be able to raise the critical concerns of such data protection issues to the Executive Committee for decision making. If such issues require greater attention at the board level, this shall be brought to being one of the agenda in the special board committee on data protection or alternatively, at the Audit Committee level.

7.1.3.1 Everyone Can Lead

Looking into the scheme of data protection leadership and its actors, I take the position and view that everyone can lead in data protection. Lead, in the sense that, it is not about power struggle and tussle. Lead, in the sense that, it is a collective accountability that mirrors and reflects the company/organisation/institution's vision and mission. Of relevance, and most importantly, the leadership should be parallel with its 'DNA', its culture and its day-to-day governance and operations.

7.2 From Outside to Inside

At the time of this writing, data protection is a new subject matter in Malaysia and also in ASEAN. There are not many experts specialising in this area, although some advocates and solicitors tend to specialise based on their prior and existing industrial relations, capital market, corporate and commercial (which includes banking and finance), and perhaps, the nearest; technology, media and telecommunications' practice. This is a positive sign that takes place. For company, organisation and institution, it is worthwhile to get engage with these professionals in order to gauge the comprehensive understanding on how PDPA works. Subject to the size of the company, organisation and institution, appointing an independent professional (whether it is a legal firm, consulting firm or information security expert firm) requires cautious consideration too, as follows:

7.2.1 Consideration 1

If your company, organisation or institution has had its panel of professionals, ensure that they are continuingly equipped with the breadth of understanding on data protection. It may not be restricted to the laws, regulations/guidance only, but also extendable to the understanding of technologies and its interrelationship with your data processing activities within a commercial transaction setting.

7.2.2 Consideration 2

Careful consideration should be given to professionals who claim they are expert, but not qualified to deliver a legal advice, or consult your company, organisation or institution not only from the PDPA's viewpoint, but also from the viewpoints of the EU, US, APEC and the OECD. A good and commendable data professional should be able to have the global breadth of understanding, at least, on comparative jurisdictional approaches of data protection, besides the local/regional content and expertise derived from his or her local/regional experience.

7.2.3 Consideration 3

To further enhance the transfer of knowledge and skills, it's recommended to consider 'secondment' engagement between the professionals and your company, organisation and institution. On the one hand, this may help to appreciate the diversity of issues, challenges and practice faced and on the other hand, this shall equally determine whether the required professionals possess the right knowledge and skills in data protection. If the secondment route may not be practicable, consider to retain the professionals based on ad-hoc basis and if the quality of advice/consultation is exceptionally well, consider retaining the professionals on a retainer basis.

7.2.4 Consideration 4

Professionals are also people like us (in a career context). They need to attend training and be retrained. They need to be certified in a specialised data protection professional certification. It's best to consider their professional learning development, certification plans and match the same with your company, organisation and institution's plan too. At present, the leading certified data protection professional is managed by the International Association Privacy Professionals (IAPP), based in the US. It is highly recommended to be certified by IAPP to being a Certified Information Privacy Professional (CIPP). For future planning, consider to identify potential members who should be able to get certified. This consideration could also be extended to the professionals who have not secured certification.

7.2.5 Consideration 5

Consider to having a diversity of professionals, instead of one. A diversity of legal firm, consulting firm, information security expert firm and in some cases, academic consultant is the best combination. Subject to your company, organistion and institution's budget, and the complexity of the subject matter in data protection, a diversity of professionals deemed to be invaluable. This is due to the 360-degree viewpoints that you may secure from their professional advice and opinion.

7.2.5.1 The Public Relations in Data Protection

Data protection leadership is partly incomplete without the role of Public Relations (PR)/corporate communications. Company, organisation and institution with PR budget and pre-planned data protection campaign may not face such hindrance to effectuate. The best practice is to design the campaign through stages. Strategically, they are:
- *Stage 1:* data protection campaign in the working place;
- *Stage 2:* data protection accountability statement and commitment in existing products and services; and

- *Stage 3:* data protection accountability statement and commitment in all marketing collaterals (brochure, website and existing branding platform)
Start-up or medium-sized company may consider these:

7.2.6 Consideration 1

Outsource the function to an independent Public Relation (PR) consultant and highlight your positioning in relation to data protection leadership. For instance, if the products and services are related to data processing activities, such branding collaterals (brochure and website) should highlight whether they are data protection compliant and friendly.

7.2.7 Consideration 2

Partially outsource the function to the PR consultant if cost and resource is a key constraint. In certain instance, you may periodically position your business' undertaking in relation to the operations, products and services that may affect data protection. This could be done through existing social media platform or reasonable marketing collaterals that suits the business.

7.2.8 Consideration 3

Engage and communicate effectively with your client, business partners and associates in relation to new products and services' offerings that may affect data protection. Such updates may be useful to be consistently communicated throughout. This may lead to potential impression to your client, business partners and associates' on how pivotal data protection is, in your business,

7.3 Global Engagement

Inevitably, it's best to develop potential regional and global engagement to raising potential policy based issues in data protection. Although this seems to be quite high level, company, organisation and institution, which have deep interest in data protection within their business models, products and services may consider to establishing the engagement.

The APEC Electronic Commerce Steering Group is the potential platform. This may be done through public policy engagement with the Commissioner or any related governmental ministries or agencies that may have the similar interest. The OECD Directorate for Science, Technology and Industry is also another regional platform that may be considered for engagement. These two organisations shape the influence amongst its members towards any policy-based discussions and consultations relating to data protection. Although the outcome of such position and strand is partly not binding, nonetheless, it's advisory and influential. It may also potentially shape the regional and global data protection's trend.

For the Commissioner, relevant governmental agencies, ministries and officials, the yearly international conference of data protection and privacy commissioners is a global platform that must not be missed. At the time of this writing, the forthcoming conference will be held from 23rd October to 24th October 2012 at Punta Del Este, Uruguay.[1] This yearly conference gathers all data protection commissioners, authorities, professionals, experts and interested stakeholders to get engage, articulate, discuss and debate on topical issues relating to data protection across the globe. Invariably, such developments from the European and American parts should also add the value to the engagement. Global platforms and engagements organised by the IAPP are also worthy to consider.[2] These global engagements shall enable company, organisation and institution to:

- **Keep abreast** with the global issues relating to data protection;
- **Explore** specific data protection issues that may potentially arise from, and contributed by, existing and new technologies;
- **Learn** the best practices on formality and enforcement approaches of different jurisdictions;
- **Develop** potential ideas and opportunities to implement the lessons learned from the engagements;
- **Expand** the network of data protection experts globally;
- **Engage** in continuing training and development by potentially collaborating with the relevant officials, experts and consultants towards capacity building engagement; and
- **Contribute** the necessary knowledge and skills through potential transfer of knowledge.

7.3.1 Grooming More Data Protection Experts

It is exceedingly daunting to groom more data protection experts especially when the subject matter is new to Malaysia and ASEAN. As I pointed out in **Sect. 7.2** above, due to the evolutionary development in this part of the region, data protection professionals are in scarcity. To be called an expert, I am of the view that he or she should be able to fulfill the necessary grounded knowledge on data protection fundamentals, not only at the local level, but also at the global level. In addition, he or she should be able to appreciate the interrelationship of existing technologies, business and compliance at the same time. To reach this level, it requires

---

[1] See 34th International Conference of Data Protection and Privacy Commissioner's website. http://www.privacyconference2012.org/english/home/. Accessed 1 July 2012.

[2] See IAPP https://www.privacyassociation.org/. Accessed 1 June 2012.

multidisciplinary understanding and exposure. In view of the present landscape, I propose these:

- **Creation** of a local data protection certification in Malaysia that is generally transferrable and recognisable in ASEAN;
- **Complement** the existing international certifications that is issued by the IAPP, once, and if, such certification is introduced; and
- **Consult** the relevant professional-based bodies in Malaysia and ASEAN that may have potential interest in data protection to regionally harmonise the certification.

Although the above proposal sounds idealistic and perhaps, viable in 5 years time (or more), if considered, it may boost Malaysia and ASEAN data protection leadership as a whole. This, however, could not be materialised without the involvement of the Commissioner, relevant governmental agencies, ministries and interested stakeholders who may want to contribute to this capacity building. Malaysia and ASEAN requires more talents in data protection. In order to do groom these talents, it must begin from the top to the bottom of the company, organisation and institution. Likewise, from the outside to the inside's contributions of professionals who have the breadth expertise in data protection.

7.4 Brief Guidance to Malaysian and ASEAN Companies Having Establishment in the EU and the US

There are some Malaysian and ASEAN companies, which have had investments and operations in the EU and the US. Depending upon the business structure; whether it is project based or as a subsidiary, unincorporated joint venture or an incorporated joint venture, the need to understand the local data protection laws is paramount. It is unmissable. These are the strategic guidance for consideration:

7.4.1 Strategic Guidance 1: Apply the Local Data Protection Laws

If the company has business operations in several member states of the EU, the rule of thumb is that, the local data protection laws apply. Nonetheless, there are certain conditions that must be complied with in relation to, transfer of, personal data and sensitive personal data from Malaysia and ASEAN countries to the EU; whether the company is a data controller, data processor or acting as a data importer or an exporter. In this respect, it is best to consult the local laws and the relevant provisions on data transfer.

If the company has business operations in some states in the US, cautious consideration should be made to the nature of data processing in the respective areas of businesses. The states in the US have different legislation governing sector-specific legislation. On a broader scale, the company must also consider the adoption of the US Safe Harbor, being the self-regulatory requirements in relation to data privacy.

7.4.2 Strategic Guidance 2: Appoint Local Data Protection Professional(s)

The appointment of data protection professional(s) to coordinate and advice on such formality, requirements, enforcement and governance issues of the local laws is vital. The professionals should be able to work closely with the company's data protection team, its in-house counsels and local-based advocate and solicitor to addressing the required subject matter relating to its business and data protection compliance. The appointed professional(s) will be the key contact or the lead to act on the company's behalf whilst dealing with the formalities, governance and compliance required under the national laws. If and when necessary, they will also act on your behalf to coordinate such data protection matters with the data protection authorities and advise on potential issues relating to data transfer agreement or any preferred options that may be relevant to the business' needs and objectives.

7.4.3 Strategic Guidance 3: Pursue Periodic Data Protection Audit with the Data Protection Professional(s)

To further improve the company's business operations, products and services that affect data protection, it is recommended to commence a periodic (quarterly) audit with the data protection professional(s). The company's data protection team, its local professionals and advocate & solicitor may also be involved to this audit (if necessary). The rationale of the proposed periodic audit is to exercise the recommended best practice—certain national data protection authorities of the EU require audit trails (if severe security breach happened). In the US, the requirements differ form one state to another state. Subject to the business model, project structure and involvement of the company in its data processing activities, it is still indispensable to pursue periodic audit as pre-emptive measure.

7.4.4 Strategic Guidance 4: Review and Improve Data Protection Management and Governance

Throughout the business operations in the EU and the US, it is also prevalent to review and improve the company's data protection management and governance. In the interest of data protection leadership, the outcome of review, proposed rectification strategies and plans should be tabled at the board and executive level of the company. This may benefit the year-on-year operations and potential strategic and consultative engagement with the relevant data protection professionals.

List of Materials

Asia-Pacific Economic Cooperation (APEC) CBPR System – Policies, Rules and Guidelines (2012) Purpose: Consideration. Submitted by: DPS Chair. http://aimp.apec.org/Documents/2011/ECSG/DPS2/11_ecsg_dps2_009.pdf. Accessed 30 May 2012

ComputerWeekly (2012) You Can Outsource Responsibility, But Not Accountability – Identity, Privacy, Trust. http://www.computerweekly.com/blogs/the-data-trust-blog/2010/08/you-can-outsource-responsibili.html. Accessed 30 June 2012

Data Protection Accountability: The Essential Elements (October 2009) A Document for Discussion. http://www.ftc.gov/os/comments/privacyroundtable/544506-00059.pdf. Accessed 1 April 2012

Hunton & Williams Centre for Information Policy Leadership, Accountability-based Privacy Governance (2012) http://www.informationpolicycentre.com/accountability-based_privacy_governance/. Accessed 28 March 2012

IAPP: Demonstrating Privacy Accountability (2012). https://www.privacyassociation.org/publications/demonstrating_privacy_accountability/. Accessed 8 February 2012

IAPP Certification – Certified IAPP Privacy Professional (2012). https://www.privacyassociation.org/certification/. Accessed 15 February 2012

International Chamber of Commerce Discussion Paper on Data Protection Principle of Accountability (2012). http://www.iccwbo.org/Advocacy-Codes-and-Rules/Document-centre/2012/ICC-discussion-paper-on-data-protection-principle-of-accountability/. Accessed 28 March 2012

Nymity (2012) Privacy Interview with Experts, Interview on Demonstrating Accountability. http://www.nymity.com/About_Nymity/~/media/Nymity/Files/Interviews/2011-04-McQuay.ashx. Accessed 15 March 2012

Office of the Privacy Commissioner Office of Canada (2012) Walk the Talk and Show It: Demonstrable Accountability for Data Protection. http://www.priv.gc.ca/media/sp-d/2012/sp-d_20120417_pk_e.asp. Accessed 18 June 2012

The Scope of Application of EU Data Protection Law and Its Extraterritorial Reach

Eduardo Ustaran

> *In this globalised world, data knows no borders. Therefore we have to make sure that companies can easily transfer data to third countries while not compromising the level of data protection for individuals when they leaves the EU*

(Viviane Reding, Vice President of the EC, EU Justice Commissioner, Spring Conference of European Data Protection Authorities, 3rd May 2012, Luxembourg)

Abstract

One of the most radical changes to European data protection to be introduced by the new EU Data Protection Regulation proposed by the European Commission is the criteria to determine the applicability of EU data protection law. Under the current data protection directive, the rules are twofold. If the controller is based in an EU Member State, that controller will be subject to the law of that Member State and to the scrutiny of the regulator of that country. However, if the controller is based outside the EU but uses equipment in the EU to collect information, that controller will be subject to the laws of every single Member State and to the scrutiny of each and every regulator. In the case of non-EU controllers, linking the applicability of the law to the location of equipment produces bizarre situations as in a densely networked world, the use of data processing equipment is literally ubiquitous. Therefore, the European Commission is trying to introduce a completely different approach. Under the proposed Data Protection Regulation, if the controller is based in an EU Member State and it has one main establishment, then it will still be subject to the Regulation but it

---

E. Ustaran (✉)
Field Fisher Waterhouse, 35 Vine Street, London EC3N 2AA, UK
e-mail: eduardo.ustaran@ffw.com

will only be subject to the scrutiny of one regulator. But a controller that is based outside the EU will be subject to the Regulation and to the scrutiny of each and every regulator where it offers products or services to EU residents or monitors the behaviour of EU residents. This chapter analyses the existing EU rules and proposed changes, and considers its practical implications for the future of data protection.

8.1 The Importance of Determining the Applicability of the Law

8.1.1 Difference Between Applicable Law and Jurisdiction

The concepts of Applicable Law and Jurisdiction are two legal concepts that are often misconstrued as meaning the same thing. However the distinction is crucial and each concept plays an essential role in the interpretation and governance of legal relations. In general terms, Applicable Law refers to the system of laws (i.e. the laws of Country A) that determine whether or not a party's actions are lawful, and the consequences of any unlawful activity. Jurisdiction, in this context, does not refer to a specific territory, rather it is a term used to describe the courts or regulators of a certain country (or countries) that have the competence to enforce the applicable laws when unlawful activity has occurred.

The important point here is that "applicable law" and Jurisdiction do not necessarily relate to the same territory. The applicable laws may be those of Country A, but the authorities and regulators of Country B may be competent to enforce them.

8.1.2 Approaches to the Application of the Law

From a legal compliance perspective, identifying whether a particular law or regulatory framework applies is always the starting point. In order to determine if a legal entity is required to comply with any obligations set out by a given law or regulatory instrument, it is essential to ascertain whether such law or regulatory instrument is applicable to the activities of that legal entity in the first place. There are two common factors that determine the applicability of the law: one has to do with the sector or line of activity in which the entity operates and the other is purely geographical.

In the context of privacy and data protection law, different frameworks rely on different approaches to establish their own geographical applicability. Typically, these approaches belong to one of the following categories:
- Applicability based on the location of the organisation responsible for the processing.
- Applicability based on the location of the processing itself or on the location of the equipment used to carry out the processing.

- Applicability based on the location or residency of the individuals to whom the data relates.

8.1.3 Impact on Organisations

Being subject or not to data protection law, in particular EU data protection law, is not a small matter. EU data protection law is one of the strictest in the world and any organisation that is subject to it will need to comply with a whole range of practical requirements. It will also be subject to the scrutiny of one or several data protection supervisory authorities. The kind of obligations that apply under EU data protection law include:

- *Notice*—personal information must be processed fairly and lawfully and only for specified and lawful purposes. This obligation requires organisations to be transparent about how and for what purposes information are collected; information should not be used for new or additional purposes unless such use is fair (i.e. within the reasonable expectations of the individuals).
- *Proportionality*—personal information should be adequate, relevant and not excessive. Therefore organisations must ensure that the information they hold/use is sufficient for the purpose(s) they are holding it for but that they do not hold more information than is required.
- *Data quality*—personal information should be accurate and kept up to date.
- *Data retention and deletion*—personal information should not be kept for any longer than is necessary.
- *Data security*—personal information should be kept securely using appropriate technical and organisational measures to protect the information against unauthorised or unlawful processing and against accidental loss, destruction or damage.
- *International data transfers restrictions*—personal information should not be transferred to a country outside of the EU unless adequate measures are put in place to protect the information.
- *Honouring individuals' rights*—the rights of individuals to whom the information relate must be upheld. Such rights include:
  - A right of access to a copy of the information.
  - A right to object to uses of the information that are causing or are likely to cause damage or distress.
  - A right in certain circumstances to have inaccurate personal data rectified, blocked, erased or destroyed.
  - A right to object to decisions being taken by automated means (i.e. a decision that is taken wholly without human involvement that has a significant effect on the individual concerned).
  - A right to object (opt-out) to the information being used for direct marketing purposes. There may be additional obligations requiring specific consent (opt-in) for certain types of marketing, for example telephone or email marketing.

8.2 EU Data Protection Directive: Current Criteria

8.2.1 Legislative Background and Aim

8.2.1.1 The Commission's Original Proposal

On 27 July 1990, the European Commission (the "Commission") introduced its proposal for a directive concerning the protection of individuals in relation to the processing of personal data to the Council of the European Union (the "Council").[1]

Recital 10 of the Commission's original proposal read:

(10) Whereas any processing of personal data in the Community should be carried out in accordance with the law of the Member State in which the data file is located so that individuals are not deprived of the protection to which they are entitled under this Directive; whereas, in this connection, each part of a data file divided among several member States must be considered a separate data file and transfer to a non-member country must not be a bar to such protection.

Article 4(1) of the Commission's original proposal read:

1. Each Member State shall apply this Directive to:
   (a) All files located in its territory;
   (b) The controller of a file resident in its territory who uses from its territory a file located in a third country whose law does not provide an adequate level of protection, unless such use is only sporadic.

In relation to the draft article 4, the Explanatory Memorandum[2] accompanying the proposal stated:

This article specifies the connecting factors which determine the application in each Member State of the Directive's provisions. The choice of factors in paragraph 1 is motivated by the desire to avoid a situation in which the data subject is completely unprotected owing, mainly, to the law being circumvented. The factual criterion of the place in which the file is located

---

[1] OJ C/1990/277/3.
[2] COM (90) 314 final—SYN 287, pp. 21–22.

has therefore been adopted. In this connection, each part of a file which is geographically dispersed or divided among several Member States must be treated as a separate file. [...]. This article is also designed to avoid any overlapping of applicable laws.

8.2.1.2 The Commission's Amended Proposal

Following consultation with the European Parliament (the "Parliament"),[3] on 16 October 1992 the Commission submitted an amended proposal.[4] The amendments included a new Recital 12 (replacing Recital 10 of the original proposal), which stated:

(12) Whereas, in order to ensure that individuals are not deprived of the protection to which they are entitled under this Directive, any processing of personal data in the Community must be carried out in accordance with the law of one of the Member States; whereas, in this connection, processing carried out by a person who is established in a Member State should be governed by the law of that State; whereas, the fact that processing is carried out by a person established in a third country must not stand in the way of the protection of individuals provided for in this Directive; whereas, in that case, the processing should be governed by the law of the Member State in which the means used are located, and there should be guarantees to ensure that the rights and obligations provided for in this Directive are respected in practice;

Article 4(1) was amended as follows:

1. Each Member State shall apply the national provisions adopted under this Directive to all processing of personal data:
   (a) Of which the controller is established in its territory or is within its jurisdiction;
   (b) Of which the controller is not established in the territory of the Community, where for the purpose of processing personal data he makes use of means, whether or not automatic, which are located in the territory of that Member State.

---

[3] The Parliament submitted its amendments in Session Document A3-0010/92, 15 January 2002 (EP//148286/JUR/FIN).
[4] OJ C/1992/311/30.

In its Explanatory Memorandum[5] the Commission stated in relation to article 4:

> This article lays down the connecting factors which determine which national law is applicable to processing within the scope of the Directive, in order to avoid two possibilities:
> - That the data subject might find himself outside any system of protection, and particularly that the law might be circumvented in order to achieve this;
> - That the same processing operation might be governed by the laws of more than one country.

The Commission went on to explain that the main criterion for determining the applicable Member State law had been changed from the place where the data "file" was located to the place of establishment of the controller on the grounds that the location of a file or of a processing operation will often be impossible to determine. Where the controller is not established in the EU but makes use of means located in the territory of a Member State, the law applicable is to be the law of that Member State. The Commission also pointed out that, as suggested by the Parliament, the reference to 'sporadic use' had been removed as this was a vague term open to various interpretations.[6]

8.2.1.3 The Final Text

On 13 April 1995, the Parliament and the Council agreed a common position with a view to adopting the Directive.[7] This was followed by a Decision of the Parliament on 15 June 1995.[8] The Directive was promulgated on 24 October 2009.[9]

The final version of the Recitals concerning applicable law read:

> (18) Whereas, in order to ensure that individuals are not deprived of the protection to which they are entitled under this Directive, any processing of personal data in the Community must be carried out in accordance with the law of one of the Member States; whereas, in this connection, processing

---

[5] COM (92) 422 final—SYN 287.
[6] See the Explanaory Memorandum, p.13.
[7] OJ C/1995/93/1.
[8] OJ C/1995/166/105.
[9] OJ L/1995/281/31.

carried out under the responsibility of a controller who is established in a Member State should be governed by the law of that State;

(19) Whereas establishment on the territory of a Member State implies the effective and real exercise of activity through stable arrangements; whereas the legal form of such an establishment, whether simply branch or a subsidiary with a legal personality, is not the determining factor in this respect; whereas, when a single controller is established on the territory of several Member States, particularly by means of subsidiaries, he must ensure, in order to avoid any circumvention of national rules, that each of the establishments fulfils the obligations imposed by the national law applicable to its activities;

(20) Whereas the fact that the processing of data is carried out by a person established in a third country must not stand in the way of the protection of individuals provided for in this Directive; whereas in these cases, the processing should be governed by the law of the Member State in which the means used are located, and there should be guarantees to ensure that the rights and obligations provided for in this Directive are respected in practice;

(21) Whereas this Directive is without prejudice to the rules of territoriality applicable in criminal matters;

The final text of article 4(1) read:

1. Each Member State shall apply the national provisions it adopts pursuant to this Directive to the processing of personal data where:
   (a.) The processing is carried out in the context of the activities of an establishment of the controller on the territory of the Member State; when the same controller is established on the territory of several Member States, he must take the necessary measures to ensure that each of these establishments complies with the obligations laid down by the national law applicable;
   (b) The controller is not established on the Member State's territory, but in a place where its national law applies by virtue of international public law;
   (c) The controller is not established on Community territory and, for purposes of processing personal data makes use of equipment, automated or otherwise, situated on the territory of the said Member State, unless such equipment is used only for purposes of transit through the territory of the Community.

(d) Aim of article 4(1) on The Basis of the Legislative History of the Directive

It is clear from the evolution of the text of the Recitals and of article 4(1) as well as from the Commission's Explanatory Memoranda accompanying earlier drafts of

the Directive that throughout the legislative process the overriding intention of the drafters was to avoid positive and negative conflicts of law and to ensure:
- That the data subject will not find himself outside any European system of protection and that the law will not be circumvented in order to achieve this; and
- That the same processing operation will not be governed by the laws of more than one Member States.

In other words, it is evident from the documentation that accompanied the drafting of the Directive that article 4(1) has two basic purposes:
- To ensure that gaps on protection do not arise, by requiring that any processing of personal data in the Community must be carried out in accordance with the law of one of the Member States. EU law must not be circumvented (e.g. by a controller who avoids to open an establishment in the EU); and
- To prevent conflicts of Member States laws from arising, by specifying which particular Member State law would apply in a particular instance.

Both aims were clearly stated in the Commission's Explanatory Memoranda. The first aim is also manifest in Recital 20 of the Directive.

8.2.2 Controllers Established in the EU

Article 4(1)(a) sets out the default rule that the law of a member State applies when the data processing is carried out in the context of the activities of an establishment of the controller on the territory of the Member State. The other provisions of article 4(1) are designed to apply a Member State's law only where article 4(1)(a) does not apply.

8.2.2.1 "Establishment"

The concept of "establishment" is left undefined by the Directive, although Recital 19 states that "establishment" implies "the effective and real exercise of activity through stable arrangements'. This appears to build upon case law of the European Court of Justice on this point.[10] Recital 19 goes on to say that 'the legal form of such an establishment, whether simply branch or a subsidiary with a legal personality, is not the determining factor in this respect."

It is unclear whether a website would constitute "effective and real exercise of activity through stable arrangements". It has been suggested that at first sight and despite the fact that it can be argued with some force that effective and real exercise of activity as per Recital (19) can be carried out through a website, it would be

---

[10] C-221/89, *The Queen v. Secretary of State for transport, ex parte Factortame Ltd and others* [1991] ECR, p. I-3905, para 20: "the concept of establishment within the meaning of Article 52 et seq. of the Treaty involves the actual pursuit of an economic activity through a fixed establishment in another Member State for an indefinite period".

difficult to argue that a website can satisfy the need for stable arrangements as per Recital (19).[11]

The definition of an "established service provider" of Directive 2000/31/EC (the "E-Commerce Directive") lends support to this approach: "a service provider who effectively pursues an economic activity using a fixed establishment for an indefinite period. The presence and use of the technical means and technologies required to provide the service do not, in themselves, constitute an establishment of the provider".

The E-Commerce Directive, therefore, requires more than just the technical means and technologies necessary for the operation of a website in order for a service provider to acquire the status of an "established" provider. This is made clear by Recital 19 of the E-Commerce Directive which states that "the place of establishment of a company providing services via an Internet website is not the place at which the technology supporting its website is located or the place at which its website is accessible but the place where it pursues its economic activity". The Article 29 Working Party has also followed this line of analysis.[12]

If the same concept is applied to article 4(1)(a) of the Directive, it follows that a data controller with a website in Member State A who pursues its economic activity in Member State B or in a third country will not be subject to the data protection law of Member State A as it will not have an establishment there.

However, the interpretation of the requirement is a matter for Member State law and, as noted above, there are substantial variations between Member States. An academic commentator notes that it seems that in some countries any economic activity by a company might lead to the company being considered established for the purpose of article 4(1)(a).[13] He goes on to state that such attempts should be resisted as the Directive's definition of establishment does not contain a concept of piercing the corporate veil which would enable a Member State to assert jurisdiction over a non-EU based entity merely on the basis of that entity's ownership of or participation in an entity established in the EU.

Furthermore, such an overreaching implementation would be contrary to one of the two main purposes of article 4, because it increases the likelihood of conflicts between Member States' laws. Consider for example a controller established in a Member State that has properly implemented the Directive. The controller also has an economic interest in another Member State adopting the approach discussed in the previous paragraph. The same processing would be potentially governed by the laws of more than one Member State, which is precisely one of the pitfalls that the drafters of the Directive intended to avoid.

---

[11] Bygrave (2000).

[12] Article 29 Data Protection Working Party, Working document on determining the international application of EU data protection law to personal data processing on the Internet by non-EU based web sites, 5035/01, EN/Final, WP56, 30 May 2002.

[13] Kuner (2007).

Therefore, in accordance with the purpose and letter of the Directive in such instances a Member State should not apply its law pursuant to article 4(1)(a). Similarly, a Member State should not apply its law when the relevant data processing is performed not by a European entity but by a group entity located outside the EU.

8.2.2.2 "In the Context of the Activities" of an Establishment

The language of article 4(1)(a) of the Directive is clear that a Member State can apply its law where an entity has an establishment in a Member State plus the relevant processing takes place in the context of the activities of that establishment. This means that, in any event, the establishment should also play a relevant role in the particular data processing.

Some academic commentators suggest that the processing must be carried out in the course of the activities and, furthermore, within the control of the relevant establishment.[14]

Taking into account both the language and purpose of article 4(1)(a) as well as the broader purpose of the Directive, it is clear that the article will only apply to an EU-based entity if that entity (a) is involved in the actual processing of personal data, and (b) does so as a controller.

8.2.3 Controllers Not Established in the EU

Article 4(1)(c) is widely acknowledged as having caused more controversy than any other provision of the Directive. The Commission itself recognised that the criterion of "use of equipment" may not be easy to operate in practice, may need further clarification and/or may require an amendment creating a different connecting factor.[15] In addition, as with article 4(1)(a) national variations in the implementation of the Directive result in inconsistent application of the provision across the EU.

The provision is intended to allow a Member State to apply its national data protection law to a controller who, although not established in the EU, makes use of equipment situated in that Member State unless that equipment is used only for the purposes of transit through the EU.

There exist at least two major concerns in relation to article 4(1)(c). First, the central concepts of "equipment", "situated" or even "transit" could have worked well at the time of adoption of the Directive but do not necessarily fit the reality of instantaneous global transactions on decentralised infrastructures such as the internet or cloud computing; because of their obsolescence those concepts are open

---

[14] Jay and Hamilton (2003).
[15] First report on the implementation of the Data Protection Directive (95/46/EC).

8 The Scope of Application of EU Data Protection Law...

to numerous interpretations. Second, they seem to be facilitating the extraterritorial application of EU law.

As mentioned, one of the two main purposes of the Directive is to attempt to ensure that the data subject will not find himself outside any European system of protection and that the law will not be circumvented in order to achieve this. This is the main intention of the drafters behind article 4(1)(c) as seen above. However, given the widespread use of new technologies and decentralised networks, in theory the provision could result in the application of European data protection law to non-EU law entities who have no material connection to Europe other than the fact that they communicate electronically with European users.

8.2.3.1 "Equipment Situated" in a Member State

It is probably not unreasonable to assume that at the time of the adoption of the Directive, the concept of "equipment" would have generally be thought to refer to a computer network or other physical object which could be located in the EU and operated remotely.[16] In any event, the interpretation of article 4(1)(c) should be based on the purpose of the article, which, as discussed above is to ensure that data subjects in Europe are not left without any protection as a result of controllers avoiding the application of EU law by establishing their corporate activities in a third country.

It is also worth considering the legislative history and Recitals to the Directive. In the Commission's amended proposal both the relevant provision and recital referred to "means" as opposed to "equipment". However, in the final version of the Directive, although article 4(1)(c) refers to "equipment", recital (20) refers to "means". It is not clear why both terms were retained and whether they are intentionally used interchangeably.

A semantic analysis indicates that perhaps "equipment" is narrower than "means", in that it may be taken to refer to a tangible or physical apparatus. Even so, the inclusion of the word "means" in the recitals suggests that the discrepancy is intentional. It could be seen as showing the drafters' intention not to restrict the applicability of article 4(1)(c) by reference to the technical or physical characteristics of particular processing methods, but rather to adopt a broad approach generally capturing methods of processing irrespective of such characteristics. Therefore, the terms "means" and "equipment" should be construed broadly for the purposes of article 4(1)(c), as this appears to have been the intention of the drafters.[17]

The computer of a European user could qualify as equipment, provided of course that the computer is being used by the controller as opposed to the user (see following sub-section on "makes use"). In theory, a communications network (such as a WiFi or perhaps a 3G network) located in the EU could also qualify as

---

[16] See Kuner (2007), p. 120, with further references to academic publications.

[17] Note that Italian law actually uses the term "means" ("mezzi") rather than equipment, see Korff, in Kuner's discussion at p. 48.

equipment. However, if this position were accepted it could result in making the entire internet or, theoretically, the "cloud" subject to EU data protection law, which would be absurd. It is also worth noting that the ECJ has ruled that the international data transfers restrictions enshrined in article 25 of the Directive should not become rules of general application to the internet without the controller taking a positive step to transfer personal data outside the EU.[18]

However, a corporate subsidiary in the EU is normally unlikely to be considered to be "equipment" of the parent company if the subsidiary is a separate legal entity. If, however, the subsidiary is a branch without legal personality, it is conceivable, although improbable, that it could be deemed to be equipment.

Software may or may not constitute "equipment". To begin with there may exist a mismatch between the electronic form of software and the requirement that the equipment is situated somewhere. If software used for a data processing is installed on a computer situated in a Member State, it can be argued that software amounts to equipment "situated in a Member State". In the context of cloud computing, however, it would be more difficult to demonstrate the link between a piece of software and a particular Member State.

In summary, it follows that, in principle, almost any hardware, software or system could qualify as "equipment situated" on the territory of a Member State. What would them become material is whether it is in fact the controller who makes use of such equipment.

8.2.3.2 "Makes Use"

Article 4(1)(c) requires that it must be the controller as opposed to another user of the equipment situated on the territory of a Member State in order for the law of that Member State to apply to the data processing.

It follows that in the user PC example mentioned above, in the vast majority of cases it would be the user, as opposed to the controller, who will make use of the equipment. This will be so in many cases of "normal" computer use (e.g. where an EU user visits a foreign website or e-mails a non-EU based controller).[19] However, malicious or bona fide "taking over" of the user's PC from a distance is already a common occurrence: distance working and online collaboration tools often enable a remote user to take over a PC. There seems to be some ambiguity around whether "makes use" has in article 4(1)(c) the normal colloquial sense or whether a certain degree of control by the non-EU based controller is required. This approach seems

---

[18] C-101/01 Bodil Lindqvist [2003] ECRI-12971, para. 69.

[19] See recital 47 of the Directive: "Whereas where a message containing personal data is transmitted by means of a telecommunications or electronic mail service, the sole purpose of which is the transmission of such messages, the controller in respect of the personal data contained in the message will normally be considered to be the person from whom the message originates, rather than the person offering the transmission services; whereas, nevertheless, those offering such services will normally be considered controllers in respect of the processing of the additional personal data necessary for the operation of the service".

to be in accordance with the purpose and spirit of the Directive: after all, the controller is the person who determines the means of processing.

8.2.3.3 "Transit"

Where it is established that the controller makes use of equipment situated in a Member State, article 4(1)(c) applies unless the controller uses the equipment merely for purposes of transit via the EU. There is no authoritative guidance (from the European legislator or otherwise) as to what "transit" means exactly in the context of processing of personal data. It seems however, that it would not be inappropriate to refer to one of the fundamental technical characteristics of the Internet—the automatic forwarding of internet packets from one server to another.

So much so, if the equipment used in the processing is used merely to receive and automatically transmit data (a mere conduit) then such equipment is likely to be seen as equipment being exempt as merely serving transit purposes. A typical example is likely to be telecoms equipment.[20] However, servers or other equipment that store, manipulate and further process the data will not be exempt. In the absence of any interpretative guidance, a determination would have to be made on a case-by-case basis taking into account the purpose, function and actual use of the equipment.

8.3 The Need for Change

8.3.1 The Role of Local Offices

The language of article 4(1)(a) of the Directive suggests that where an entity has an establishment in a Member State but the relevant processing does not take place in the context of the activities of that establishment, the Member State should not apply its law. However, there is a degree of uncertainty as to how to interpret the role of a local establishment in relation to any processing of personal data which may be carried out by an international group of companies or legal entities.

In the context of its examination of data protection issues related to search engines, the Article 29 Working Party submitted that an establishment clearly plays a relevant role in a processing operation where:
- It is responsible for relations with users in a particular jurisdiction;
- It establishes an office in a Member State that is involved in the selling of targeted advertisements to the inhabitants of that state;
- It complies with court orders and/or law enforcement requests by the competent authorities of a member State with regard to user data.[21]

---

[20] WP 56.

[21] Article 29 Data Protection Working Party. Opinion 1/2008 on data protection issues related to search engines, 00737/EN, WP 148, 4 April 2008.

These arguments are questionable because whilst in these three examples the relevant establishment of the search engine provider may operate within a Member State for all sorts of business purposes, the types of activities described may not necessarily involve processing of user data. For example, the practice of selling targeted advertising is unlikely to require any actual processing of user data by the entity arranging the sale.

There may also be instances where the local establishment will only process a very limited amount of user data that excludes search-related information—for example, a local EU-based entity may interface with users of that country in order to deal with enquiries about the service, but that relationship may be restricted to helpdesk-type functions. In addition, there may be cases where all processing of user data by the local EU-based entity will be carried out in its capacity as a processor for an overseas-based controller.

As a result, clarification is needed in connection with the relationship between the criterion that relies on the relevant processing that takes place in the context of the activities of an establishment in a Member State and the actual role of that establishment.

8.3.2 Cloud Computing

Applying the rules under article 4(1) can also be problematic in the context of cloud computing, because of its distributed and truly international nature. There is one particular problem that was highlighted by the Article 29 Working Party in its opinion on cloud computing of 1 July 2012.[22] The Working Party pointed out that in the light of article 4(1)(c) which, as seen above, refers to how data protection legislation applies to controllers who are not established in the EU but use automated or non-automated equipment located in the territory of the Member State, if a cloud client is established outside the EU, but commissions a cloud provider located in the EU, then the provider exports the data protection legislation to the client.

8.3.3 Cookies

The link between the use of Internet cookies and equipment in the sense of article 4(1)(c) has generated much attention including from the Article 29 Working Party, which has taken the position that the storing of a cookie on an

---

[22] Article 29 Data Protection Working Party, Opinion 5/2012 on Cloud Computing, 01037/12/EN, WP196, 1 July 2012.

EU user's computer will trigger the application of article 4(1)(c).[23] In this type of case, it is possible to challenge the Article 29 Working Party's analysis on the basis that the wording of the Directive is being stretched to cover new technologies that were not envisaged when it was adopted in 1995. Given the nature of cookies and other similar applications that rely on internet connectivity to enable a service provider to recognise a particular user, concluding that a non-EU controller is subject to the laws of every Member State as a result of the existence of a file in the terminal equipment of its EU-based users seems very far fetched and beyond the aims of the Directive. In fact, a more logical conclusion would be to state that the use of cookies fits within the transit exception mentioned above.

In addition, although not in relation to article 4, the decision of the ECJ in Lindqvist[24] suggests that as with the rules of article 25, article 4 should similarly not be applied to activities that could result in EU data protection law being applied to the entire Internet, unless the non-EU based controller has taken a positive step to target EU-based individuals.

8.3.3.1 The Working Party's Recommendations

In anticipation of the EU data protection legislative reform and in order to contribute its views to the debate, on 16 December 2010, the Article 29 Working Party adopted a formal Opinion on applicable law.[25] In this Opinion, the Working Party provided its own analysis of article 4(1) of the Directive but also highlighted a number of areas for further improvement.

In particular, the Working Party acknowledged that the wording used in the Directive and the consistency between the different parts of article 4 would benefit from further clarification as a part of the revision of the general data protection framework. Accordingly, the Working Party identified a need for addressing existing shortcomings and made the following recommendations:

> a. There is a need to address the inconsistencies in the wording used in Articles 4(1)a and 4(1)c with regard to "establishment", and the notion that the controller is "not established" in the EU. To be consistent with article 4(1)a which uses the criterion of "establishment", article 4(1)c should apply in all cases where there is no establishment in the EU which would trigger the application of article 4(1)a or where the
> *(continued)*

---

[23] Article 29 Data Protection Working Party, Working Document Privacy on the Internet – An integrated EU Approach to On-line Data Protection, 5063/00/EN/FINAL, WP37, 21 November 2000, p.28.

[24] See the discussion in WP37.

[25] Article 29 Data Protection Working Party, Opinion 8/2010 on applicable law, 0836-02/10/EN, WP179, 16 December 2010.

processing is not carried out in the context of the activities of such an establishment.
b. Some clarification would also be useful with regard to the notion of "context of activities" of the establishment. The Working Party has emphasised the need to assess the degree of involvement of the establishment(s) in the activities in the context of which personal data are processed, or in other words to check "who is doing what" in which establishment. This criterion is interpreted taking into account the preparatory works of the Directive and the objective set out at the time to keep a distributive approach of national laws applicable to the different establishments of the controller within the EU. The Working Party considers that article 4(1)a as it stands now leads to a workable but sometimes complex solution, which seems to argue in favour of a more centralised and harmonised approach.
c. The change envisaged in order to simplify the rules for determining applicable law would consist of a shift back to the country of origin principle: all establishments of a controller within the EU would then apply the same law regardless of the territory in which they are located. In this perspective, the location of the main establishment of the controller would be the first criterion to be applied. The fact that several establishments exist within the EU would not trigger a distributed application of national laws.
d. This could only be acceptable however, if there are no significant differences between the laws of Member States. Any effective application of the country of origin principle would otherwise result in "forum shopping" in favour of Member States whose legislation is considered as more permissive towards data controllers. This could obviously also harm data subjects. Legal certainty for data controllers and for data subjects would only be guaranteed if a comprehensive harmonisation of national legislation is reached, including harmonisation of security obligations. The Working Party therefore supports a strong harmonisation of data protection principles, also as a condition for a possible shift to the country of origin principle.
e. Additional criteria should apply when the controller is established outside the EU, with a view to ensuring that a sufficient connection exists with EU territory, and to avoid EU territory being used to conduct illegal data processing activities by controllers established in third countries. The two following criteria may be developed in this view:
    – The targeting of individuals, or "service oriented approach": this would involve the introduction of a criterion for the application of EU data protection law, that the activity involving the processing of personal data is targeted at individuals in the EU. This would need to consist of substantial targeting based on or taking into account the effective link between the individual and a specific EU country. The following

examples illustrate what targeting could consist of: the fact that a data controller collects personal data in the context of services explicitly accessible or directed to EU residents, via the display of information in EU languages, the delivery of services or products in EU countries, the accessibility of the service depending on the use of an EU credit card, the sending of advertising in the language of the user or for products and services available in the EU. The Working Party notes that this criterion is already used in the field of consumer protection: applying it in a data protection context would bring additional legal certainty to controllers as they would have to apply the same criterion for activities which often trigger the application of both consumer and data protection rules.
- The criterion of the equipment/means: this criterion has shown to have undesirable consequences, such as a possible universal application of EU law. Nonetheless, there is a need to prevent situations where a legal gap would allow the EU being used as a data haven, for instance when a processing activity entails inadmissible ethical issues. The equipment/means criterion could therefore be kept, in a fundamental rights perspective, and in a residual form. It would then only apply as a third possibility, where the other two do not: it would address borderline cases (data about non EU data subjects, controllers having no link with EU) where there is a relevant infrastructure in the EU, connected with the processing of information. In this latter case, it might be an option to foresee that only certain data protection principles—such as legitimacy or security measures—would apply. This approach, which obviously would be subject to further development and refinement, would probably solve most of the problems in the current article 4(1)c.
f. As a last recommendation, the Working Party calls for more harmonisation in the obligation of controllers established in third countries to appoint a representative in the EU, with the objective of giving more effectiveness to the role of the representative. In particular, the extent to which data subjects should be able to effectively exercise their rights against the representative should be clarified.

8.4 EU Data Protection Regulation: Proposed Criteria

8.4.1 A Change of Approach

The kind of issues highlighted above demonstrate that the applicability criteria under article 4 of the Directive are no longer fit for purpose. Therefore, as part of the data protection legislative reform aimed at replacing the Directive with a General Data Protection Regulation (the "Regulation"), the Commission has suggested a different approach which still relies on the location of the organisation responsible for the processing in certain cases but that introduces for the first time the idea of applicability based on the residency of the individuals to whom the data relates.

8.4.2 The EU Legislative Reform

By way of background, the Commission has undertaken a process of reviewing the general EU legal framework on the protection of personal data. As stated in its Communication on *A comprehensive approach on personal data protection in the European Union*[26] (the "Communication"), the main policy objectives for the Commission are to:
- Modernise the EU legal system for the protection of personal data, in particular to meet the challenges resulting from globalisation and the use of new technologies.
- Strengthen individuals' rights, and at the same time reduce administrative formalities to ensure a free flow of personal data within the EU and beyond.
- Improve the clarity and coherence of the EU rules for personal data protection and achieve a consistent and effective implementation and application of the fundamental right to the protection of personal data in all areas of the Union's activities.

Accordingly, the Commission has sought to amend the applicability criteria under article 4 of the Directive. The Communication explained the Commission's intentions in this respect as follows:

> The Commission's first report on the implementation of the Data Protection Directive as early as in 2003 highlighted the fact that the provisions on applicable law were "deficient in several cases, with the result that the kind of conflicts of law this Article seeks to avoid could arise". The situation has not improved since then, as a result of which it is not always clear to data controllers and data protection supervisory authorities which Member State is responsible and which law is applicable when several Member States are concerned. This is particularly the case when a data controller is subject to different requirements from different Member States, when a multinational enterprise is established in more than one Member States or when the data controller is not established in the EU but provides its services to EU residents.
>
> Complexity is also growing due to globalisation and technological developments: data controllers are increasingly operating in several Member States and jurisdictions, providing services and assistance around the clock. The Internet makes it much easier for data controllers established outside the European Economic Area (EEA) to provide services from a distance and to

---

[26] COM(2010)609 final.

process personal data in the online environment; and it is often difficult to determine the location of personal data and of equipment used at any given time (e.g., in "cloud computing" applications and services).

However, the Commission considers that the fact that the processing of personal data is carried out by a data controller established in a third country should not deprive individuals of the protection to which they are entitled under the EU Charter of Fundamental Rights and EU data protection legislation.

The Commission will examine how to revise and clarify the existing provisions on applicable law, including the current determining criteria, in order to improve legal certainty, clarify Member States' responsibility for applying data protection rules and ultimately provide for the same degree of protection of EU data subjects, regardless of the geographic location of the data controller.

8.4.3 Initial Proposal by the Commission

Following a period of formal and informal consultations that took place during 2010 and 2011, the Data Protection Unit of DG Justice at the Commission prepared a draft proposal that was circulated as part of its interservice process in December 2011. The interservice version of the draft Regulation stated in Article 2:

1. This Regulation applies to the processing of personal data in the context of the activities of an establishment of a controller or a processor in the Union.
2. This Regulation applies to the processing of personal data of data subjects residing in the Union not carried out in the context of the activities of an establishment of a controller in the Union, where the processing activities are directed to such data subjects, or serve to monitor the behaviour of such data subjects.

The key departure from the Directive was in respect of the applicability criteria to situations where the controller is not established in the EU and the emphasis was on whether the processing activities were directed to EU residents. This appeared to follow some of the Article 29 Working Party recommendations in this area.

8.4.4 Commission's Final Proposal

On 25 January 2012, the Commission published its final proposal for a Regulation which separated the material and territorial scope of application. With regard to the latter, article 3 stated:

> 1. This Regulation applies to the processing of personal data in the context of the activities of an establishment of a controller or a processor in the Union.
> 2. This Regulation applies to the processing of personal data of data subjects residing in the Union by a controller not established in the Union, where the processing activities are related to:
>   (a) The offering of goods or services to such data subjects in the Union; or
>   (b) The monitoring of their behaviour.
> 3. This Regulation applies to the processing of personal data by a controller not established in the Union, but in a place where the national law of a Member State applies by virtue of public international law.

Again, the key departure from the Directive is in respect of the applicability criteria to situations where the controller is not established in the EU, but in the final draft of the Regulation, the Commission abandoned the reference to the processing activities being directed to EU residents in favour of a reference to the offering of goods or services to such EU residents.

8.4.5 Controllers Established in the EU: Role of Main Establishment

Putting aside the reference to processors, the reference to "the processing of personal data in the context of the activities of an establishment of a controller or a processor in the Union" under the draft Regulation is the equivalent to the reference to the processing carried out "in the context of the activities of an establishment of the controller on the territory of the Member State" under the Directive. Therefore, it can be assumed that the issues regarding the presence of an establishment in the EU are identical under the two frameworks.

8.4.6 Controllers Not Established in the EU: Offering Goods and Services in the EU

As mentioned above, in the final draft of the Regulation, the Commission abandoned the reference to the processing activities being directed to EU residents in favour of a reference to the offering of goods or services to such EU residents. This departs from the recommendation made by the Article 29 Working Party but provides a greater degree of certainty as to the kind of EU-bound activities that would trigger the application of the law.

8.4.7 Controllers Not Established in the EU: Monitoring of Behaviour

Recital 21 of the proposed Regulation points out that in order to determine whether a processing activity can be considered to "monitor the behaviour" of data subjects, it should be ascertained whether individuals are tracked on the internet with data processing techniques which consist of applying a "profile" to an individual, particularly in order to take decisions concerning her or him or for analysing or predicting her or his personal preferences, behaviours and attitudes. Taking this explanation into account, the reference to the monitoring of the behaviour is likely to prove controversial if it remains in the final version of the Regulation for two reasons.

First, it is not clear whether the monitoring of someone's behaviour in a way that triggers the application of the law is restricted to the Internet or not. This criterion was not recommended by the Working Party and there is no explanation for its rationale other than Recital 21 which refers explicitly to tracking individuals on the internet. However, it is not inconceivable that the concept may be applied in other cases, not least because EU data protection law is meant to be technologically neutral.

Secondly, there is a risk that, for example, ascertaining an internet user's potential interest on the basis of his or her browsing patterns in order to deliver targeted advertising to that user will trigger the application of EU law irrespective of the impact of such practices on the privacy rights of individuals. This kind of practice has become global and cannot be said to have adverse consequences for the individual as the only effect is to present the user with an ad about one particular product or service instead of another. So it seems somewhat disproportionate to apply universally the Regulation's stringent framework to that kind of entirely innocuous practice.

8.5 The Future and Practical Implications

Whilst the proposed article 3 of the Regulation setting out the criteria for its application represents an improvement from the existing regime under the Directive, there are some aspects of the proposed criteria that create uncertainty. The first one relates to the fact that it is not clear what is meant to be captured by the reference to the monitoring of an EU-based individual's behaviour and why this triggers the application of the Regulation. There is a danger that given today's technology, all sorts of normal uses of technology and activities that take place on the Internet may be caught by this criterion. For example, web analytics, used by the operators of websites around the globe that may be visited by individuals from the EU, should not by themselves fall under the monitoring of EU residents' behaviour. Therefore, it is necessary to make the territorial scope provision more relevant to the effective protection of EU data subjects' rights.

In addition, the ability of international organisations with a presence in the European Union to benefit from the proposed new rules concerning the competent data protection supervisory authority would be compromised if Articles 3(1) and 3(2) were to be applied cumulatively. In order to bring about more clarity and legal certainty, policy makers should ensure that the rules dealing with the applicability of the law deal with this issue, so that if there is already an EU based controller within a corporate group, that controller should be responsible for compliance in respect of the relevant data processing [as per Article 3(1)].

The EU data protection legislative process is likely to continue until at least 2014, so there is currently an opportunity to ensure that the scope of application of EU data protection law and its extraterritorial reach achieves the right balance and the policy objective sought by the EU policy makers. The success of this aim depends on the ability of the EU legislators to be realistic and on their understanding that no particular technology should determine the outcome, as otherwise the adopted framework will be impractical and ineffective.

References

Article 29 Data Protection Working Party, Opinion 5/2012 on Cloud Computing, 01037/12/EN, WP196, 1 July 2012

Article 29 Data Protection Working Party, Opinion 8/2010 on applicable law, 0836-02/10/EN, WP179, 16 December 2010

Article 29 Data Protection Working Party, Working Document Privacy on the Internet – An integrated EU Approach to On-line Data Protection, 5063/00/EN/FINAL, WP37, 21 November 2000, p. 28

Article 29 Data Protection Working Party, Working document on determining the international application of EU data protection law to personal data processing on the Internet by non-EU based web sites, 5035/01, EN/Final, WP56, 30 May 2002

Article 29 Data Protection Working Party. Opinion 1/2008 on data protection issues related to search engines, 00737/EN, WP 148, 4 April 2008

Bygrave LA (2000) Determining applicable law pursuant to European data protection legislation. Comput Law Secur Rep 16:252–257, http://dx.doi.org/10.1016/S0267-3649(00)89134-7

Jay R, Hamilton A (2003) Data protection law and practice, 2nd edn. Sweet and Maxwell, London

Kuner C (2007) European data protection law, corporate compliance and regulation, 2nd edn. Oxford University Press, Oxford

Information Security in the Internet Age

Eva Rose Rahim

> The concern is over what will happen as strong encryption becomes commonplace with all digital communications and stored data. Right now the use of encryption isn't all that widespread, but that state of affairs is expected to change rapidly

(Dorothy E. Denning, Distinguished Professor, Department of Defense Analysis, Naval Postgraduate School & Fellow of the Association for Computing Machinery)

Abstract

This descriptive chapter aims to impress the readers on various latest technologies that relate to critical information security. It is based on my analysis, observation and experience whilst dealing with this. The demanding technology's offerings, deployment and its usage have had pushed Internet users like us to be more cautious and considerable whilst managing personal data. Each section of this chapter highlights some practical guidance for readers and proffers useful explanations that could be potentially considered in our daily life and business.

9.1 Cloud Computing and Challenges

Cloud computing is a hot topic and will continue to be so. Due to its agility and long term benefits outweighing its drawbacks, many organisations are following. However, the lack of international standards in cloud compliance has probably slowed down the top decisions in entirety. Security is another issue in the slow adoption.

E.R. Rahim (✉)
Demand QC Global Ltd., 52 Penderry Rise, London SE6 1HA, UK
e-mail: Miss.raz.rahim@gmail.com

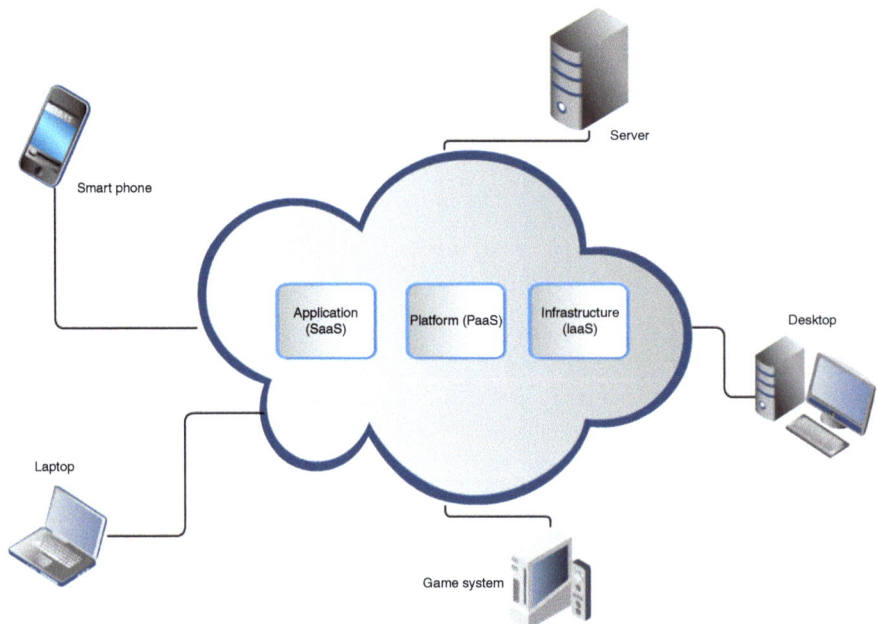

Fig. 9.1 Schematic diagram of cloud computing

Though cloud security has been proclaimed highly improved, yet—the cases of Salesforce.com phishing attack in 2007, the RSA SecurID and Sony PlayStation's network accounts compromised in 2011, and more recently with the distributed denial of service (DDoS) attacks into the CIA and the UK's Serious Organised Crime Agency websites in early 2012[1]—cloud vulnerabilities and cyber threats are still a growing concern. No surprise that IT experts have coined 2011 as the year of the cloud as well as the year of hack. It was also an eventful year that privacy was ill-fated,[2] majorly due to Facebook ever-changing privacy policy.

9.1.1 Brief History and Overview

Cloud computing roots back to the 1960s when John McCarthy pioneered the time-sharing system,[3] where systems remotely shared computing resources and applications. The term "cloud" refers to a schematic cloud—in the same way how the Internet is perceived—where all shared applications, platforms and infrastructures sit, ready to be consumed as services by clients as shown in Fig. 9.1.

---

[1] Agencies (2012).

[2] Arthur (Arthur 2011).

[3] Wikipedia (2012a).

Cloud computing has won media attentions since Amazon Web Services (AWS) was introduced in July 2002.[4] This triggered the collaboration between IBM and Google in October 2007,[5] in order to address computing challenges with web applications, particularly when social networking had begun to emerge. Essentially, cloud is all about web-based services. Users no longer need to install software onto their computers, but simply able to access and use the applications directly from browsers, after which they have been securely authenticated. We are already consuming cloud services such as Google Docs, web-based emails, and Microsoft Office 365 via the Internet. The amass take-up of cloud computing is mainly due to a steep rise in Open Standards and Open-Source software.

The National Institute of Standards and Technology (NIST) defines cloud computing as, "… a model for enabling ubiquitous, convenient, on-demand network access to a shared pool of configurable computing resources (e.g., networks, servers, storage, applications, and services) that can be rapidly provisioned and released with minimal management effort or service provider interaction."[6] On-demand service and rapid provisioning of shared computing resources are the keys to the cloud.

9.1.2 Why the Cloud?

For businesses, simply put, it reduces overall IT spend for when they need to provision and manage hardware, software, and applications within a complex infrastructure. Three fundamental cloud service models are:

- *Software as a Service* (*SaaS*)
  It is a delivery of software applications hosted centrally by service providers. SaaS stems from a class of centralised computing called Application Service Providers (ASP) and usually accessed via web browsers. Recently, Database as a Service (DaaS) has emerged as an entity of SaaS. Examples include Salesforce.com, Google Docs, and Microsoft 360.
- *Platform as a Service* (*PaaS*)
  The model utilises computing platforms to deliver services. Providers typically provision the hosting capabilities by facilitating deployment of services, where customers control software configurations and development. Examples include Microsoft Azure and Amazon Elastic Beanstalk.
- *Infrastructure as a Service* (*IaaS*)
  With this, storage space is leveraged within servers and data centres. Providers facilitate one or more virtual machines based on business demands, and thus bill

---

[4] (Amazon 2012a).
[5] (Haikes & Murchinson 2012).
[6] (Grance & Mell 2011).

the customers based on the amount of resources allocated and consumed. Examples include Rackspace Cloud, VMWare and Amazon Simple Storage Service (Amazon S3).

The cloud business model of pay-per-usage, in the similar way how utility companies charge the households, makes cloud a promising route. With the use of resource pooling—that contributes to performance optimisation—businesses empower cloud strategy in their mission critical on-demand applications. With businesses attempting to reach their audiences via different means such as mobile phones, tablets, digital televisions, and gaming consoles, the cloud further brings out its long term benefits and return on investment (ROI). Forrester projects the global cloud market will grow to more than $241 billion by 2020,[7] while Gartner forecasts it to be worth of $150 billion in 2013.[8] Mimecast, provider of cloud email management, reveals that seven in ten companies that are already using cloud will move all new applications into the cloud.[9] To date, migration of IT into cloud computing has been a business pattern; however as with other hosted systems, it presents challenges within traditional security, trust and privacy.

For end users, the cloud favours ease of use. Also, saving data in the cloud would mean that users can access this anytime using any web enabled devices, on top of storing the same data on their own computers. Dropbox, for instance, allows users to store data in the cloud storage and their synchronisation service does all the magic. In fact, I am writing this chapter using Dropbox as a storage mechanism so that I can always access it on-demand regardless of where and when I continue writing. Thankfully, I never have to carry USB flash drives anymore.

Maintaining software fixes and upgrades in the cloud is next to nothing since cloud providers have this ready in place. Like businesses, end-users pay the service based on the usage and space consumed. Ease of use is the name of the game; however, it comes at the expense of not knowing where the data physically resides. For all you know, your data could temporarily be in Iceland or in Australia. When users find out how easy it is to do everything in the cloud, by human nature, they will eventually start storing their sensitive data without realising the impact of doing so. Privacy and data protection requirements vary by country and therefore you need to consider the privacy rules that cover each of the jurisdictions they operate in as well as the rules that govern the treatment of data at the locations where the cloud service providers provision their services.

Four cloud deployments are:
- *Public cloud*
  Services are public and are generally free to use by the general public. Businesses would also consume services from it for their own purposes, via

---

[7] (Ried & Kisker 2012).

[8] (Ingthorsson 2011).

[9] See Ingthorsson's analysis.

in-house or third party Web applications, facilitating pay-per-use pricing model. Examples include Facebook, Twitter, and other social-driven sites. It is housed within massive but scalable data centres owned by providers.

- *Private cloud*

  It is solely built for one organisation consumed internally by private cloud users. Infrastructure is owned and managed by the organisation itself, or by a trusted third party supplier, and all services are internally hosted. If virtualisation is enabled, then it is referred as a *virtual private cloud*, where services are generally accessible via VPN or other secure protocols. Naturally, private cloud can reside within a public cloud centre, but with the exception of secure access connections (including physical access). It is best suited for highly sensitive data where security is paramount.

- *Community cloud*

  This cloud stems from the specific sets of shared requirements (such as security, application types, legislative issues, compliance, and efficiency demands) among a group of users. It is a "closed" private cloud that supports a specific community. This type of deployment has become more adapted by government bodies; hence generally known as Government Cloud. Due to legislative issues, this cloud may be the answer to country specific judicial concerns.[10]

- *Hybrid cloud*

  Public and private clouds are composited to logically separate data and application, hence hybrid. Data is housed in private clouds, with defined security policies, while applications are made accessible via public clouds. Search engines, emails, blogs are one of many examples of a hybrid cloud.

Cloud service providers usually have security compliance built into the infrastructure. This needs to be assessed in detail by you, as a business or an organisation, taking into account of the type of users that will be accessing the cloud services. Reliability, security and data protection should always be assessed. For instance, Amazon Simple Storage Service (Amazon S3) guarantees SLAs with 99.99 % availability, solid security [with Identity and Access Management (IAM) and Server Side Encryption (SEE)] and complies with regulatory standards such as PCI and HIPAA.[11]

With hybrid cloud, more likely you will use multiple vendors depending on your compliance requirements. The more vendors you have, the more security compliance you need to assess, since no vendors will have exactly the same compliance at any one time. Each vendor has their own APIs that can be consumed by other vendors in the cloud, with each to their own security protocols, as portrayed in Fig. 9.3.

---

[10] (Nisvold 2012).

[11] Amazon (Amazon 2012b).

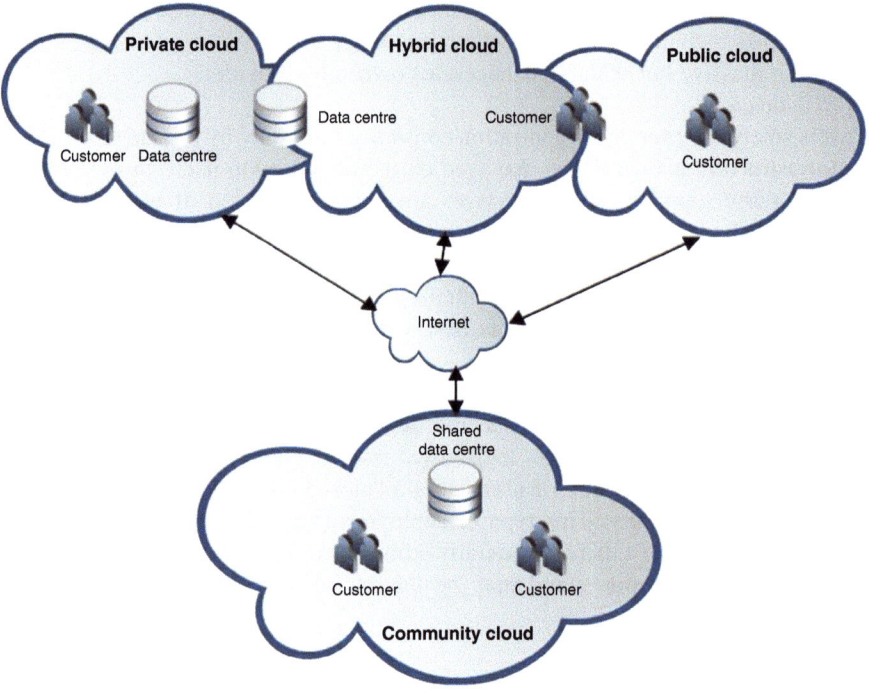

Fig. 9.2 Cloud deployment models

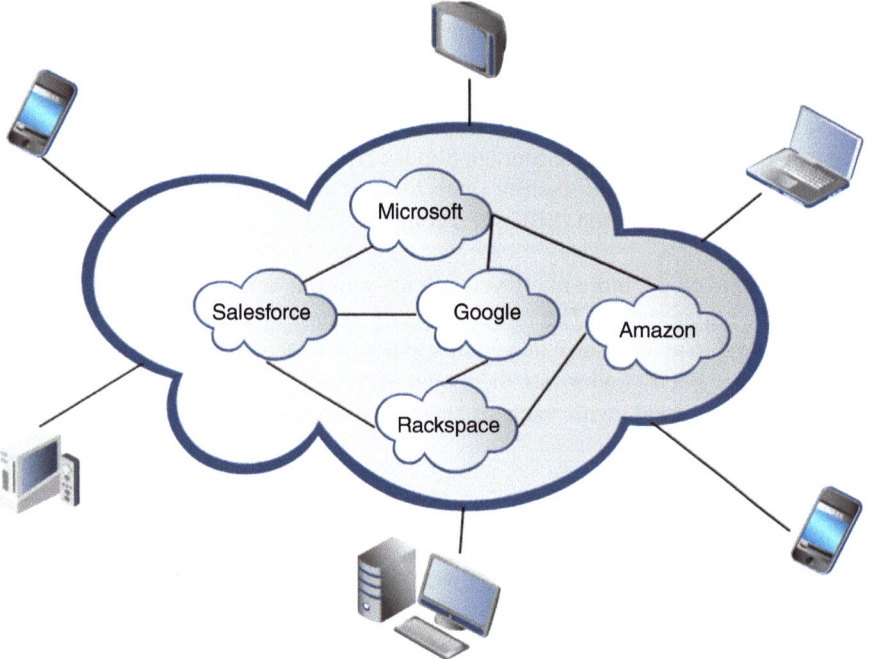

Fig. 9.3 Multiple providers in the cloud

9.1.3 Security Vulnerabilities

Bring Your Own Device (BYOD) is a trending concept. It is about bringing consumer technologies into workplace, where they use own devices such as mobile phones and tablets in order to access company data. The consumerization of IT[12]— sparked by the wide usage of iPhone and Android—claims to have freed up corporate IT departments to do more critical tasks, but at the expense of exposing cloud endpoints with malicious software. The trend is so challenging that some IT coined BYOD as Bring Your Own Disaster or Bring Your Own Danger.[13] If not properly aligned with enterprise standards and practices, then BYOD could result in End Node Problem, where trusted devices could access an "un-trusted" network by means of say, a web application from which script injections could happen. Even if the device itself is trusted by a network, the user accessing the device needs to be properly authenticated. And even if the user is authenticated, and the device already has some form of keyloggers installed, this still does not guarantee the security of endpoints. The real potential issue here is therefore not within cloud network, but lies within the user devices accessing the service, where the endpoints reside. Most user devices are rarely configured to any security standards, which is therefore problematic. Some companies have banned Dropbox in a corporate network, realising employees may upload corrupted files onto it, or legitimate files that contain sensitive data. IBM bans Dropbox after fearing that sensitive data could be let loose by employees through smart phones.[14] If the endpoint is not properly secured (i.e. no strong authentication and encryption), then data could potentially be leaked into the hands of irresponsible people. Even if the environment is secure, there is also a risk of someone accessing the device and do something malicious. Simple example is when you upload a file onto Dropbox via a laptop, and your smart phone is synchronising this file instantaneously. You forget to set the phone to "sleep mode". During this time someone else could potentially get onto the phone and accessing those sensitive data. Whilst security is in place, it is the person's responsibility to abide by the policy.

Almost every website has Facebook, Google, or LinkedIn login widget to allow users to use their existing social credentials. This is what Single Sign On (SSO) is all about. For example, you can login into YouTube by using your GoogleID without having to create a new YouTube login. Similarly, Pluck provides social platform solutions that allow customers to use its SSO feature for consumers to use existing social logins in order to leave comments on their sites. SSO is easy to manage in a cloud. But, it becomes tricky when you have multiple cloud environments with multiple providers. This is true when you need to manage diverse standards and third-party access to your data and applications. While this

---

[12] (Reed 2011).

[13] (Hardy 2012).

[14] (Bergstein 2012).

is possible, it still remains challenging. SSO is largely constructed through Web Application Programming Interface (Web API) and Software Development Kit (SDK), and some use OpenID protocols for authentication. While vulnerabilities are not an issue at protocol levels, they pose risks by the system that allows each SSO element—for example, Microsoft research team found out that Adobe's Flash cross-domain feature totally crippled Facebook SSO security.[15] Provisioning SSO this way is seen as convenience, rather than having security in design, which OneLogin claims to resolve with the implementation of Security Assertion Markup Language (SAML).[16] SSO is a feature that has become a trend, but you, as a business should assess its greater impact on security.

The recent case of LinkedIn member passwords being compromised[17] has triggered a huge media response on how far one can rely on SSO. Some argue that it is mostly down to users creating weak passwords. But how strong is strong and how weak is weak? When most of us cannot remember complicated long passwords, we revert to something more memorable such as favourite car, pet's name, birthdays, and so on. Surprisingly, those entities are also used as a common set of password reminder questions. Google provides two-step verification which enhances another security layer. Google further provides application-based verification on mobile devices. By doing so, the industry has begun to think and act on how to tackle user's weak password problems, which I strongly think should be utilised by all SaaS-based applications.

It is a standard practice for all providers to implement intrusion detection system. With different setups of cloud deployments, there are few guidelines written by Phil Cox,[18] which he feels that the ultimate responsibility comes down to both providers and you (as a business). In other words, solid SLAs should be drawn between both parties. Providing intrusion detection system is not an option, rather it is a must-have list for cloud deployment.

Cloud computing empowers virtualisations, that is when virtual machines are used to consolidate hardware, computing powers and resources. It also drives multi-tenancy environment where a software application is designed to virtually partition its data and configuration, and each client works with a customised virtual application instance. While this is done in a controlled manner, there is potential to compromise a virtual machine (VM) hypervisor—hypervisor VM manager (VMM) that allows multiple operating systems, termed *guests*, to run concurrently on a host computer. If the hypervisor is vulnerable, it will become a primary target and all its guests will be affected. At the scale of the cloud, such a risk would have broad impact if not otherwise mitigated. This requires an additional degree of network isolation and enhanced intrusion detection by security monitoring.

---

[15] (Chen et al. 2012)
[16] (Pederson 2012).
[17] (Silveira 2012).
[18] (Cox 2012).

9 Information Security in the Internet Age

However, hypervisors are purpose-built with a small and specific set of functions. Though attacks have not been reported against hypervisors so far due to its small functions and that they are not used to run third-party applications, it is to note that hypervisors should be monitored frequently, seeing that is completely transparent to network traffic.

To address security concerns with virtualisations, certification matters. Several products have undergone formal security evaluations and received certification. It is also vital to acquire independent audit to inspect how vulnerable a virtualisation is.

Do not to dismiss cloud outright simply because you have concerns over security. As technology matures, most vendors have improved security. With many industry standards to comply, it is you, as a business, to decide whether what they have in place agrees with your security requirements. If not, additional layer of security and measures will need to take place.

9.1.4 Compliance Challenges

Gartner Field Survey reveals that back in early 2010,[19] "Data location, privacy and access concerns" was a top issue after "Security of service" among companies planning to adopt cloud. Two years on and the same concerns still stay on top. Security and data compliance are not directly related, but they are inter-connected. Weak security means weak compliance, and thus risks the danger of sensitive data being exploited.

The flexibility of what cloud provides—where it can be created, dismantled, reconfigured, grown, and shrunk on-demand—is its core characteristics. But, the big question here is—can it incorporate necessary regulatory requirements? Being in the cloud means you would expect a lot of traffic and data going back and forth, and the processing and storage of data therefore needs to comply with regulations. Simple, but it is an understatement. So, with the cloud setups, who are data controllers and who are data processors? Who is responsible of what?

All UK businesses holding personal data must comply with Data Protection Act (DPA) 1998. With the cloud computing, data can be transferred and held outside of the European Economic Area. Since privacy and data protection requirements vary by country, the UK governance body states that it is actually your business that is ultimately responsible for that data.[20]

In Sweden, whoever makes use of a cloud service for processing of personal data is the controller of personal data, even if the processing is carried out by a cloud service provider or its sub-contractors.[21] It is the controller that must ensure that the processing of personal data is in compliance with the DPA and other legislations,

---

[19] (Laczynski 2011).
[20] (Business 2012).
[21] (Datainspektionen 2012).

such as government agency-specific records statutes and the Public Access to Information and Secrecy Act.

In Germany, the business (as a cloud customer) acts as a data controller, must therefore comply with the DPA such that these minimum requirements shall be met[22]:

- Open, transparent and detailed information by the cloud service provider on the technical, organisational and legal framework including a security concept;
- Transparent, detailed and clear contractual provisions governing the processing of the data in the cloud, especially concerning the location of the data processing including the notification about any changes thereto, as well as concerning the portability of the data and interoperability;
- The implementation of the agreed data protection and data security measures the provider as well as the cloud customer; and
- Up-to-date and meaningful evidence regarding the cloud infrastructure; e.g., certificates by recognised and independent auditors.

In Italy, the most challenging provisions of compliance with cloud computing is the appointment of cloud providers as data processors, while consumers and operators shall remain autonomous data controllers.[23] A guide on cloud computing published on May 24, 2012 by the Italian Data Protection Authority (Garante) further states that those who have chosen (or about to choose) cloud computing should solidly place adequate measures of security and staff training in order to ensure compliance enforced by the Act.

It is obvious from the above that jurisdictions are operated differently between countries in the EEA, let alone other countries outside of the region. Compliance within cloud computing should be founded on the basis of data protection definitions on who data controllers and data processors are, and definitive and clear agreements shall be constructed between the providers, third-party suppliers and the customers (that is you as a business or an organisation). Failure to do so would cause further disagreements along the line, and ultimately would hinder the growth, hence the benefits of cloud computing.

9.1.5 Future Trends and Paths

Many companies are now at the planning stages with regard to cloud deployment. Growth in private and hybrid cloud deployments are expected in the next few years.

BYOD is a trend that has been increasingly adopted by many large companies to date. While it helps IT department strategically, you will need to think about what long term impact it will impose. Tightening the security, pairing with industry compliance would help, but it still comes down to education among employees.

---

[22] (Moos 2012).

[23] Data Guidance (2012).

Contracts should be drawn, agreed, and signed with the employees about the importance of securing their own devices and installed applications. This is extremely challenging in its own right, but ensuring that IT policies are constantly monitored at every endpoint is one wise step ahead.

Some useful pointers to follow:
- Sign contract directly with cloud providers, on behalf of your customer;
- Always have security measures written clearly in the contract and ensure you understand the implication of each. Get an independent audit report and/or certification verification;
- Ensure the provider's employees have qualifications in the industry. Vetting their backgrounds helps in determining that you are not dealing with someone with past criminal records;
- Get details of people or a group of people who have access to your customer's data. Ask your provider when and why they are accessing it. A provider's employee snooping on sensitive data in the cloud would present greater risks;
- Verify access control to your data and environment, which includes physical access to the provider's premises;
- When deploying private or community clouds, stay in control with your user's devices, since these are endpoints to your system;
- Vetting your provider's financial background helps in determining that if anything should happen with the provider financially, mitigation procedures are in place. Should your provider disappear, you will need to ensure the no sensitive personal data is lost;
- In the event of service cancellation with current provider, ensure that all of your customer data are returned according to compliance requirements. Some providers do not tell you that your data is actually housed in a common shared network and the risks they carry; and
- Following the return of your data, make sure your provider sets out complete procedures on data deletion in their system. You will need to check this at the point of signing the contract, not when you are already in contract.

Ultimately, should you decide to migrate your current IT infrastructure into the cloud, it is your responsibility to arm yourself with the deep knowledge of cloud models and service deployments, their security and compliance challenges, long before you seal the deal. It could be a long-winding exercise, but it is a worthwhile investment.

Your requirements will also change depending on the criticality of your data. If it is regulated or highly sensitive and contains personally identifiable information, you need to impose more stringent security and privacy requirements. If your cloud provider does not offer a specific control, say, encryption-at-rest and access controls, either you ask your provider to implement that controls, which may result in a higher fee, or you have to simply walk away. But a set of deal-breaker assessment criteria, like the ones based on protection of critical data, is exactly what you need to quickly eliminate services that are not a good fit.

9.2 Demystifying Scripting Technologies

Long gone all web pages that do nothing apart from displaying static text and images via web browsers. Since the inception of ECMAScript,[24] web pages have become dynamic with user interactions, by use of JavaScript, Document Object Model (DOM), Asynchronous JavaScript and XML (Ajax). They are used in a way that web applications can send data to, and retrieve data from, a server asynchronously (i.e. in the background) without interfering with the display and behaviour of the existing page. Because of this nature, most web developers constantly use scripting technologies to transfer data from web browsers to web servers, and back.

While the use of scripting technologies enhances user experience—for example, user will not have to wait for a username validation to come back by pressing a submit button, since validation occurs as when a user types in few characters in the input box—attackers can exploit it to inject malicious scripts. Maybe not intended by a web developer, but without secure web programming, then this can become a big setback for nearly all parties involved, including those confined as data controllers and processors. This explains the Principle 7 of the DPA 1998—*appropriate technical and organisational measures shall be taken against unauthorised or unlawful processing of personal data against accidental loss or destruction of, or damage to a personal data*. It implies that technical measures shall start from application development itself, working from bottom to top.

9.2.1 Web 2.0, Ajax, APIs, Web Services

Web 2.0 is about interoperability, sharing, user engagement and collaboration via the Web. Social networking sites stems from Web 2.0, where two-way interactivity happens. Web 1.0 is passive viewing, where websites create content and users are only able to read them. Web 2.0 characterises three important entities[25]:

- Rich Internet Applications (RIA)—web applications mimicking desktop application for rich and interactive user experience. This is often achieved via Ajax, Flash, and Adobe Flex framework;
- Web-Oriented Architecture (WOA)—the technique to maximise browser-server interactions with web services and APIs. RSS feeds are one of many examples that use this architecture; and
- Social Web—where social relations are created as a result of richer applications. Examples are Facebook, Twitter, and LinkedIn.

Much of Web 2.0 development revolves around client-side scripting, where Ajax is often used. Asynchronous communication happens in the background. HTML

---

[24] Wikipedia (2012b).

[25] Wikipedia (2012c).

9 Information Security in the Internet Age   169

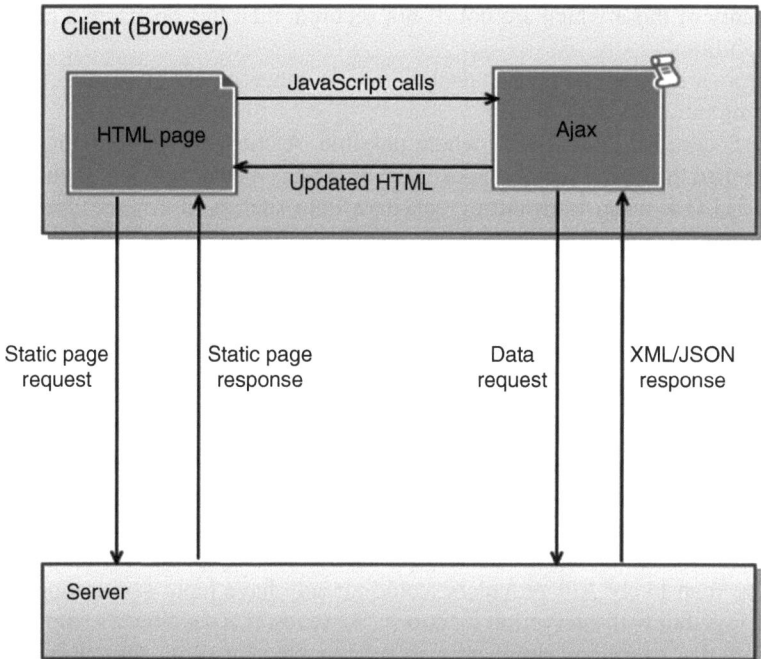

Fig. 9.4 Schematic Ajax interaction

pages are static by design, and it is Ajax techniques that make HTML pages constantly being updated, as schematically shown in Fig. 9.4.

Some developers use this technique to transfer sensitive data depending on what an application needs to process and return. Should this be the case, such data needs to be in a format that is not readable by packet sniffers. If you use Ajax, the server usually responds with data formats that JavaScript can parse and use. By inspecting the response, an attacker can craft injection strings to break the format, and consequently place arbitrary content onto the HTML page. This content could appear legitimate to the end users, but what they may not realise is that injections already happen in the background. Though input validation checking may already exist to counteract the injections, it may not detect the same injection in a new data format—say in raw text format. Therefore, developers should inspect Ajax requests using web debugging tools such as Fiddler, Firebug, or Chrome's Developer tools.

In addition to client-side scripting, Web 2.0 often uses server-based communication protocols such as REST or SOAP. Server side scripting promotes SEO friendly results, i.e. search engines will only index content that is rendered statically in the HTML source view page. LinkedIn, for instance, exposes both JavaScript API and REST API that allows developers to build rich applications. Demand Media, via its Pluck social products, offers REST APIs and SDKs to optimise SEO content. Many of today's APIs are secure, but you will be surprised to find out that plenty of those which are not. If not secured, then this opens up a number of vulnerabilities.

If you are using APIs that deal with a number of sensitive data, then the following practices apply:

- Use Secure HTTP (HTTPS) where possible. A client-server communication is tunnelled through a Secured Socket Layer (SSL). Web developers should always use HTTPS when transmitting sensitive data such as usernames, emails and passwords. With strong encryptions, a packet sniffing program will not be able to see this in plain text, hence secure its transmission layer;
- Never transmit sensitive data in plain text, ever! Plain, human-readable text is a recipe for disaster. If not using HTTPS, developers should always encrypt the data by block cipher, such as MD5, SHA-2 or AES, in order to build a cryptographic hash function; and
- Sanitise input data. Most websites use databases to store data. Injections can happen at scripting level and/or at database level. Input therefore has to be sanitised prior to processing the data. Sometimes, an attacker would attempt to inject arbitrary code directly into parameterised URLs. Therefore, input sanitisation has to happen at every possible data entry point.

More than likely API providers would already have input sanitisation built in SDKs, together with encryption functions. However, it is developer's responsibility to ensure that every precautionary step is accounted for. With some Rapid Application Development (RAD) tools such as Microsoft Visual Studio products and open source programs, developers should use their built-in testing tools (or as a plug-in) in order to validate user inputs. Test codes are usually developed before the actual code is written, which what test-driven development (TDD) is. Traditional software development adopts TDD in its lifecycle. Web development has also adopted the same; in order to ensure that the application is fully tested.

Developers may argue their applications are already secure, but most times attackers use less obvious, indirect and creative techniques to exploit vulnerabilities. What are those techniques? There are many, but CWE has compiled a great list of 2011's top 25 most dangerous vulnerabilities,[26] which includes cross-site scripting, cross-site request forgery, SQL injections, buffer overflow and many others.

9.2.2 Injection Techniques and Attacks

Cross-site scripting (XSS) is a well-known technique that exploits user input by means of altering content received from the server back to the browser. Once received, attackers would usually use JavaScript to redirect user to an HTML page hosted elsewhere, or to render the page with legitimate content. This is usually

---

[26] Christey et al. (2011).

used for phishing scam, which is a method to gather victim's personal data. XSS commonly starts with embedded links in emails that genuinely appear as if they come from legitimate sources. Recently, XSS was used to gain admin access privilege on a victim's computer.

A user identified as "Security Obscurity" explains step-by-step method to launch an example of XSS attack on Orange—a French telecom giant—website through a social commenting platform.[27] The aim of this attack was to gain access to a victim's computer by getting admin privileges. By simply injecting a parameterised URL on the site, "Security Obscurity" was able to craft a malicious link to be embedded in an email. A user who falls prey to the link would be tricked into believing that the email was genuine—seeing that the link contains a legitimate URL (for instance, it is denoted as http://www.orange.co.uk/xxx). But, unbeknownst to the victim, the link was actually masked as XSS character encoding, which when clicked, would compromise the victim's machine. From this scenario, it is evident that starting from XSS, user's machine is compromised as a result. Imagine if the victim is in a secure corporate network, the impact is unimaginable!

XSS works via SSL connection as well, simply because browsers cannot differentiate between malicious and legitimate content served by a web application—i.e. HTTPS is just a secure channel, nothing else. With the case of "Security Obscurity", XSS succeeded by phishing even though SSL was in place.

So, how do you avoid this creatively crafted XSS attack? Always sanitise the input! And test, test, and more tests—by this, it means that tests are to be carried out continuously not just at the time of application release, but also when and after patches are applied. One simple (but dangerous) test assumption is that most developers would test the application after the patch release, assuming that anything prior would work. This, in fact, is a security hole that is often explored by attackers to start challenging vulnerability. And this is when test-driven development (TDD) is preferred, since test automation is taken care of during its lifecycle. Microsoft has introduced Security Development Lifecycle (Microsoft SDL), since 2004, in an effort to securely build software applications that align with security standards and compliance requirements.

Cross-site request forgery (XSRF) is almost the opposite of XSS. If XSS exploits the trust that a user has on a website, then XSRF is the exploit of a trust that a site has on a user (i.e. the browser that a user is using). This type of attack forces the victim unwillingly (also unbeknownst to him) to execute an action in which he has already been authenticated on a site by the browser through a previous request. Take an example where an attacker can perform a fund transfer of a victim's bank account without the victim knowing this happening in the background. All the attacker needs to do is to craft the request via a link sent through a viral email. A little social engineering technique would almost guarantee the success of this attack. This was evident in the XSRF vulnerability exposed by researchers from

---

[27] Security Obscurity (2012).

Princeton University in 2008, with a detailed step written in their research paper.[28] Thankfully, it was fixed before the research paper was published.

There are many other examples how XSRF works programmatically. The most important thing here is to prevent such attacks in the future, both from application development perspectives as well as from the end users themselves. Developers should therefore follow these general guidelines:

- Use CAPTCHA to ensure that the response is generated by a person;
- Re-authentication. When an important action is required such as a fund transfer, then the application needs to re-authenticate the user; and
- One time token. Currently most financial institutions have provided each customer with a security token dongle, where a customer must enter randomly generated 6 digits code before they can proceed with the request. The code is time-based, and therefore the same digit will never be used again.

As with the end-users, these are useful to note:

- Logoff immediately at the end of every active session;
- Use protected-mode sessions (also known as private-browsing mode) provided by browsers when accessing sites such as banks or membership-driven sites;
- Never allow your browser to save usernames and passwords and avoid "remember me" feature at any cost; and
- If possible, use different browsers to access different applications at the same time. For instance, use Firefox to access your web-based email, and Chrome to check your bank balance. If you are only using one browser, use tabbed-browsing, one of which has privacy mode session enabled.

When developers are asked whether their databases are prone to SQL injections, the common answer would probably be, "it's already taken care of by our secure database system, so this is filtered per incoming request". The vulnerability is well understood and security analysts have warned retailers and organisations about it for several years. Yet, it still continues to date, with the most recent case of Wurm Online, a 3D Massively multi-player online (MMO) role-playing game, whose social pages and main website have been compromised by SQL injection attack in May 2012.[29] This caused the immediate shutdown of the site while their developers were deciding on shifting PHP-based to a different solution, which is at cost.

SQL injection is a technique to pass arbitrary SQL commands or queries through a web application for execution by a backend database. Take, for example, a website that displays product information on a page, with the following URL:

`http://www.mysite.com/products/product.php?id=8187`

The ID is then passed into a database, and all associated data will be returned. An attacker would inject malicious SQL statement like this:

---

[28] (Felten & Zeller 2012).

[29] (Reahard 2012).

```
http://www.mysite.com/products/product.php?id=8187
UNION SELECT Username, Password FROM Users
```

This writes up the corresponding SQL statement like this:

```
SELECT ProductName, [Product Description] FROM Products
WHERE ProductNUmber = 8187 UNION SELECT Username, Password
FROM Users;
```

The result of this query reveals list of all usernames and passwords in the system. Of course, this works directly if the attacker knew the exact names of tables and columns. However, it is not a rocket science either to find the database table names and columns if further injections are tried and tested.

So, how do you mitigate this? This can be viewed in three categorisations:

- *Coding and web application configuration level*

  All inputs are to be sanitised. This includes escaping special characters such as apostrophes and mark-ups as well as quote-safe the input. Modern programming languages usually provide such checks and make the necessary alterations before the value is passed into the database. However, developers will still need to inspect every possible input data to ensure that it is clean and properly validated. In addition, error reporting should never be shown on the page this gives clues to attackers on how your application responds to invalidated data. Many websites out there still show these errors. It is only a matter of time when an attacker would gather this error and start injecting malicious codes into your database application.

  Also, consider prepared statements (or parameterised queries) when writing database queries in the code. Prepared statements can harm performance, which is an issue when building a complex web application. To counteract this, developer can choose to create SQL stored procedures as an alternative.

- *Database application level*

  It is always a good practice to encrypt sensitive data inside the database itself. Passwords and credit card numbers are often good candidates to be stored as a "salted-hashed" format. When a user creates a password, a randomly generated "salt" value is created by the application and appended to the password, and the password-and-salt are then passed through a one way encryption routine. The result is a salted hash, which is stored in the database along with the clear text salt string.

  Within database level, developers can create SQL stored procedures in order to eliminate the use of SQL statements in the code altogether. Stored procedures are a set of SQL queries written as a subroutine inside the database itself. Furthermore, stored procedures can be used to validate input, which adds additional layer of coding practices.

A database administrator can limit permissions and segregate users, which help control the access level for application uses only. Web application usually runs as a specific user and so does a database application.

- *Server infrastructure level*
  Separating web server and database server is another good practice to add a security layer in your web application. For instance, putting the machine in a DMZ with extremely limited pinholes "inside" the network means that even getting complete control of the web server does not automatically grant full access to everything else.

9.2.3 Security Breaches to Date

The largest ever-breach was in 2008 where the Heartland Payment Systems was hacked, compromising an estimated 134 million customer credit card accounts. The attackers launched SQL injection attack, which resulted in them being sentenced to 20 years in federal prison.[30] Heartland eventually paid more than $110 million to Visa, MasterCard, and other card associations to settle claims related to the breach. Most recently in April 2012, Global Payments, a company that processes card transactions went public with a report on estimated 1.5 million card numbers were at risk due to detected hacking intrusions. At the time of writing, in which the case is still under further investigation—the root cause of the intrusion yet to be determined—the company further claimed that their customer data may also have been stolen.[31] This prompted Visa and MasterCard to remove Global Payments from their Payment Card Industry (PCI) compliant service providers.

Armerding[32] compiles the top 15 worst data security breaches of the twenty-first century which reveals that most of the breaches were the results of scripting injections (either XSS or SQL injections). It is almost certain that despite all the warnings, guidelines that security analysts have published in the past, the hacking trend is still on the up. Giants such as Sony's PlayStation, RSA, and ESTsoft (of which all made to the list) would have had to invest more time and resources to fix the vulnerabilities, but it is clear that the consequences they had to bear far outweighed the damages.

Symantec recently published that even though there were 4,989 vulnerabilities identified in 2011—compared to 6,253 in 2010—the general trend over time is still upward considering the fact that approximately 95 new vulnerabilities discovered every week.[33] The numbers are worrying, and even more so when cloud deployment and the consumerisation of IT are on the up. While external threats will

---

[30] (Zetter 2010).
[31] (Mills 2012).
[32] (Armerding 2012).
[33] Symantec (2012).

continue to multiply, insider threats will still need to be accounted for since employees may act intentionally—and unintentionally—to leak or steal valuable data by means of accessing services via multiple devices in particular when BYOD policy is adopted.

9.2.4 Web 3.0 and Beyond

Web 3.0, also termed as "Semantic Web", is a movement collaborated by W3C to promote common formats of data by defining it to mean something. It provides a framework to make data more meaningful. Simply put, Web 2.0 is all about user-generated content in a read-write mode (Web 1.0 is read-only mode), i.e. users are consuming as well as contributing. Web 3.0, on the other hand, is about personalisation based on what that data means to the users. Apple's iPhone 4S with its Siri—a powerful voice recognition engine—is one example where data is processed and returned by semantic user instructions. For instance, you would issue a voice command, "Tell my husband that I am going to be half an hour late". The Siri app will analyse this command, finds your husband in your contacts list, and then sends a message to him that you are going to be 30 minutes late.

9.2.4.1 Cool, You Say? Indeed, I Respond

Web 3.0 enables applications to behave and respond like a human would, as if you have your own personal assistant. The next generation of Web 3.0 browsers could be used to search something general in order to get something specific. For instance, "Where can I watch the latest Oscar winning movie in my area?" As a result, the search engine will return this year's movies that have won Oscar nominations, locate your area and find the nearest cinema that shows the list of movies, complete with showing times and prices. All you have to do is to book and pay online. Better still, you can book it first and use pay-as-you-wave technology to validate the booking as soon as you are in the cinema.

9.2.4.2 Fantastic, You Say? Indeed, I Respond

These technologies have become more sophisticated, which also means they introduce further vulnerabilities and pose a new wave of security threats. Web 3.0 and cloud computing come hand-in-hand, and whatever security concerns that you have in cloud, the same concerns should be accounted for with Web 3.0. As the Web matures, it is hard to keep track of each. The NIST's National Vulnerability Database (NVD) compiles a vulnerability management data repository from which you can refer to, and plan necessary investment to your coding. The NVD includes databases of security checklists, security related software flaws, misconfigurations, product names, and impact metrics.[34] On top of this, there are a

---

[34] (NIST 2012).

number of security vendors and specialists that provide useful guidelines and references, such as Trend Micro and Outpost24.

9.3 Cookies and LocalStorage

Cookies are used to store the "state" of your browser, i.e. if you visited a site for the first time, the site's web application will create a simple piece of text file and place it in your browser. The next time you visit the same site; it recognises you as a repeat visitor. For e-commerce sites, cookies are largely used to help track your shopping items until you purchase them. Once purchased, these data are destroyed since you have completed the transaction as intended.

As of May 26, 2011, the new EU cookie law was introduced to govern web users the right to choose what information gets stored in their browsers, and thus have the options to opt out. The Information Commissioner's Office (ICO) is to fine all UK website owners up to £500,000 for serious breaches in the law. The websites were given a year from the law coming into effect to ensure that they comply. Whilst this is a good move to protect online privacy, to date there are still a number of websites which are yet compliant simply because their online behavioural advertising largely depends on cookies. Furthermore, the change in law means the change on how cookies are constructed by developers, which also means a large number of time and resources are needed for that change to happen. Developers choose cookies as a means of authentication and identification engines and this practice has allowed developers to do more than just storing temporary data.

9.3.1 Authentication and Cookies Encryption

Cookies cannot carry viruses, install malware or execute malicious programs. Yet, cookie security often becomes a topic. This is due to the fact that the kind of information stored by cookies that make it unsecure. This is particularly true when a cookie is predominantly used as an authentication medium, when it is sent back and forth between a server and a browser in plain text format. Consider the following cookie that is sent by a server to a browser:

```
Set-Cookie:user_key=firstName.lastName;
user_email=myname@mydomain.com;   domain=.mydomain.com;
path=/; expires=Sat, 31-Dec-2012 11:30:00 GMT; secure
```

The flag `secure` means that cookie is only usable for when you are using SSL connection. To a degree, yes it is secure since you are counteracting packet sniffing—i.e. an attacker cannot intercept traffic through a secure tunnel. But, the fact that user key is exposed in human-readable format; then security matters. With email value is also being exposed, it becomes almost identifiable data.

There are many ways in which you, as a developer, can ensure cookies are encrypted. Too little done means you are introducing risks. Too much done, then your web application suffers from performance degrading, in particular when you are building large sites with expected high number of traffic.

Some guidelines to follow include:

- Determine the exact purpose of using cookies. If you are using it to retain user sessions, then make sure that this cookie is automatically destroyed for when user closes his/her browser. This is done by not setting an expiration date and time to the cookie. The browser itself will recognise that this cookie is session only cookie and will destroy it as soon as user closes the browser. But, if the user session is terminated by means of logging out, then you have to programmatically remove it from browser—since browser will not know that user has ended the application session and therefore would still retain that cookie. This comes to a point where, as a user, it is important to *always* log out from a site;
- Secure cookie with HTTPS. To manage a cookie via a secure connection, you will need to purchase SSL certificates, at a cost. But, with HTTPS you counteract packet sniffing. All banks and financial institutions already have SSL implementation in place;
- Secure cookie with encryption. This is usually done with a hashing method, i.e. you will set a combination of values, such as username, IP address, time of login, or email into a string and then apply hashing algorithm. This method does not need SSL to work. Even if someone sniffs the packet, they will need to know the algorithm first plus how everything is put together;
- Use HttpOnly cookie. With HttpOnly flag, it tells the browser that this particular cookie should only be accessible strictly via HTTP or HTTPS protocols. This means managing it via JavaScript (with `document.cookie`) will not work. HttpOnly is supported by modern browsers and is one effective mechanism to mitigate XSS attack—any attempt to access the cookie from client script is strictly forbidden—though not completely eliminate its possibility;
- Double authenticate the user. In other words, you are re-validating the current logged-in user. You do this for when a user needs to perform a highly sensitive action, such as transferring fund or changing password. Many sites to date have this implemented in a way that login form is displayed where user will need to re-enter credentials before he/she can proceed with the action; and
- Make full use of cookie attributes. In addition to HttpOnly and Secure flags, cookie attributes come with domain, path, expiration date and max age. Domain and path, for instance, tells the browser that cookies should only be sent back to the server for the given domain and path. By explicitly specifying the domain, you are rest-assured that these cookies are only meant for the domain specified, i.e. cross-domain is not allowed under the Same Origin Policy (SOP).

9.3.2 HTML5 with LocalStorage: Cookies Alternative?

HTML5 is the fifth revision of Hypertext Mark-up Language (HTML) introduced as a response to improve interoperability. It is to allow design and layout extensibility and an attempt to making data semantically meaningful. As of the time of writing, HTML5 is not yet fully supported by all browsers. If you are interested in checking whether your current browser is fully supported by HTML5, html5test. com is the first place to go.

HTML5 comes with localStorage, web database, and offline application cache mechanisms. These are particularly useful to replace—or in some cases to complement—cookies. Cookies have limitations such as maximum size of 4KB (localStorage comes with 5KB) and the transmission challenges of cookie data via HTTP headers. localStorage is intended to overcome the limitations.

Localstorage works with key-value pairs, in the same way as a cookie does. Therefore, you can store the exact same data. It is stored locally on user's machine, and can be retrieved just like cookies. Large sites usually need to persist session data, which eventually can become bigger. As cookie only limits to 4KB, then localStorage is a good option. Also, depending on how your application is designed, cookie interacts with server from time to time, and therefore it is likely to execute a number of round trips, which degrades performance. localStorage interacts on the client/browser exclusively and is not transmitted to the server.

You can also use other offline storage mechanisms in HTML5 such as web database and application cache, locally within a user's browser. Thus, you do not depend on localStorage entirely, and make full use of the other two features. As a result, this will improve overall performance.

All in all, localStorage, web database, and application cache are new, as with HTML5. While developers are still testing the features, it is hard to say that they are a good alternative to cookies. Also, security and privacy presented by HTML5 are still yet to be deemed effective. It is not about HTML5, but it is do with browser vendors that would maximise HTML5 offline storage mechanisms to set easy policies for users to be able to manage their privacy. Firefox Android, for instance, has an option of "Tell sites not to track me"—this somehow makes privacy controllable. But, what's missing is a clear statement to purpose of the tracking. And the type of data they need from user in order to lawfully allow the sites to help them track.

9.3.3 When Privacy Is Violated

Online behavioural advertising collects user's data through browsing habits, search queries, and web site history, via third-party cookies. Simple example is when you are using Google, you will notice a number of advertisements being displayed based on what you have previously searched. Google makes use of third-party cookies to enable this to happen. It is the same technique where all web portals such as Yahoo, AOL and MSN.com use to gather user's data and send those to an Ad Server, a system designed exclusively for delivering and tracking advertising. In most cases, the Ad Server is actually a network of cloud servers owned and maintained by a separate company.

Keynote Systems reveals that 86 % of websites have third party trackers.[35] Trackers are provided by businesses other than a website that you are currently on to record your browsing history and personal data. How do they violate the privacy?

- 27 % of trackers do not promise to anonymise data,
- 41 % of trackers do not offer an opt-out,
- 56 % of trackers do not have industry oversight or regulation.

Though nearly 100 % of websites include privacy policy statements, most are not written in day-to-day conversational language. It is therefore hard to understand. Because of this, users tend to agree to the policy without being made understood what exactly it means to their personal data and how they are meant to be used.

In my observation through an Android phone I own, every mobile application that I download has a list of items that tells me the kind of personal data being exposed and processed. Some applications explicitly want to use my contacts list, my phone number and my geographical location—from which I decided not to proceed with the installation. Because I value my privacy and that not knowing how, who, and where my personal data goes, the transparency given by these applications helped me make my decision.

This, I believe, should be adopted by modern web browsers, which I have yet seen happening.

9.4 Social Media and the Transfer of Data

Social networking sites and social networking services (both abbreviated as SNS) are the two terms used interchangeably to describe methods and engines that support social activities and relations among living people in a virtual world. However, "sites" and "services" are two different things—"sites" commonly refers to websites while "services" are the engines that drive social connections via various media. This means that people can still connect to each other via other methods than just a website, i.e. through mobile devices, and gaming consoles, for as long as SNS (the services) are made available.

The principal idea behind this is for two people or more to share interests, activities, ideas, or anything that matters based on trust elements—"trust" is a

---

[35] TechJournal (2012).

loosely termed here, simply based on how people have used Facebook, Twitter, LinkedIn, and other networking sites to create social relations.

Today, SNS is not only used for connecting people around the world, but businesses are also using the technology to reach out their audience in the shortest time possible. Why SNS? Quite simply, it is the trusted relationships that exist among the social networkers. That is, in the name of trusts, users tend to share more than just their names and email addresses. They are more than happy to share their likes and dislikes, photos, videos and even their reviews and comments left on third party websites. And these types of data are often more useful, articulated, and accurate when compared with offline consumer researches that could take months to complete, compile and published.

9.4.1 Businesses Conducted via SNS

First, let's see few social media stats for small businesses in 2011[36]:
- Brands that post at least once every day will reach *22 percent* of their social fans in a given week;
- *44 percent* of small-to-medium business decision makers use social media, of which *86 percent* use Facebook, *41 percent* LinkedIn, and *33 percent* Twitter;
- Nearly *60 percent* of all small business decision makers spend less than $100 on social media and *74 percent* of businesses do not employ anyone to manage their social media marketing;
- *50 percent* of small business owners reported gaining new customers through social media—most notably through Facebook and LinkedIn; and
- *51 percent* of Facebook users and *64 percent* of Twitter users are more likely to buy from the brands they follow.

One thing for sure is that, social media will never cease. The trusts that are created within the social community are in fact a valuable commodity to use. After all, friends tend to purchase products from their trusted friends who already left reviews and comments on the products. The Facebook "Like" button is a direct way to share interests and this small plug-in has been used by majority of today's brands and publishers. In fact, it is a social marketing vehicle to reach audience in a massive scale. Having a Facebook Fan page would help, but adding Facebook Like button, it draws in their friends into the equation. As of July 2011, comScore reported that big brands such as Coca Cola, Starbucks and Disney each boasted more than 20 million fans.[37]

The question of security and privacy when doing business via SNS still remains to date. If my Facebook friend clicked on a malicious link which was consequently posted on my wall, and I clicked it as a result, should I then be worried about the

---

[36] (Mershon 2011).

[37] (Bruich et al. 2011).

possible threat getting into my corporate network? How this sharing of data gets transferred and how will it compromise my network and servers?

9.4.2 Transfer and Sharing of Data

Facebook, LinkedIn, and Twitter distribute their social APIs for developers to integrate with their websites. It is at this point where the transfer of data happens. After a user is authenticated via social login (i.e. a user can use their existing Facebook account in order to login to another site, without having to create a separate account on the originating site), the APIs will expose personal data such as name, gender, email and physical location. LinkedIn further exposes other identifiable data such as job, your professional career networks, which will also expose the people inside that network. In a recent job interview that I had with LinkedIn in early 2012, I was shown an intuitive application whereby an airline reservation system could offer seats to business customers where they can know who will be sitting next to them, knowing beforehand that this person is in the same career or having the same job interests. I instantly raised privacy concerns, from which they replied about an opt-out feature. However, from my own experience, the opt-out was never made to the level that I would expect it to work. After all, I am still hounded by recruiters sending job vacancies directly into my mailbox, by addressing my previous name, as opposed the new name I have chosen to profile my data in LinkedIn.

Security concern is another matter. With malicious social apps, clickjacking, and thefts of accounts, there is every chance that shared content carry unfortunate side effects. While existing web filters and corporate anti-virus will help, it still addresses the endpoint security. Some web-based endpoint web filters can intercept traffic after encryption. That means, even though social sites provide SSL connection at the point of authenticating users, there is still a chance of eavesdropping, in particular if a user is accessing the sites via their own mobile phones or tablets.

With cloud computing and SNS, data can reside in any data centres located in various parts of the world. Where data are strongly encrypted and the decryption keys securely managed, the data location should be irrelevant.[38] This is true to an extent. However, if the data is decrypted in a country where DPA is not harmonised, then this data is clearly identifiable and deemed not protected. So, how do you counteract this problem? In addition to encryption, tokenisation[39] can be the answer. The security approach to tokenisation is to replace highly sensitive data, such as credit card number, with a surrogate value called token, without having mathematical relation to the original data like encryption and decryption. Tokenisation is unique in that it completely removes the original data from the

---

[38] (Hon & Millard 2012).
[39] (PerspecSys 2012).

systems in which the tokens reside. Tokens cannot be reversed back to their original values. This, therefore, a worth investment to look into.

9.4.3 Social Engineering

You may have invested a lot in cloud infrastructure, network security and applications compliance, but some acts of manipulating social users into giving confidential information—also called social engineering—could still raise yet another security concern. It is common nowadays to convince users to visit some random websites, without realising that these websites are known to be targets for XSS, XSRF and other forms of security attacks.

Social engineering deals with human-based decisions, not something to do with technical by any means. There are many techniques come into picture on how this is crafted. Phishing is one common technique where emails are embedded with links that redirect to malicious sites. Some may argue that by hovering a mouse over an embedded link in an email, it is a sure-way to ensure that link is legitimate. However, with scripting techniques, explained in previous section, all is made possible. Someone once said, "Why exists the effort of someone cracking a user's password where you can easily trick a user into a phishing site to get all the data that you need?"

Pretexting—the act of engaging a victim into surrendering information by inventing a scenario or a series of events—has become one of the most popular techniques in social engineering. An attacker would usually do some research into understanding the victim's background before approaching the victim. With SNS, all the basic information is out there for an attacker to collate and manipulate. After all, one might question, of all Facebook friends that one has, how many of them are your real friends that you can trust? Is it fashionable to have more than 1,000 friends online, not knowing who they really are? And how many have you actually met face to face? And even if you do know your friends personally, how many friends of your friends can actually see your whereabouts, your tagged photos and your latest updates?

Something to ponder.

9.5 What the Future Holds

Cloud computing, dynamic content, social networks—all have paved their ways in the emergence of today's World Wide Web. And they will continue doing so in next years to come. The fact that users have become sophisticated in connecting with other people via different means other than desktops, data have become dynamically big, in particular when content is constantly created and generated by general public like us.

9.5.1 "Big Data" and Dynamic Content

Moving forward, developers increasingly favour HTML5, Ajax, CSS, XML, and script toolkits to build engaging and desktop-like RIAs. No more multiple clicks to check your shopping carts, or even to see which friends who bought the same product and liked it. This high degree of interaction creates dynamic content in a massive scale. And the fact that users can interact via smart phones, tablets, and gaming consoles, the tidal wave of data is coming. To hold this type of data, cloud technology comes into a perfect place.

Forrester reveals that most enterprises are not yet aligned with the demand of dynamic data.[40] Majority of enterprise websites manage static content for storage and retrieval, not in two-way interactions. If this current trend continues without enterprises starting to look into it, then the data growth will crush the existing infrastructure.

9.5.2 Security Measures and Data Preventions

As explained in this chapter, security and data protection are common top issues that have slowed down the decision into cloud computing. When deciding, the following factors should give you a good guidance:

- Threats of opportunist attacks. Spamming, phishing, distributed malware, and DDoS are examples of long-standing and constantly growing types of exploits. Attackers usually look for highly sensitive data such as credit cards and personally identifiable information. You should work with your security providers with protecting data as well as data centres;
- Threats of targeted attacks. Usually aimed at stealing government and commercial data, the threats are strategic and stealth. This takes time to plan and execute. Types include spear-phishing and SQL injection. Again, your security providers should detail on how data is protected from it. Security of data centres, including personnel should be measured too;
- Trends in virtualisations. Virtualisation does not equal security even though it provides restrictions. All virtual machines (VMs), hypervisors and guests are to be sufficiently protected in software, hardware and infrastructure;
- Trends in consumerization of IT. In other words, if you are enabling on BYOD, you will need to impose security policy and data compliance at endpoints such as mobile devices. This includes the policy where sensitive corporate data being encrypted and properly managed by the employee responsible;
- Trends in cloud computing. SNS speeds up the deployment of cloud computing, and you surely do not want to fall behind. Everything within the cloud needs to be solidly protected and compliant, including the applications that sit within;

---

[40] (Forrester 2012).

- Trends in safe Web 2.0 and growth in Web 3.0. Developers are leading indicators of the trends. And more businesses are using of SNS to maximise audience and impressions. In parallel, a number of privacy concerns has surmounted with social APIs. Therefore, if you wanted to enable SNS, make sure you can control application access, downloads, and posts. Building a secure community channel would be one way to realise the potential of Web 2.0 and Web 3.0;
- Protecting information. Some vendors offer purpose-built solutions for data at rest, in motion, and in use. This is a starting point, but you will also need to look into data deletion and elimination policy. Monitoring data reveals how they are moved across network. There are specific vendors dealing with data loss and data leak prevention software, which is another investment worth looking into, in order to achieve compliance. Also, get independent auditors that can check whether your service providers are compliant with numerous security regulations, such as HIPAA, ISO 27001, and PCI DSS;
- Securing modern data centres. Data centres are often aimed by targeted attacks. You will need to ensure that data centres have all the security your business needs, which includes physical security access, certifications and personnel qualifications. Data centre architectures must also be built atop a flexible framework that can facilitate new and emerging trends;
- Setting priorities as a business enabler. If your business takes a full advantage of cloud power, SNS features, with BYOD deployment, then it is time to ensure you are ahead of the game by putting security, data compliance, and data integrity at every point where data resides, which includes endpoints. Consumers are now increasingly aware of their data and will always have higher confidence knowing that their services are provided with those businesses acted as enablers; and
- Setting priorities to achieving on-demand always-on connectivity. You need security that protects a virtual network of people, data, applications, infrastructures, and services, that can be anywhere at any given moment. This means unified strategy, where you can reduce complexity to the point where it is operationally feasible to achieve true connectivity.

In an attempt to combat hacking trends, information security and vulnerabilities, the Online Trust Alliance (OTA) has designated the yearly Online Trust Honor Roll to recognise those companies worldwide who are doing the right thing. Their mission is to develop and advocate best practices and policy concerning security and privacy. If your business is planning to join the ride of technology emergence with compliance as a defence, then I would strongly advise on following the OTA guidelines. Who knows, your company will be next on the list?

References

Agencies (2012) LulzSec's Ryan Cleary and Jake Davis plead guilty to hacking. The Guardian, 25 June 2012. http://www.guardian.co.uk/technology/2012/jun/25/lulzsecs-ryan-cleary-guilty-hacking. Accessed 30 June 2012

Amazon (2012a) Amazon Media Room: History & Timeline. http://phx.corporate-ir.net/phoenix.zhtml?c=176060&p=irol-corporateTimeline. Accessed 23 June 2012

Amazon (2012b) Amazon Simple Storage Service (Amazon S3). http://aws.amazon.com/s3. Accessed 1 July 2012

Armerding T (2012) The 15 worst data security breaches of the 21st Century. http://www.csoonline.com/article/700263/the-15-worst-data-security-breaches-of-the-21st-century. Accessed 4 July 2012

Arthur C (2011) The technology year in review. The Guardian, 29 December 2011. http://www.guardian.co.uk/technology/2011/dec/29/2011-year-review-technology?commentpage=last#privacy. Accessed 30 June 2012

Bergstein B (2012) IBM Faces the Perils of 'Bring Your Own Device'. http://www.technologyreview.com/news/427790/ibm-faces-the-perils-of-bring-your-own-device/. Accessed 1 July 2012

Bruich S, Lipsman A, Mudd G, Rich M (2011) The power of like – how brands reach and influence fans through social media marketing. http://www.comscore.com/Press_Events/Presentations_Whitepapers/2011/The_Power_of_Like_How_Brands_Reach_and_Influence_Fans_Through_Social_Media_Marketing. Accessed 6 July 2012

Business Link (2012) Data protection and cloud computing. http://www.businesslink.gov.uk/bdotg/action/detail?itemId=1084689193&r.i=1084688657&r.l1=1073861197&r.l2=1075422920&r.l3=1084685982&r.s=m&r.t=RESOURCES&type=RESOURCES. Accessed 2 July 2012

Chen S, Wang R, Wang XF (2012) Signing me onto your accounts through Facebook and Google: a traffic-guided security study of commercially deployed single-sign-on web services, p.7 section 4.2. http://research.microsoft.com/pubs/160659/websso-final.pdf. Accessed 1 July 2012

Christey S, Brown M, Kirby D, Martin B, Paller A (2011) CWE/SANS Top 25 most dangerous software errors. http://cwe.mitre.org/top25. Accessed 4 July 2012

Cox P (2012) Intrusion detection in a cloud computing environment. http://searchcloudcomputing.techtarget.com/tip/Intrusion-detection-in-a-cloud-computing-environment. Accessed 1 July 2012

Data Guidance, Italy (2012) DPA issues cloud computing recommendations. 14 June 2012. http://dataguidance.com/news.asp?id=1801. Accessed 2 July 2012

Datainspektionen (2012) Cloud services and the Personal Data Act. http://www.datainspektionen.se/in-english/cloud-services/. Accessed 2 July 2012

Felten EW, Zeller W (2012) Cross-site request forgeries: exploitation and prevention. http://www.cs.utexas.edu/~shmat/courses/cs378/zeller.pdf. Accessed 4 July 2012

Forrester A (2012) Tidal wave of dynamic web content is coming – how will you respond? March 2012 (PDF document)

Grance T, Mell P (2011) The NIST definition of cloud computing. http://csrc.nist.gov/publications/nistpubs/800-145/SP800-145.pdf. Accessed 23 June 2012

Haikes C, Murchinson J (2012) Google and IBM Announce University Initiative to Address Internet-Scale Computing Challenges. http://www-03.ibm.com/press/us/en/pressrelease/22414.wss. Accessed 23 June 2012

Hardy M (2012) BYOD: Trend or trivia? http://fcw.com/articles/2012/04/30/buzz-byod-trend-buzzword.aspx. Accessed 1 July 2012

Hon WK, Millard C (2012) Data export in cloud computing – how can personal data be transferred outside the EEA? The cloud of unknowing, part 4. http://script-ed.org/?p=324. Accessed 7 July 2012

Ingthorsson O (2011) 5 Cloud computing statistics you may find surprising. http://cloudcomputingtopics.com/2011/11/5-cloud-computing-statistics-you-may-find-surprising. Accessed 30 June 2012

Laczynski E (2011) Managing cloud security: intrusion detection services in a public cloud (datapipe). http://www.rightscale.com/info_center/slide-decks/fall2011-managing-cloud-security.php. Accessed 2 July 2012

Mershon P (2011) 26 Promising social media stats for small businesses. http://www.socialmediaexaminer.com/26-promising-social-media-stats-for-small-businesses/. Accessed 6 July 2012

Mills E (2012) Global payments: consumer data may also have been stolen. http://news.cnet.com/8301-1009_3-57452047-83/global-payments-consumer-data-may-also-have-been-stolen. Accessed 4 July 2012

Moos F (2012) DPA guidance on cloud computing. http://www.nortonrose.com/news/63297/dpa-guidance-on-cloud-computing. Accessed 2 July 2012

NIST (2012) National Vulnerability Database. http://nvd.nist.gov/home.cfm. Accessed 4 Jul 2012

Nisvold (2012) Cloud basics – Deployment model. 12 March 2012. http://blog.visma.com/blog/cloud-basics-deployment-models. Accessed 1 July 2012

Pederson T (2012) Microsoft's study on social single sign-on protocols. http://www.onelogin.com/microsofts-study-on-social-single-sign-on-protocols. Accessed 1 July 2012

PerspecSys (2012) Data residency – where is your cloud data physically located? http://www.perspecsys.com/how-we-help/data-residency/. Accessed 7 July 2012

Reahard J (2012) Wurm Online website down after SQL attack. http://massively.joystiq.com/2012/05/11/wurm-online-website-down-after-sql-attack. Accessed 4 July 2012

Reed B (2011) Q&A: Why consumerization won't kill corporate IT. http://www.pcworld.com/businesscenter/article/241012/qanda_why_consumerization_wont_kill_corporate_it.html. Accessed 1 July 2012

Ried S, Kisker H (2012) Sizing the Cloud. http://www.forrester.com/Sizing+The+Cloud/fulltext/-/E-RES58161?objectid=RES58161. Accessed 30 June 2012

Security Obscurity (2012) From XSS to NT AUTHORITY. 30 May 2012. http://security-obscurity.blogspot.co.uk/2012/05/from-xss-to-nt-authority.html. Accessed 4 July 2012

Silveira V (2012) An update on LinkedIn member passwords compromised. http://blog.linkedin.com/2012/06/06/linkedin-member-passwords-compromised. Accessed 2 July 2012

Symantec (2012) Internet Security Trend Report: 2011 Trends, Volume 17. April 2012. http://www.symantec.com/about/news/release/article.jsp?prid=20120429_01. Accessed 4 July 2012

TechJournal (2012) Online behavioral tracking pervasive, Google privacy practices often violated. 28 June 2012. http://www.techjournal.org/2012/06/online-behavioral-tracking-pervasive-google-privacy-practices-often-violated. Accessed 6 July 2012

Wikipedia (2012a) Time-sharing. http://en.wikipedia.org/wiki/Time-sharing. Accessed 23 June 2012

Wikipedia (2012b) ECMAScript. http://en.wikipedia.org/wiki/ECMAScript. Accessed 30 June 2012

Wikipedia (2012c) Web 2.0. http://en.wikipedia.org/wiki/Web_2.0. Accessed 2 July 2012

Zetter K (2010) TJX hacker gets 20 years in prison. http://www.wired.com/threatlevel/2010/03/tjx-sentencing. Accessed 4 July 2012

Data Protection and Local Authorities in the United Kingdom

10

Indirani Viknaraja

> *At a time when councils are increasingly working with community partners, when data is shared it is vital that they uphold their legal responsibilities under the Data Protection Act. Failures not only put local residents' privacy at risk, but also mean that councils could be in line for a sizeable monetary penalty.*
>
> *We must also consider the detrimental impact these breaches continue to have on the individuals affected. Disclosing details about someone's social housing status can be upsetting and damaging for those affected. To help tackle this issue I've submitted a business case to the government to ask for them to extend my compulsory audit powers.*
>
> (Christopher Graham, Information Commissioner, Excerpt of the Information Commissioner's Office Press Release of 10th February 2012)

Abstract

This chapter is specially designed to provide you, the reader, with a lucid description of how data protection is viewed through the lens of a local authority. Within it's four sections the chapter explains why local authorities process personal information and what it does with it, how it protects it and what happens when it is not protected. Personal data is a valuable commodity. As creatures of statute, local authorities derive their powers either from the Act of Parliament, which sets them up, or from other legislation regulating their activities. In this twenty-first century's information society, organisations including local authorities are acutely aware of the power of information and their obligations to it.

I. Viknaraja (✉)
Southend on Sea Borough Council, Civic Centre, Victoria Avenue, Southend-on-Sea, Essex SS2 6ER, UK
e-mail: rani.viknaraja@gmail.com

10.1 A Brief introduction to Local Authorities

Local authorities (called municipalities in some countries) in the United Kingdom (UK) employ more than 2 million staff[1] and serve a client base of over 55 million people. The local authorities in the UK are also referred to as Councils and annually they spend billions of pounds on the provision of various services. Funded by central government, council tax and rate payers (businesses), local authorities provide services to their communities. These services are either provided directly, outsourced through external contractors, or through joint working with partners. Local authorities are legally responsible for the security of a vast array of personal data which is held for the provision of functions. The extensive range includes:

- Housing benefit claims, repairs, allocations and lettings process for social housing
- Environmental health services which include licensing, food safety, pollution and pest control
- Waste collection and street cleaning, including recycling, street furniture and fly-tipping
- General council tax enquiries, billing and recovery process for payment of council tax and national non-domestic rates
- Planning services (local planning issues) and building control
- Electoral register
- Parking permits and Parking Control Notices.

The government mandates local authorities to provide best value services to its residents and these have to be demonstrated through continuous improvement as people rightly demand high standards from public services.

As the English Information Commissioner, Christopher Graham (The Commissioner) wrote on his blog, 'The danger is that rights are seen as nice to have in good times, but a bureaucratic inconvenience when times are hard'.[2] It is in these tough times that we most need to defend the rights of the individuals from negligence and against abuse of power by organisations, both public and private.

10.1.1 The Constitution

Every local authority must have a standard Constitution. This sets out how it will operate, how decisions are made and the procedures which are followed to ensure that the local authority operates efficiently, and is transparent and accountable to the local residents. Councillors are elected for a 4 year period, and work closely with the officers of the local authority, to give advice, implement decisions and manage the day to day delivery of services to the residents in their Councils.

---

[1] Local Government Structure (2012).
[2] Information Commissioner's Office. http://www.ico.gov.uk. Accessed 2 June 2012.

10.2 Why Local Authorities Need Personal Data?

In order to meet its legal responsibilities and provide a quality service efficiently and effectively, local authorities need to collate and handle personal data about the community, past and present employees, contractors, councillors, agents and other organisations. This personal data must be handled properly, whether it is collected, recorded and processed on paper, or electronically or recorded in any other material, or even deleted.

So what is personal data: Personal data could be as basic as a living person's name and address. Quite simply, personal data has to be processed, whether it is for the provision of a library card, for support rendered by a councillor to a resident on a planning application or for a local authority representing on a child protection issue in court.

The Commissioner quoted, 'information is the currency of democracy' in his speech to mark International Right to Know Day 2011 and remarked that whoever first said that was stating an important truth. Data is one of the most important assets in all organisations and local authorities are no exception. Public service delivery relies heavily on the right information being available to the right people. Data is seen as a key corporate asset and employees should regard themselves as 'trusted stewards' of personal data with an obligation to protect it. This data is to be valued through out its lifecycle to ensure that it is maintained accurately and with clear reviews, retention and disposal policies in line with statute and regulatory frameworks. Better use of data can mean better services, through personalisation and by ensuring that people get the services to which they are entitled. But these services have to be planned and delivered whilst maintaining and respecting people's privacy. To quote the Commissioner again, 'Get privacy right and you will retain the trust and confidence of your customers and users; mislead consumers or collect information you don't need and you are likely to diminish customer trust and face enforcement action from the Commissioner's Office'.

The way in which data belonging to a local authority is managed and protected can be especially onerous, especially due to the extensive volume of data held and the number of data sources maintained for it to carry out its varied functions. These functions include the following:

10.2.1 Why Local Authorities Need Data

Customer Services
The local authority has responsibility for the maintenance of a website which also facilitates the collection of fees from rate payers or the payment of benefits. Personal information including names and bank details are maintained for these functions. Straying from traditional methods of communication the focus is shifting heavily towards Self Service Channels, resulting in less 'face-to-face' contact. This self service facility enables residents to use the latest communication technology to engage with the local authority more effectively than ever before. The community is also able to make better informed decisions about the services they receive.

This has seen an upsurge in online transactions and the increasing availability of online services also provides opportunities for fraudulent applications for the receipt of housing or tax benefit. As the advent of online facilities offer less human interaction, it could be perceived by criminals to be less well monitored or to offer more anonymity than more traditional fraud would require.

Children's Services
Sensitive adoption details, which, in line with statute requirements, have to be maintained for 100 years are stored on children's' specialists' databases. Whilst centrally held databases typically hold the Adoption Case Records with access restricted to roles and dedicated individuals, paper records are kept in locked cabinets or rooms accessible only to authorised personnel. Closed adoption cases are often archived by a third party provider away from the main local authority office.

In deciding whether or not to apply Child Protection procedures (for example to protect children from abuse), the application of professional judgement is unavoidable. This could involve sharing sensitive information with the relevant social workers, police, health and education staff or other agency staff who have dealings with the family and the legal team. Any actions decided upon as a result of investigations must be safely and securely communicated to the relevant teams at the earliest possible opportunity. Electronic copies of communications are exchanged through the use of portable media and paper records will also have to be physically transported securely from the main Council building to satellite offices.

Registrations
The local authority maintains a registration database with an index of records of births, deaths and marriages. The library holds microfiche copies of the National Index of births, marriages and deaths between certain periods. Registration of a newborn includes a log of the date and place of baby's birth, time of birth and the sex of the baby. The forename(s) and surname by which the baby is intended to be brought up by, as well as the personal details of the mother and father of the child will be recorded.

Traffic Enforcement
CCTV footages within car parks, housing estates and roads are captured for the prevention of crime and traffic enforcement. These footages could include personally identifiable images that are captured and stored securely, with a limited number of people having access to the images. Where there is a 'live feed' from the local authority's camera to the police station, both parties are made aware of their responsibilities. Where an external processor takes responsibility, the processing is in accordance with the contract applied by the data controller.

Housing

Those who satisfy the required criteria can apply to register on the local authority's general Housing Register. Sheltered housing applicants can be made by applicants who are over the age of 60. Sheltered housing is a group of unfurnished, self-contained homes designed for older people. The aim is to provide independent, secure accommodation with additional social and domestic facilities. Existing social tenants can apply to transfer to different social housing estates. Special rules apply to street sleepers, applicants in prison, the armed forces or those who owe rent to the local authority. Applications for any of these types of housing would include the submission of medical records, social care status, source and amount of income or benefits (where applicable) and the number of dependents.

Care Services

The local authority provides care services for older residents, the disabled, people with learning and physical disabilities, sensory impairment and people with mental health problems. Some of these are funded by the local authority and/or receive grants. The Adult and Community Department within the local authority carries out assessments before these services are provided. These community care assessments, which include medical records, are carried out by social care workers to establish the need for community care service and appropriate care is then made available. These assessments will consider the clients' wishes, any physical difficulties, particular health or housing needs and access to carers or family.

Payment of Benefits

The administration of benefits, which include benefits for parents and children, bereavement benefits, council tax and housing benefit is a major function undertaken by the local authority. Each entitlement is calculated based on the information supplied by the applicants. The details will enable the calculation for the entitlement to each benefit. The amount of information may include details of earnings and other income, rent or council tax and deductions for non-dependants.

10.2.2 How Do Local Authorities Manage These Varying Databases of Personal Data?

How does the authority achieve the right balance between the authority's 'need to know' and the customers 'right to privacy? Databases could be targeted by criminal hackers to overcome security measures protecting the data to steal personal data, which can then be used fraudulently, such as for identity fraud. This, together with instances of insufficient physical controls on paper records, lack of data security standards on the use of portable media and electronic records, inadequate procedures on the 'medium of secure transport', (either through the post or the internal mail delivery systems) highlight the fundamental need for the local authority to do more to protect the security of data it holds on it's customers and clients.

This comes down to the etiquette of responsible sharing. The Data Protection Act 1998 (DPA), which is based on the EU Data Protection Directive of 95/46/EC prescribes how personal data on all these databases and images can be looked after and defended. Quite simply, it is all about good housekeeping of personal data. The failure to appreciate the significance of safeguarding personal data, has not just led to hefty fines, which is especially painful in this austere climate, but also to catastrophic reputational damage.

10.2.3 You Might Wonder What 'Privacy' Means

To define it very loosely, it could mean that we have a right to a sphere of thought and action that is our own and no one else's. Privacy is more than a fundamental human right, it is also an innate human need. For instance, when you go home at night, you probably close the curtains. It is not that you are trying to hide something but is simply that you need your privacy. If you are on a bus or a plane, and someone starts reading over your shoulder, you probably feel uncomfortable. What you are reading may not be a secret, but it is just that your privacy is being invaded. If ever your car or your home had been broken into, you will know that your privacy has been violated. In fact, it can even be more painful than any material loss. And yet almost every day, that human need for privacy is being chipped away. Governments and businesses are more curious about us than ever before and everyday someone wants more information about us and has some new way of collecting it without our consent.

Article 8 of the Human Rights Act 1998 is the cornerstone of the DPA which came into force on 1 March 2000. Article 8 reads that 'everyone has a right to respect for his private and family life, his home and correspondence' and that 'there shall be no interference by a public authority with the exercise of this right except such as is in accordance with the law and if necessary in a democratic society in the interest of national security, public safety or the economic well being of the country, for the prevention of disorder and crime, for the protection of health or morals, or for the protection of the rights of freedom and of others'. Although the DPA is not a privacy law, it provides a framework in which organisations can work within.

With people becoming more aware of their privacy rights, data protection is at the top of most organisations agendas and has indeed become a fashionable subject for discussion. People are more aware than ever before that information about them could be stored online, or in the cloud and could even be there forever, as it may be difficult to erase. Adopting cloud-based solutions seems to be almost inevitable due to the competitive edge. With the increase in junk mail and unsolicited marketing text messages, incessant headlines on data losses through memory sticks left on tubes and stolen laptops or telephone hacking, media pages and airtime's lust for privacy stories is apparent. Local residents are increasingly vocal about the way their personal data is handled or shared. Although the legal right for people to have access to their records has been alive for several years, in the recent years there has been a surge in the number of requests made by residents for their personal data. Increased general awareness and the avaricious way in which the media world hound and highlight losses of personal data could most certainly be deemed as contributing factors.

So what and how does a local authority operate to ensure that the processing of its personal data is done in line with the DPA? At the heart of the processing of all personal data are the eight principles of the DPA. The eight principles (Table 10.1), with the right toolkit can be regarded as a 'critical friend'. This valuable tool helps with the compliance of what can be quite a challenging exercise to any organisation. This is especially so as a local authority is a unique organisation with a tremendous amount and variety of information flows, both internally and externally. Probably the greatest challenge for a local authority is ensuring that the exploding data flows are processed in line with the DPA.

10.2.4 Privacy Through Data Protection

Key Words
For an understanding of the DPA, it is essential to identify the definitions of some key words and the key players:
Personal data is information about a living individual, which could include any expression of opinion about the individual. This could also be information which relates to a living individual who can be identified from those data or from those data and other information which is in the possession of the data controller. This information, which includes date of birth, passport number, blood group, sexual preference, identity cards could be held in a computer or in a 'relevant filing system' (see below).
Sensitive personal data as listed by the DPA covers racial or ethnic origins of individuals, their political beliefs, religious beliefs, trade union membership, physical or mental health condition, sexual life or the commission of offences or criminal proceedings.
Relevant filing system is simply a set of manual files which are organised by reference to a particular criteria or individuals. The 'rule of thumb' check for this is commonly referred to as the 'temp test'. The 'temp test' assumes that if you employed a temporary administrative assistant who was asked to extract specific information about an individual on a filing system and he or she retrieves it with ease, it is a structured filing system.
Processing as defined by the DPA is very wide. If one 'HOARDS' information, one is processing it. The pneumonic 'HOARDS' which includes holding, handling, obtaining, organising, altering, aligning, recording, retrieving, disclosing, deleting, securing and storing defines processing.
Data subject is simply a living individual who is the subject of personal data and relates to employees, residents, customers, councillors or suppliers.

Data Controller is the organisation which determines the purposes for which personal information is to be processed. Local authorities are also data controllers.
Data Processor is any person apart from an employee, and usually third party companies used by data controllers to process their data. These third parties act on the instructions of the data controller who determine the purposes for the processing.
Recipient includes an employee or an agent.
Now the Act itself and the eight principles:

Table 10.1 The eight principles of the DPA 1998. *Source*: Information Commissioner's Office (ICO) website

Principle 1	**Fair and Lawful:** *regard to be given to the method by which data is obtained. The most common forms of compliance with this requirement are the provision of a Fair Processing Notice and the Notification in the Register of the purposes*
Principle 2	**Specific:** *data controller must specify the purpose/s for the processing. There is a clear overlap with the first two principles in that processing in breach of principle 2 will become unfair processing, and therefore a breach of the first principle*
Principle 3	**Adequate, relevant and not excessive:** *this is also known as the 'adequacy principle'. Data controllers are under obligation to only collect data that is relevant*
Principle 4	**Accurate:** *there is no definition of accurate contained within the Act, but Section (70) of the DPA*[8] *assists by stating what is inaccurate. For the purpose of this Act, data are inaccurate if they are incorrect or misleading as to any matter of fact*[9]
Principle 5	**Not kept for longer than necessary**: *only keep personal data for as long as is necessary. Statute expectations should be respected when considering disposal of personal data*
Principle 6	**Rights of data subject:** *By virtue of the Act, data subjects have certain absolute rights available to them in relation to processing their personal data*
Principle 7	**Security:** *application of appropriate technical and organisational measures to prevent accidental loss or destruction of personal data*
Principle 8	**Overseas transfers:** *transfer of personal data to anywhere outside the European Economic Area (EEA)*

10.2.5 DP Through an Information Management Officer (IMO): A Typical Day for an IMO

In this section, you are on a voyage of discovery to see how data protection is enforced in one such local authority. The IMO is to ensure that the organisation complies with the DPA and to ensure that the employees are fully informed of their responsibilities for acting within the law, and that the public (including employees) are informed of their rights under the Act. In short, as the corporate driving force the IMO plays an integral part in the compliance and promotion of information governance and the creation and development of policies and procedures which help to raise the bar for information privacy.

I am an early bird and am usually in the office by seven each morning. Each day presents its own challenges and a day rarely follows a set pattern. The day could begin with a morning appointment with the Chief Executive Officer (CEO), or a 'one-to-one' meeting with a Data Protection Co-ordinator to discuss an outstanding subject access request (SAR), a mad rush to meet a local resident with her 17 hefty files, a session on CCTV with the Head of Service, or a discussion and advice on two hybrid Freedom of Information (FOI) requests. In the time I can snatch between these meetings, I catch up on some routine like providing advice to the fraud team on the use of exemptions under the DPA, completing the Breach Management Report to the Corporate Director and offering a training session. Usually, between half past six and seven in the evening, when I am on my way home I have a chat with my daughter for an update on what my one year old grandson is up to. On that rejuvenating note, I look forward to the next day.

On this particular day, the events rolled in the stated order, commencing with an invitation to give the DP perspective to the CEO on an information sharing exercise. Although it is sometimes shunned upon that local authorities are still hideously bound by the minutiae of procedures and legislations, at times like this those processes, regulations and guidelines are the best props.

Data Sharing Exercise

There was a request for the local authority, as the data controller, to share personal data with partner organisations. This sharing of personal data was for a nationwide initiative and as the data controller had previously received consent from the data subjects, some of the key players were keen and felt comfortable for this processing to commence. The IMO however chose a more conservative slant. Understandably, whilst 'consent' had been received and whilst it is essential that the local authority should move away from working in silos and share information for the provision of a seamless service, it is wise to note that as a statutory body, the local authority must be able to point to a legitimate right that allows for any sharing, otherwise it could be acting 'ultra vires', without authority. Each organisation may have a different approach to sharing data. It is however, commonly accepted that whilst 'secondary sharing' within organisations is advocated by the Commissioner's office, it does not encourage a blanket sharing approach. The first data protection principle says that organisations have to satisfy one or more 'conditions' in order to legitimise their processing of personal data, unless an exemption applies. Organisations processing sensitive personal data, for example information about a person's health, will need to satisfy a further, more exacting condition. It is important to be clear that meeting a condition for data processing will not in itself ensure that the sharing of personal data is fair or lawful, as these issues need to be considered separately.

In this episode, it involved the sharing sensitive personal data of vulnerable young adults. Although a generic consent had been given by the data subjects, the Privacy Notice indicated that it had only been given for a particular purpose. This consent could therefore not be used by the local authority to cover all legitimate purposes.

Although it is quite easy to become 'excessively cautious' with matters of DP, the golden rule is that DP should not impede working. So a workable regime and a happy compromise were to be achieved.

If therefore the local authority had another ground for legitimate sharing, through, for example an exemption such as the prevention of crime or the prosecution of offenders, there will be no intrusion into the data subjects' privacy. As the local authority derives its power to share from statue, if the data controller can qualify that the sharing was a requirement beyond that of data protection, or indeed for a particular function, the proposed processing could be deemed justifiable.

Therefore a basic Privacy Impact Assessment was carried out and it proved that with certain 'conditions' attached to the sharing, the processing would be justified, the risk of intrusion into the privacy of the vulnerable adults would have been considered and responsible sharing promoted. The conditions included a written confirmation from the partners that any subsequent sharing of this personal data will have to sanctioned by the source of the data, deletions will be in line with the DPA and any statutory requirements and any breach would be reported in line with the local authority's policy.

Subject Access Request (SAR)

The right of access is considered to be one of the most fundamental right available to data subjects. A 'single gateway approach' has been adopted by the local authority for the efficient handling of this time consuming and rather demanding 'privilege'. Under Section 7(1), of the DPA· a data subject had written in, paid the £10 fee, which is the maximum permitted for such requests under the EU Data Protection Directive and had provided the required form of identification. As the request fell within the terms of disclosure, the local authority had the prescribed 40 calendar day timeline for the processing. Responding to this SAR was especially arduous as it involved third party details of the data subject's estranged partner and children who were now young adults and no longer needed parental support.

In line with the DPA, incorporated in the local authority's procedures on the processing of SARs was the application of a redaction system. Robust redaction had to be carried out with a fine tooth comb to 'blank' out all third party data and to ensure that it did not in any way violate the rights of the third parties. The volume of the collation, the extensive and meticulous redaction that was required and the pressure on resource did not lend favourably to meeting the legislative 40 day timeline, or the local authority's self imposed 35 day target date. Although there had been an on going dialogue with the data subject regarding extended timelines, he was no longer patient. Understandably his frustration stemmed from the delay in the processing, but it also demonstrated his lack of awareness regarding third party data. He was of the opinion that the local authority was cloaked in a degree of secrecy with his personal data.

Following discussions with the co-ordinator, it was agreed the collation was to be produced in three tranches with pre-determined deadlines. An obsequious letter detailing the reasons for the delay and the new despatch arrangements was sent.

Due to the magnitude of the collation, it was agreed that the records will be delivered directly to the data subject's residence. The conflict between his right of access and the requirement to protect third party's privacy was clearly outlined. In this instance, third party consent could not be sought, however it was deemed as reasonable in the circumstances to disclose some information as it had previously been provided to the data subject. Article 8 of the Human Rights Act and how it referred to the rights of everyone to respect for private and family life was also explained. That this right is applied to both the applicant and his family members and that it was therefore necessary to balance the rights of all individuals when deciding whether to disclose or not was clarified in detail. This confirmed that whilst he used his democratic right under the DPA, the local authority, as the data controller was also obliged to process third party data in a fair and lawful manner.

Access to Personal files
The local authority had received an access to request for a data subject's personal files. There were 17 files, which included one page letters and reports of sensitive records from a data subject's tumultuous childhood. Due to alcohol dependence, the data subject's young, single mother was hospitalised and was therefore unable to care for her 18 month old baby. Whilst a local authority errs on the side of caution regarding child welfare, in this instance it decided to take over the responsibilities for the young baby. The child remained in voluntary care, and for the next 16 years of her life she boarded with various foster parents. Although a successful young lady now, the data subject confessed that due to her history she was prone to feelings of despair, loneliness and anger. These emotions manifested themselves into difficulties with relationships and she often blamed herself for her past. As the data subject put it, 'she was now looking for the missing pieces of the jigsaw' and felt that the records she was seeking would be the only coherent records of her childhood.

Although many years ago she had read her files via her social worker, she was not given access to everything as she had been deemed as being too young to understand what could have been potentially upsetting information. She was now exercising her right to her papers to understand her past, close that chapter and to move on with her life. It is the statutory duty of the local authority to maintain case records in respect of every child in care. Full disclosure in this case would include case records, care plans, social workers notes and child protection minutes.

As is traditionally applied to all cases, the redaction process was delicately performed. Whilst maintaining third party considerations, the data subject should receive clear records as to why she was taken into care. As it was the data subjects desire not to seek the consent of her mother, and as she did not want the 'third party' to be made aware of her access to her records, the mother's details were redacted. It was however decided by the local authority that for a better understanding of the data subject's history, it would be relevant for her to be told the reason for her reception into care.

Careful consideration was given to the sensitivity of the information and the effect it would have on the third party, and although the reason for the hospitalisation was removed, the fact that the hospitalisation was the reason for the reception into care was disclosed. Decisions regarding disclosure of sibling details proved difficult as there was no consent to share those details and the data subject was not aware of any sibling, or, if any, when they may have been separated. With regards to parents' names, it was deemed that the right of the data subject to family life outweighed the right of the parents to private life and it seemed reasonable to disclose names of parents.

Third party considerations had to be applied especially to reports and letters given by doctors and the legal team. These were provided to the local authority in confidence due to the relationship between both parties. An assessment of how reasonable it was to disclose third party information was carried out. How critical it was for the data subject to have access to the third party information in preserving her privacy rights was also deliberated. Amongst the considerations was The Gaskin[3] case law which was eventually the approach adopted. In line with DPA, without identifying third parties the local authority communicated as much as it could.

To help the data subject understand and alleviate any emotional trauma, the local authority was prepared to offer the support of a social worker to be present whilst the data subject perused her papers. As is the norm all reasons for the decision to withhold or disclose were recorded and an audit trail maintained. The data subject was content with the information she had received.

Freedom of Information Request

The Freedom of Information (FOI) Act 2000[4] became fully enacted in January 2005 and is aimed to end unnecessary secrecy and to promote transparency in public authorities. Under the Act, an FOI request had been received for information surrounding the use of CCTV in mobile cars. The local authority had introduced cars fitted with cameras for road safety enforcement. Besides the improvement of road safety, it aimed at reducing congestion on the roads, allowed buses and service vehicles to operate more effectively and controlled the management of parking as part of the local authority's integrated transport strategy. These vehicles are especially used in 'hard to reach' locations and in areas where there are particular concerns on traffic. They complement existing CCTV systems and the work undertaken by civil enforcement officers by capturing images of traffic contraventions through mobile devices. Penalty Charge Notices (PCNs) are issued to vehicles for drivers who stop on 'keep clear markings', zigzag lines near schools, no parking zones and parking in bus lanes and grass verges.

---

[3] See http://hudoc.echr.coe.int/sites/eng/pages/search.aspx#{"dmdocnumber":["695368"],"itemid": ["001-57491"]}. Accessed 2 July 2012.

[4] See http://www.ico.gov.uk/for_organisations/freedom_of_information.aspx. Accessed 2 July 2012.

Whilst it offers a good mode to get the safety message across to parents and motorists by capturing images of cars that have been parked inconsiderably, it also assists local authorities to monitor and enforce public road safety. The vehicles therefore deal with illegal and dangerous parking, and play a key role in protecting young children. A resident was challenging the PCN that had been applied to his vehicle and requested all images that had been captured of his vehicle at a particular time together with the DP considerations that had been applied to this 'Smart Car' project.

This request did not satisfy the criteria of a 'primary' request. To put it simply, a 'primary' request would be generated by third parties to include the police, identification of witnesses or authorities with power to prosecute. A 'secondary' request could be defined as any request which does not fall into the category of a primary request. Therefore before complying with a 'secondary' request, the local authority has to ensure that the request does not contravene, nor breach current legislation, including the Human Rights Act, that it complies with legislative requirements of the DPA. Regard had also been given to the relevant case law of Peck v UK.[5]

The local authority decided that the release of the material would not be under the auspices of 'crime prevention' nor the auspices of 'public well being, health or safety' but a bona fide request for personal data. The DP impact surrounding the release of the images was discussed with the Head of Traffic and Parking Management. The person making the request had provided sufficient and accurate information about the time, date and place to locate the information which was sought. The requestor was only shown information relevant to that particular search and which contains his personal data. In addition to compliance with principles contained within the DPA legislation, the local authority had to be satisfied that the data was not currently and as far as can be reasonably ascertained, not likely to become part of a 'live' criminal investigation, not likely to become relevant to civil proceedings and not the subject of a complaint or dispute which has not been actioned.

Whilst the objective of the Smart Cars is to capture only images of the offending vehicle, the very nature of the filming could involve the capturing of images of identifiable persons in the vicinity. The process of the disclosure was in line with the local authority's Code of Practice. The 'raw' data from the film footages were organised into 'evidence packs' by blanking out all other personally identifiable data and the final edited version was only to disclose images of the vehicle in question.

It was also impressed that in line with Principle 4 of the DPA, only accurate data is held and that the local authorities Code of Practice on the use of Smart Cars indicates that all unclear images are destroyed. The guidelines also indicated that the security arrangements and deletion timelines are applied to the images in line with the DPA. The resident was given copies of the Fair Processing Notices which included two extensive articles in the local newspapers and a page on the local authority's website on when, how and why this project had been undertaken. A link to the Register showing the notification to the Commissioner's Office of the use of the enforcement cars and their purposes was also sent.

---

[5] http://www.law.ed.ac.uk/ahrc/script-ed/docs/privacy_comment.asp. Accessed 29 May 2012.

Freedom of Information Request
The second FOI request was for the disclosure of the highest weekly/monthly housing benefit claim currently being met by the local authority and the date the claim started. The IMO advised that the response to this request would be a judgement call to be made by the local authority.

Although it was an FOI request, it also had a DP inclination. The DPA refers to 'data which relate to a living individual who can be identified from that data and other information in the possession of the data controller'. This definition would suggest that the local authority would be disclosing personal data where it releases information which can be linked to a particular individual/s. From perusing the details in the prepared draft response, the IMO confirmed that it will not be too difficult to identify an individual from the records and that it could therefore be construed as a disclosure of personal data. In addition, the release of such information could lead to other families with a similar housing background being 'stigmatised'. It was therefore deemed that disclosure would not be in the spirit of the FOIA and that it would also be a breach of the DPA. The request was therefore refused under Section 40 of the FOIA, which covers exemptions regarding the release of personal information.

This briefly sums up some of the IMO's responsibilities in ensuring compliance with the DPA.

10.3 Toolkit for Security

Information Security *Principle 7 of the DPA states that 'appropriate technical and organisational measures shall be taken against unauthorised or unlawful processing of personal data and against accidental loss or destruction of, or damage to personal data'.*

The lucid description of how data protection is viewed through the lens of a local authority focuses on the seventh Principle of the DPA.

In the wake of the facts that 2011 was dubbed the year of the cloud and also the year of the hack, there is now a statistical certainty that any organisation could be hacked and a panicked response is no longer an option. No organisation is immune to this threat as in 2011, the RSA, the company that issues security and encryption solutions was hacked!

This section will concentrate on how a local authority controls and manages its information through its people, processes and technology. As information is a key strategic asset, the way it is handled and exploited presents both benefits and risks. At the time of the writing, 12 local authorities in the UK have already been subject to hefty fines for data breaches. So, why the lamentable litany of data losses in the public sector? Perhaps it reveals what may be the obvious: weaknesses in the organisational, physical and technical controls of information management. Rapid technological change presents both opportunities and threats for organisations.

It appears that whilst we may have soared in the way we process and store information, we may not have maintained an equal pace with managing and controlling the threats.

One cannot argue that the complexity and getting to grips with the huge amount of information held by a local authority is in itself daunting. The never ending need for information sharing for the provision of effective and joined up services add to the challenge.

10.3.1 To Share or Not to Share Personal Data?

Local authorities need to work closely with a wide range of public bodies and therefore exchange information for legitimate and often essential reasons in the interests of providing effective services.

The Victoria Climbe and Ian Huntley cases are cited as examples which highlight the significance of responsible sharing, retention, deletion and use of data. In 2000, 8 year old Victoria Climbe died, despite the child having been known to four social services departments, three housing departments, two specialist child protection teams of the Metropolitan Police, two hospitals and a families centre managed by the National Society for the Prevention of Cruelty to Children (NSPCC). The DPA was blamed for preventing the sharing of personal information. An independent inquiry led by Lord Laming produced a report into the murder of this child abuse victim and it suggested that:

> There must be a balance struck between the protection of a child and the right to privacy and that the Government should issue guidance on the DPA 1998, the Human Rights Act 1998, and the common law rules of confidentiality.[6]

In a case in 2003, in Soham, in Cambridgeshire, in the UK, Ian Huntley was convicted of killing two school girls. In this case, the Humberside Police suggested that the DPA was the principal reason for the information about Ian Huntley's previous allegations of sexual offences not being made available to Cambridgeshire police. Ian Huntley had moved to Soham from Humberside, but previous allegations of sexual offences against him had not been revealed when he was appointed as a school caretaker in Soham. Sir Michael Bichard who was appointed to carry out an Inquiry into the 'child protection procedures in Cambridgeshire Constabulary, stated in his report'[7]:

> It is evident that police officers were nervous about breaching the legislation, partly at least because too little was done to educate and reassure them about its impact. But I do not believe that the current DPA needs to be revised as a result of these events. It is, as a member of the judiciary said recently, an 'inelegant and cumbersome' piece of legislation, but the legislation was not the problem. I suggest, however, that better guidance is needed on the collection, retention, deletion, use and sharing of information, so that police officers, social workers and other professionals can feel more confident in using information properly.

---

[6] See The Victoria Climbie Inquiry Report of an Inquiry by Lord Laming (2012).

[7] See Bichard Enquiry Report (2012).

In May 2011, the ICO published a Data Sharing Code of Practice, which states that:

> Under the right circumstances and for the right reasons, data sharing across and between organisations can play a crucial role in providing a better, more efficient service to customers in a range of sectors – both public and private. But citizens' and consumers' rights under the Data Protection Act must be respected. Organisations that don't understand what can and cannot be done legally are as likely to disadvantage their clients through excessive caution as they are by carelessness. But when things go wrong this can cause serious harm. We want citizens and consumers to be able to benefit from the responsible sharing of information, confident that their personal data is being handled responsibly and securely.[8]

10.3.2 The Information System

In a standard working day no one works in total isolation. There is exchange of information and sharing of data. There are conversations between colleagues; discussions with line managers; face to face conversations with members of the public and other professional organisations; the processing of information received through telephone, fax, letters and emails. These are all basic methods of handling information which form part of what can be simply known as the 'Information System' (Fig. 10.1). The concept of availability of information needs to be balanced by information integrity and confidentiality.

The local authority is attentive to achieving an appropriate balance between the benefits that are delivered through processing personal data and management of the residual risks. To rise to this challenge, the right culture has to be created, with the right policies and procedures to provide for accountability and scrutiny. No local authority can ever say it will never lose information, but by ensuring that the standards in the local authority are equivalent to, or exceed, the best practice identified in each of the above sections, the public will be reassured that all reasonable steps are taken to protect their information.

10.3.3 The Transformation

Increasing awareness in DP should be a culture changing exercise. There is never a flash bag awareness campaign. It is not about one big campaign, but a continual commitment to reach 'Nirvana' in privacy and it is a farce to believe that by signing up to one DP course, one would achieve all one needs to know on privacy and processing personal data. The mantra is to 'educate and to enforce'. The local authority impresses that the overall approach to the secure management of information should include the following complementary elements:

---

[8] ICO (2012).

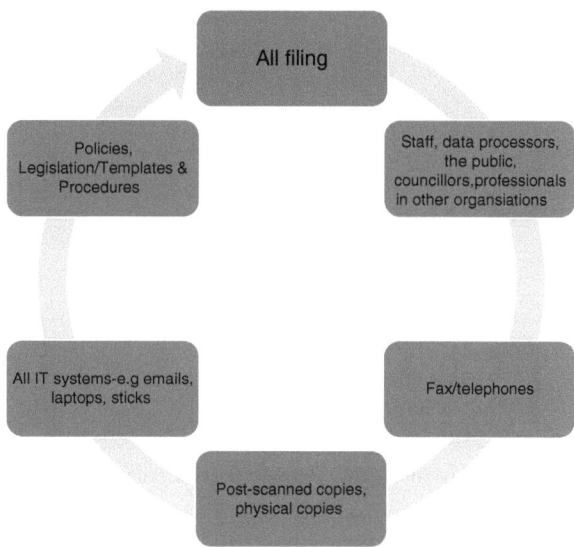

Fig. 10.1 The information system. *Source*: QTC Ltd in Bedford

10.3.3.1 Forced Compliance

Technical and procedural measures that almost force users to adopt proper data management practices in order to physically operate the systems; Information security focuses on these three ingredients: confidentiality, availability and integrity. Although as it suggests confidentiality relates to information being kept confidential, it relates to 'access controls'. This could refer to access to the computer system, a restricted area or even given access to work on particular information in an 'authorised capacity'. Other controls include the following:

- Use of basic level passwords for login
- Encryption of portable electronic devices
- Vetting of staff using the system and the allocation of permissions
- Firewalls
- Smart Cards (known as Logical Access) to monitor personnel
- Two factor authentication
- Data backup
- Access controls to computer network or a restricted area
- Proving awareness of appropriate legislation prior to access information e.g. online exam before access to system
- Physical controls to include cupboards and locks

An integral part of security is the accuracy and the reliability of the information that is processed. It is imperative to ensure that it is information that can be trusted and that the contents are up to date. Ensuring that this information is available to those who have a right of access to that information sums the definition of availability. Therefore to maintain confidentiality, integrity and availability, the data controller has to have measures in place to ensure sufficient security to prevent any unauthorised or unlawful processing, accidental loss, destruction or damage to information.

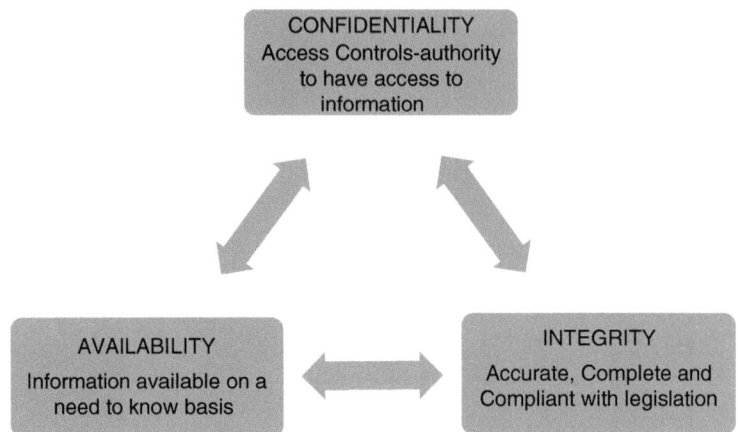

Fig. 10.2 Confidentiality, integrity & availability. *Source*: QTC Ltd in Bedford

Organisational measures including physical security, reliability of employees through identification checks, background checks in the form of Criminal Records checks for those working with children and vulnerable adults and the necessary vetting through interviews and CVs are equally significant security measures.

10.3.3.2 Soft Power

It's a concept developed to describe the ability to attract and co-opt rather than coerce and rather than using force or money as a means of persuasion.

A serious breach in Data Protection could affect the whole organisation at almost every conceivable level. It therefore requires strong leadership from the top to establish the policy parameters and action plans for the processing of personal data to be carried out in accordance with the principles of the DPA.

10.3.4 Some Beautifully Simple Steps to Help Comply with the DPA

Due to demanding business needs, there seems to be a burgeoning appetite and requirement for personal information. In the information management cycle, it is inevitable to accept that the 'human factor' is the final part of the jigsaw. Therefore the power to influence people's behaviours through increasing awareness in the management of personal data is almost critical. With the shifting privacy landscape and the redefined new challenges, training and 'education' for staff sit high on the local authority's agenda.

10.3.4.1 Evolution and Not Revolution

Increasing awareness in DP should not be a 'revolution but an evolution'. The gradual 'drip feed' mechanism through frequent gentle reminders and integrated

Table 10.2 Local authorities that suffered monetary penalties and causes. *Source*: media reports available in the public domain

Period	Local Authority	Fines	Breach
Nov 2010	Hertfordshire County Council	£100,000	Fax with highly sensitive information to wrong recipients
Feb 2011	Ealing Council	£80,000	Laptop with sensitive personal data stolen from employees home
Feb 2011	Hounslow Council	£70,000	Laptop with sensitive personal data stolen from employees home
Jun 2011	Surrey County Council	£120,000	Sensitive personal information emailed to the wrong recipient on three separate occasions
Nov 2011	Worcestershire County Council	£80,000	Five emails with highly sensitive data sent to the wrong recipient
Nov 2011	North Somerset Council	£60,000	Sensitive personal information emailed to 23 unintended recipients
Dec 2011	Powys County Council	£130,000	Child protection papers sent to the wrong recipient
Jan 2012	Midlothian Council	£140,000	'Looked after care review' sent to unintended recipients
Feb 2012	Croydon Council	£100,000	Bag containing papers relating to the care of a child sex abuse victim stolen
Feb 2012	Norfolk County Council	£80,000	Allegations against a parent and welfare of child sent to wrong recipient
Feb 2012	Cheshire East Council	£80,000	Email containing personal data sent to 180 unintended recipients
May 2012	Barnet Council	£70,000	Sensitive paper records of children stolen from social worker's home

and sustained awareness programmes through workshops and 'events' assist in instilling the DP message and stabilising the authority's defences.

> Insanity is the repetition of something over and over again, believing that the outcome will eventually change[9]

Staff need to be made aware of why it is important to take personal responsibility for processing personal data before they are encouraged to do so. In today's economic climate, while it is challenging enough to remain in employment and settle their household bills each month, information security may not feature high on the list of priorities for staff. Surprisingly, many also deem that 'information security' is a corporate function and not their own! When staff are empowered with responsibility, the urge to protect whatever is at stake is almost instinctive. Increasing awareness of cybercrimes and the loss of personal data due to human error will

---

[9] Albert Einstein's Quotation. http://www.brainyquote.com/quotes/quotes/a/alberteins133991.html. Accessed 1 May 2012.

achieve more to improve security and reduce 'mistakes' than any sophisticated technical solution alone can accomplish.

10.3.4.2 Empower Through Training

Training in DP and compliance is an integral part of induction. Regular class room style training sessions, at corporate and team levels help to promote excellence in data processing and assists the local authority to maintain its promise to its residents regarding the control it has on their personal data. There is a 'three line whip' (strict instruction) regarding attendance at corporate training sessions. These sessions are 'tailor made' to suit hard and soft skill audiences and in keeping with the organisations commitment to equality and diversity policies. To stimulate interest and increase awareness, these training sessions broach on current national and global news in the information governance world, guidance from the regulator and disseminate best practices from other local authorities. These face-to-face training sessions also provide open forums and a platform for questions. Feedbacks from all training sessions are evaluated to improve the training modules. An e-learning tool to further encourage the DP message across the local authority is also available and is mandatory to all members of staff. Staff are also empowered and equipped with knowledge and skills on secure information handling through workshops and forums, which are 'bespoke' sessions for a variety of skill levels ranging from social workers to lawyers.

10.3.4.3 Compliance Framework

The compliance framework, which is made up of a suite of policies, processes, tools, templates, registers, and systems define and support compliance management activities and are available to staff. The local authority can boast that they are produced in simple language and avoid jargon to make it as penetrable as possible to everyone. Whilst being 'user-friendly', they allow users to provide feedback to inform future iterations. Version controls are in place to make notings of any changes as and when they occur.

10.3.4.4 Caldicott Principles

To complement the overarching corporate policies there are operational specialist guidances produced at service area levels, to cater for the particular requirements of the service area. This is especially applicable to service areas that process health or records of care and support offered to young people, families, the disabled, the elderly and vulnerable adults and children. Caldicott Guardians are the nominated individuals in the local authority who are responsible for making decisions about sharing identifiable social care information. They are responsible for balancing the public interest of protecting sensitive information with the public interest for sharing information to enhance citizen care. The six key Caldicott Principles, which bear resemblance to the eight DP Principles, highlight the safe and secure handling of social care files.

10.3.4.5 'Transmission'

To add to security arrangements, guidelines on despatch are available in service areas. Whenever it is necessary to send any part of an Adoption Case Record for example within the Council offices, the information is placed in a sealed plain envelope and marked 'Personal and Confidential'. This mail is then double-enveloped and an audit trail of the whole 'transmission' is recorded making it possible for 'track and trace' of the documents. When external post is necessary, then arrangements are made for copies of relevant documents to be sent by recorded or special delivery. Any sensitive personal data that is sent electronically is either sent through the secure email network, is password protected, and encrypted.

10.3.4.6 Secure Remote Working

With the technology enablers, a new business driver for the local authority is 'remote working'. Although one big factor that drives remote working amongst local authorities is the rationalisation of office space, in an attempt to make efficiency savings by closing 'unfit for purpose offices' and making better use of office space in smaller purpose built offices, this also encourages flexible working for staff. Remote working is seen to offer staff a better work/life balance and therefore improve overall productivity. This enthusiasm and appetite for remote working is only a success for the organisation and staff, if it is well supported. Remote workers who are gravely exposed to information security risks have to satisfy rigorous safeguarding measures before they are allowed to work remotely. Successful completion of an online DP course is a prerequisite for all home or remote workers.

A two-factor authentication with hard-tokens and passwords are then provided; secure logging-in to prevent unauthorised access; encryption of all remote transmissions; and physical protection on the central server ensures that any data accessed remotely will not leave traces of the data. The flow of data from one point to the next is through a Citrix gateway. There are strict controls on the onward copying and storing of any data that is accessed or downloaded remotely. Due to the inherent risk in carrying large volumes of personal data, only the physical 'transportation' and carriage of data that is essential for remote working is encouraged. These are some of the steps taken by the local authority to offer security and integrity to the personal data that is accessed remotely.

10.3.4.7 Literature and Communication

There are publications in various editions of 'in house' newsletters, bulletins and ad hoc 'everyone emails' on topical DP updates. This 'campaign' acts as a good source of breach management tool and provide informative overview and quick response to queries frequently raised by staff.

Quite simply, good communication which include effective use of the intranet for posting messages; leading by example; physically sticking posters in frequently visited places and gentle reminders through 'pop up' messages on computers are also used extensively.

10.3.4.8 Internal Audit
At regular intervals, the internal audit team carry out reviews on the security and safeguards surrounding data. The findings and recommendations inform the gaps in the compliance universe which are then identified and improved; the requirement for education and training needs are identified and other deficiencies or inefficiencies are flagged up and acted upon as necessary.

10.3.4.9 Contractors
The local authority deals with third parties/data processors for the provision of goods and/or services. For efficiency savings, the local authority traditionally outsources it's cleaning and garbage collections for example. The formal agreements and contracts, which are drawn by the data controller include consideration of responsibility for data security and breaches. Whilst the data processor processes personal data on behalf of the data controller, the liability lies with the data controller. It is therefore essential that the local authority as the data controller is satisfied that a data processor is processing personal data in line with the Act and contractually complying with security and the obligations under the seventh principle of the Act.

10.3.4.10 Penetration Test
Besides the host of Information Technology Security policies, which support the IT system in the local authority, this department also carries out an annual detailed penetration test of the organisations information communications network. This involves an external organisation using tools and mechanisms that could be used by a hacker, to 'test' the local authority's network to explore the weaknesses of the system. The results from the penetration tests and an accurate assessment of the potential impacts to the organisation provide an outline of a range of technical and procedural countermeasures to reduce risks.

10.3.4.11 Deletion Programme
One element of simplicity is ensuring that staff handle and store only the very minimum amount of personal data required to carry out their daily functions. A document retention and disposal guideline, which includes advice on secure archiving, sets the path for ensuring that data is disposed when it is redundant and prevents the risk of data compromise. Keeping information for longer than is necessary does afford staff more time to forget about its existence, which in turn has the potential for a breach. Quite often, redundant data is at a bigger risk of being carelessly thrown away by staff.

10.3.4.12 Incident Reporting
Partners, stakeholders and staff are educated on incident reporting in line with the Breach Management Procedures and are made aware of the escalation structure that is available. They are informed that in the event of a breach, timely and well-executed communication could lessen the impact of the 'loss' and the reputational damage to the organisation. Managing compliance effectively requires continuous

Hard Power

This involves censure and punishment for improper management of data and loss of personal data. Through the Breach Management Procedure, the local authority impresses that if there is evidence of serious compromises or irresponsible handling of personal data, disciplinary action could be taken. Invoking 'appropriate punishment' emphasises the seriousness of losses and creates a deterrent effect.

10.4 What Happens When Compliance Fatigue Occurs!

What is a Breach: "an act or omission where the organisation has not met it's compliance, process or behavioural obligations"

Whatever the nature of the breach in the local authority, it is dealt with based on the following four important elements. These are considered immediately by the IMO in liaison with the relevant Group Manager or Head of Service:

Containment and recovery[10]: breaches will require not just an initial response to investigate and contain the situation but also a recovery plan including, where necessary, damage limitation. This will often involve input from the Information Technology, Human Resources and Legal departments and in some cases contact with external stakeholders and providers.

Assessment of ongoing risk: assess the risks that may be associated with the breach. Most important is an assessment of potential adverse consequences for individuals, how serious or substantial these are and how likely they are to happen. Certain data security breaches will not lead to risks beyond possible inconvenience to those who need the data to do their job. An example of this is where a laptop is irreparably damaged but its files were backed up and can be recovered, albeit at some cost to the business.

Notification of breach: informing staff in the affected area of the breach is an important element of the breach management plan. However, informing people about a breach is not an end in itself. Notification should have a clear purpose, whether this is to enable individuals who may have been affected to take steps to protect themselves or to provide advice and deal with complaints.

Evaluation and response: a log is maintained of all security incidents and is monitored regularly, allowing for any trends to be picked up and preventative measures to be put in place. It is important not only to investigate the causes of the breach but also to evaluate the effectiveness of the response to it. If the breach was caused, even in part, by systemic and ongoing problems, then simply

---

[10] See Procedures on data Security Breach Management of Southend-0n-Sea Borough Council.

BREACH REPORTING STRUCTURE					
Breach Level	Very High	High	Medium	Low	Very Low
IMO/Group Manager/Head of Service	x	x	x	X	x
CEO/Senior Information Risk Officer (SIRO)	x	x	x		
Senior Management Team	x	x	x	X	x

Fig. 10.3 Breach management structure. *Source*: local authority

containing the breach and continuing 'business as usual' is not acceptable. If the response was hampered by inadequate policies or a lack of a clear allocation of responsibility then it is reviewed and amended in light of the weaknesses identified. In order to maximise what can be learnt, the IMO debriefs the team, through tailored round table discussions, for the service area with organisational responsibility for the breach or corporately for the organisation, after the incident, to identify and mitigate their risks.

If the security incident was caused by staff and there is evidence that there has been contravention of the local authorities policies, procedures or guidance, the organisation will take appropriate disciplinary action. This will depend on the severity of the risk and the risk classification level ascribed to the incident.

The risk management plan will include a series of controls which will include structured training in DP and the maintenance of data logs which should be systematically monitored. Data logs also act as an invaluable tool in allocating liability. These controls should either reduce further risk of such a breach or reduce the impact.

All breaches and potential breaches are escalated to the Senior Management Team which is ultimately responsible for the effective management and compliance with the regulatory and business compliance requirements of the organisation (Fig. 10.3). For example, the DP Act would be a regulatory requirement and the local authority's Breach Management Procedure would be deemed a business compliance requirement. All breaches are fed into the monthly management reporting process, by means of measuring performance against predefined Key Performance Indicators (KPIs).

10.4.1 Privacy Incidents

The common adage 'the best laid plans of mice and men often go awry' seems to fit right. The number of incidents that have been reported are worrying. The recently reported data breaches reveal that they are commonly caused by human behaviour. Extensively publicised high profile data losses undermine the public's faith and confidence in the organisation's competency to process personal data. This also reduces the public's trust in sharing their personal data. It might seem in the distant past, but most people and especially privacy experts will vividly recall a major data breach on 20 November 2007, which caused widespread apprehension regarding security surrounding personal data. Two computer discs holding the personal details of all families in the UK with a child under 16 had gone missing. The Child Benefit data on them included names, addresses, dates of birth, National Insurance numbers and, where relevant, bank details of 25 million individuals and 7.25 million families. Junior officials at Her Majesty's Revenue and Customs (HMRC),[11] had sent information to the National Audit Office (NAO) for auditing. Two password protected discs containing a full copy of HMRC's entire data in relation to the payment of child benefit was sent to the NAO, by HMRC's internal post system operated by the courier TNT. However the package was not recorded or registered and it appears the data had failed to reach the addressee in the NAO.

The HMRC debacle has been followed by several other breaches in government organisations. Information security continues to remain a much shared concern by government departments. In May 2012 Barnet Council was fined £70,000 after details including the names, addresses and sexual activities of 15 vulnerable children were stolen from a social worker's home.

10.4.2 Complaints

The UK public is up in arms that their data is still not being protected by organisations as their complaints to the Information Commissioner's Office (ICO) demonstrate:

10.4.2.1 2010
10,598 complaints made in relation to breaching DPA
1,722 complaints made related to disclosure of data
657 complaints related to security
3,781 companies were specifically complained about, with financial organisations and government bodies heralding amongst in the top 10 worst offenders

10.4.2.2 2011
10,074 total complaints requesting assessment under the DPA
1,834 complaints related to disclosure of private data
620 complaints involved security breaches
4,036 companies were specifically complained about for alleged breaches of DPA

10.4.2.3 2012: April 2012
771 complaints about a breach of the DPA raising concerns over personal data
231 complaints concerning security of personal data

---

[11] UK's families put on fraud alert. http://news.bbc.co.uk/1/hi/uk_politics/7103566.stm. Accessed 2 July 2012.

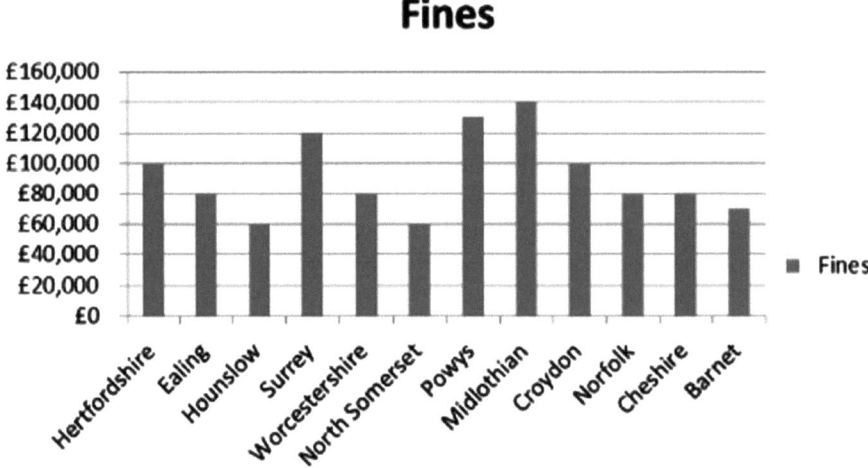

Fig. 10.4 Monetary penalties suffered by local authorities in the UK from March 2010 to May 2012. *Source*: media and reports available in the public domain

10.4.2.4 Key Facts

This year alone the ICO received 1002 complaints that raised concerns over the disclosure of personal data or breaches of the DPA—an average of eight a day. Since its inception, the ICO has received 26,227 data protection complaints that resulted in serving 14 monetary penalties, equating to a mere £1,171,000 in total fines.

10.4.3 Trends in Data Breaches

Since April 2010, the Information Commissioner has had the power to issue monetary fines for serious breaches of the DPA. Breaches that cause substantial damage or distress to individuals can attract civil monetary penalties. The UK Commissioner comments that 'failure to respect an individual's privacy can lead to distress and in certain circumstances can cause that individual real damage, mentally, physically and financially'.[12]

10.4.4 Monetary Penalties

In the period April 2010 to May 2012 12 local authorities have attracted monetary penalties, totalling £1,110,000 due to data breaches (Table 10.2 and Fig. 10.4). A glaring fact is that these monetary penalties are becoming more frequent. So far,

---

[12] Ofcom (2012).

every single breach that has attracted a fine has been in relation to data in transit. These include emails sent to the wrong people, despatch of paper records to incorrect recipients, a fax sent to an unintended number or due to the loss of an unencrypted laptop. It seems apparent that the breaches have been due to the negligent 'insider', as opposed to the external 'hacker'.

10.4.5 Undertakings

Data breaches that led to undertakings being signed by local authorities have soared in the last few years. From June 2010 to April 2012, the Information Commissioner's Office has secured undertakings from 26 local authorities in relation to various breaches of the DPA (Tables 10.2 and 10.3). These include thefts of unencrypted laptops with sensitive personal data, loss of documents containing children's records, dumping of computer with personal information in a skip and the mishandling of a subject access request. In September 2011, Walsall Council gave an undertaking to comply with the seventh data protection principle following the accidental disposal of hundreds of residents' postal votes in a skip. The votes, which were dumped by one of the Council's contractors, included names, addresses, dates of birth and signatures. The local authority breached the Act as it did not have a written agreement with the contractor processing the personal data. In addition, the local authority also failed to provide the data processor with instructions as to how the information should be kept secure. The ICO stated that 'whilst Councils can hire contractors to process personal information on their behalf, they must remember that they are still ultimately responsible for ensuring people's information is kept secure' (Fig. 10.5).

The threat of ICO intervention should not be the business driver. Concentrating on protecting data, no matter where it lives, is paramount in today's world. However, local authorities like various major multinational organisations have suffered privacy issues and have recently drawn the attention of the regulator, the media and of course their clients. Although they are grasping the nettle and tackling the security of their information, the staggering number of monetary penalties, which came into force in April 2010, calls for stronger data security.

It is incorrect to say that errors of this nature are limited mainly to public sector organisations. Most of us would imagine that an organisation such as NASA would have an impenetrable security system. However NASA had 5,408 computer security lapses in 2010 and 2011, including the loss of a laptop in March 2011. 'Some of which resulted in the unauthorized release of sensitive data including export-controlled, Personally Identifiable Information (PII), and third-party intellectual property.'[13]

---

[13] Stolen NASA Laptop Had Space Station Control Code. http://news.discovery.com/space/stolen-nasa-laptop-had-space-station-control-code-120301.html. Accessed 12 June 2012.

Table 10.3 List of LAs who signed undertakings due to data breaches from April 2010 to May 2012. *Source*: media and reports available in the public domain

Period	Local authority	Nature of breach
Jun 2010	West Berkshire Council	Loss of a USB stick with sensitive personal information of children
Jul 2010	**London Borough of Barnet**	Theft of a laptop and unencrypted USB sticks from home of an employee
Jul 2010	**West Sussex County Council**	Theft of unencrypted laptop with sensitive data stolen from employee's home
Jul 2010	Buckinghamshire County Council	Loss of documents containing sensitive personal data of two children
Nov 2010	Stoke-on-Trent City Council	Loss of personal details of children in care
Nov 2010	Portsmouth City Council	Council gives out personal details by mistake
Feb 2011	**Doncaster Metropolitan Borough Council**	Personal details of 39 employees provided without relevant redactions in place
Feb 2011	The Isle of Anglesey County Council	Contractor mistakenly sent letters with financial information to wrong individuals
Feb 2011	Cambridgeshire County Council	Loss of memory stick containing sensitive data
Mar 2011	Wolverhampton City Council	Confidential records dumped in skip
Apr 2011	The City of York Council	Accidental disclosure of personal data to a third party following a printer mix-up
Apr 2011	Borough of Poole	Faxes containing personal data sent to the same incorrect fax number thrice
May 2011	Somerset County Council	Social care records sent to the wrong family
Jun 2011	North Lanarkshire Council	Theft of a home support worker's bag containing sensitive personal records
Jul 2011	Kirklees Metropolitan Council	Care workers contracted by data controller left client sensitive personal data in their cars whilst on visits
Sep 2011	Walsall Council	Accidental dumping of postal vote statements in a skip
Oct 2011	Dumfries and Galloway Council	Accidental publishing of names, salaries and dates of birth of employees on website
Nov 2011	Southwark Council	Computer and papers with personal information in a skip
Nov 2011	Rochdale Metropolitan Borough Council	Loss of an unencrypted memory stick with personal details of over 18,000 residents
Feb 2012	Basingstoke and Deane Borough Council	Mistakenly sent personal information relating to 29 people who were living in supported housing
Feb 2012	Dacorum Borough Council	Theft of computer hard drive containing sensitive personal data
Feb 2012	Staffordshire County Council	Mishandling of a subject access request
Feb 2012	Bolton Council	Theft of sensitive personal data from a keyworker's car

(continued)

Table 10.3 (continued)

Period	Local authority	Nature of breach
Feb 2012	Brighton & Hove City Council	Theft of an unencrypted personal laptop with sensitive and personal data stolen
Feb 2012	Craven District Council	Theft of unencrypted laptop containing a database with details of 2,300 individuals
Apr 2012	Leicestershire County Council	Theft of a briefcase containing sensitive personal data from a social worker's home

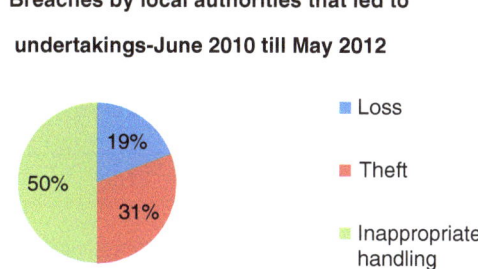

Fig. 10.5 Percentages of data breaches in local authorities from April 2010 to May 2012 that attracted undertakings. *Source*: media and reports available in the public domain

Non compliance—Why does it happen?

This twenty-first century's information industry is continually faced with threats of breaches. Complacency in organisations regarding security should be replaced with a proactive rather than reactive approach. Organisations should be empowered with an understanding of their responsibilities regarding the handling of personal data.

References

Bichard Enquiry Report (2012) http://www.dh.gov.uk/prod_consum_dh/groups/dh_digitalassets/documents/digitalasset/dh_110711.pdf. Accessed 8 July 2012

ICO (2012) Data Sharing Code of Practice. http://www.ico.gov.uk/for_organisations/data_protection/topic_guides/data_sharing.aspx. Accessed 8 July 2012

Local Government Structure (2012) http://www.direct.gov.uk/en/governmentcitizensandrights/ukgovernment/localgovernment/dg_073310. Accessed 20 May 2012

Ofcom (2012) What price privacy? The unlawful trade in confidential information. http://www.ofcom.org.uk/data-protection/what-price-privacy-the-unlawful-trade-in-confidential-personal-information/. Accessed 20 June 2012

Procedures on data Security Breach Management of Southend-0n-Sea Borough Council (2012) http://www.southend.gov.uk/downloads/file/3971/procedures_on_data_security_breach_manage%20ment. Accessed 20 May 2012

The Victoria Climbie Inquiry Report of an Inquiry by Lord Laming (2012) http://www.dh.gov.uk/prod_consum_dh/groups/dh_digitalassets/documents/digitalasset/dh_110711.pdf. Accessed 8 July 2012

List of Materials

Living World. http://livingword.co.uk/case-studies/information-is-the-currency-of-democracy/. Accessed 28 May 2012

Research. ICO urges easy opt-out of online tracking, but EU demands opt-in. http://www.research-live.com/news/government/.../4003097.article. Accessed 5 June 2012

Data Protection Enforcement: The European Experience—Case Law

11

Dan Manolescu

> *I am concerned that not all EU institutions and bodies are performing as well as they should. Implementation of data protection principles is not only a matter of time and resources, but also of organisational will. Ensuring compliance is a process that requires the commitment and support of the hierarchy in all institutions and bodies*
>
> (Peter Hustinx, European Data Protection Supervisor (EDPS), Brussels, 30th January 2012, excerpt of the EDPS Press Release 03/12)

Abstract

This chapter will firstly describe the concepts of personal data and privacy, how these are similar and different in the same time, and what is the regulator aim with regards to the protection of the individual rights and freedoms. Subsequently, two most representative case law will be described and analysed in order to understand the applicability of the EU legal framework in regards to privacy and data protection.

11.1 The Concept of Data Protection and Privacy

The EU approach to data protection aims to confer a uniform protection among its Member States considering data protection as a fundamental right. The EU legislation is based on a set of rights and principles for personal data treatment (processing), without considering that the data is held in the public or private sector, and it protects just natural persons not legal entities.

D. Manolescu (✉)
E-crime expert, Rue du Noyer 230, Ap.3, Brussels 1030, Belgium
e-mail: dmanolescu@gmail.com

The EU regards the relation between data protection and the economic value as a proper balance between fundamental rights and free flow of information (which has economic value). By granting data protection as a fundamental right, the aim is to protect the individuals but also to encourage the free flow of information, which has strong economic value, giving data subjects legal certainty and encouraging them to not negatively affect the exchange of information and data "...the transmission of such data from the territory of one Member State to that of another Member State [...]to the pursuit of a number of economic activities at Community level..."[1]

The concept of privacy and data protection is not the same. The protection of privacy is a fundamental right that is mainly protected by Article 8 of the European Convention on Human Rights when the concept of data protection, which is also a fundamental right, sets forth the basic principles for data subjects' protection.

Data protection has a privacy dimension, but it is narrower in scope than the privacy concept, "as the privacy encloses more than personal data".[2] From a different angle, it encloses a wider area, "since personal data are protected not only to enhance the privacy of the subject, but also to guarantee other fundamental rights, such as the right to freedom of expression".

Furthermore, data protection gives individuals the right to know what (private) data is collected, on what legal grounds, how it is used, for how long it used and kept, and by whom. Also, it specifically grants data subjects with the rights to access, modify, update or ask for deletion of such data.[3]

11.1.1 Right to Privacy

In the EU, the European Convention on Human Rights (ECHR) grants the Right to Privacy

Article 8: "Right to respect for private and family life which reads:
1. *Everyone has the right to respect for his private and family life, his home and his correspondence.*[4]
2. *There shall be no interference by a public authority with the exercise of this right except such as is in accordance with the law and is necessary in a democratic society in the interests of national security, public safety or the economic well-being of the country, for the prevention of disorder or crime, for the protection of health or morals, or for the protection of the rights and freedoms of others"*.

Furthermore, in the Charter of Fundamental Rights of the European Union, Article 7—Respect for private and family life provides:

---

[1] Directive 95/46/EC. Preamble. (7). 1995.

[2] EDPS. The processing of personal data related to the use of the communication network in EU Institutions and bodies: ensuring compliance with Regulation (EC) 45. 2001, p. 5.

[3] Directive 95/46/EC. Article 10: Information To be Given to the Data Subject and Article 12: Right of access.

[4] Council of Europe. Article 8 of the European Convention on Human Rights 1950.

> Everyone has the right to respect for his or her private and family life, home and communications.[5]

The ECHR is binding not only for individual states but also indirectly for the European Union as the Article 6(1) of the Treaty on the Functioning of the European Union reads:

> The Union recognises the rights, freedoms and principles set out in the Charter of Fundamental Rights of the Europeans, which shall have the same legal value as the Treaties[6]

The Article 6(2) reads: "The Union shall accede to the European Convention for the Protection of Human Rights and Fundamental Freedoms".[7]

Article 6(3) stipulates:

> Fundamental rights, as guaranteed by the European Convention for the Protection of Human Rights and Fundamental Freedoms and as they result from the constitutional traditions common to the Member States, shall constitute general principles of the Union's law.[8]

11.1.2 Right to Data Protection

The fundamental human right to data protection is granted individually and separately under the Charter of Fundamental Rights of the European Union (Charter), Article 8—*Protection of personal data:*

1. *Everyone has the right to the protection of personal data concerning him or her.*
2. *Such data must be processed fairly for specified purposes and on the basis of the consent of the person concerned or some other legitimate basis laid down by law. Everyone has the right of access to data which has been collected concerning him or her, and the right to have it rectified.*[9]

The Charter has granted two different fundamental rights to privacy and to personal data and not just one to privacy, aiming to confer protection to personal data as well. The case law of the European Court of Justice (ECJ) recognises the principles laid down in the Charter as general principles of law.[10]

From a practical perspective on how the ECJ and the **Civil Service Tribunal (First Chamber)** enforced the right to data protection. Following will be presented two representatives case law one on the applicability of the Directive 95/46/EC (for the private sector) and the other on the applicability of the Regulation 45/2001 (for the EU Institutions and bodies).

---

[5] Article 7 of The Charter of Fundamental Rights of the European Union 2000.

[6] The Treaty on the Functioning of the European Union. Treaty of Lisbon. Article 6(1), 2007.

[7] The Treaty on the Functioning of the European Union. Treaty of Lisbon. Article 6(2), 2007.

[8] The Treaty on the Functioning of the European Union. Treaty of Lisbon. Article 6 (1),(2),(3), 2007.

[9] Article 8 of The Charter of Fundamental Rights of the European Union 2000.

[10] Judgment of the European Court of Justice in Case C-101/01. Bodil Lindqvist. 2003.

11.2 Enforcement through Case Law

11.2.1 Case C-101/01: Criminal Proceedings Against Bodil Lindqvist (Reference for a preliminary ruling from the Göta hovrätt (Sweden)

11.2.1.1 Community Legislation: Directive 95/46/EC
Scope:
- Publication of personal data on the internet
- Place of publication
- Definition of transfer of personal data to third countries
- Freedom of expression
- Compatibility with Directive 95/46 of greater protection for personal data under the national legislation of a Member State.

11.2.1.2 Court Composition
Composed of: P. Jann, President of the First Chamber, acting for the President, C.W.A. Timmermans, C. Gulmann, J.N. Cunha Rodrigues and A. Rosas (Presidents of Chambers), D.A.O. Edward (Rapporteur), J.-P. Puissochet, F. Macken and S. von Bahr, Judges,
- Advocate General: A. Tizzano,
- Registrar: H. von Holstein, Deputy Registrar,

11.2.1.3 Participants to the Hearings
- Mrs Lindqvist, by S. Larsson, advokat,
- The Swedish Government, by A. Kruse, acting as Agent,
- The Netherlands Government, by H.G. Sevenster, acting as Agent,
- The United Kingdom Government, by G. Amodeo, acting as Agent, assisted by J. Stratford, barrister,
- The Commission of the European Communities, by L. Ström and X. Lewis, acting as Agents.[11]

11.2.1.4 Summary of the Case
Mrs. Bodil Lindqvist worked as a catechist in a parish of Alseda in Sweden.

She took a course in data processing where she learned how to set up websites, to upload their content, and also to manipulate the content of her websites. In late 1998, Mrs. Bodil Lindqvist setup an Internet page, using her home computer.[12] She was the only person having access to the website in terms of uploading, manipulating and updating data. The purpose of that particular website was to present useful

---

[11] Decision of the Court in the Case C-101/01 (2003).
[12] Case C-101/01 Bodil Lindqvist v Åklagarkammaren i Jönköping – reference to the ECJ under Article 234 of the Treaty by Götta Hovrätten (Sweden) for a preliminary ruling in the criminal proceedings before that court against Bodil Lidqvist.

information for future parishioners to get prepared for their confirmation.[13] Her website contained information about herself and private information such as names, family circumstances and telephone numbers of her colleagues from the parish. In one occasion, Mrs. Bodil Lindqvist mentioned on her website how one of her colleagues got an injured leg and for that reason she was working part-time. Also, mentioned on the website was a humoristic approach to describing her colleagues' hobbies. Mrs. Bodil Lindqvist did not inform her colleagues about the existence of this website and her comments and that their personal contact details were posted, nor did she inform or seek for advice from the Supervisory Authority on data protection in Sweden. When her colleagues found out, they were not happy about their personal contact details and name being posted on this website and also about Mrs. Bodil Lindqvist personal comments referring to them. With that occasion, Mrs. Bodil Lindqvist removed their personal details and contact information from her website. Soon after, the Public Prosecutor, brought prosecution against Mrs. Bodil Lindqvist, regarding her breach of the national Swedish legislation on data protection and privacy as transposed into the national legislation of the Directive 95/46 EC. The prosecution stated that Mrs. Bodil Lindqvist breached the above-mentioned legislation by processing personal data without prior approval from the Swedish Supervisor Authority as stated in the national legislation and in the Directive 95/46/EC. Also, Mrs. Bodil Lindqvist processed sensitive data by mentioning one of her colleagues, which had at that time a broken leg. The public prosecutor made reference to the disclosure of personal medical data without approval. The last allegation was regarding Mrs. Bodil Lindqvist transferring personal data to a third country without having authorization, beside the National Act and the Directive 95/46/EC stipulate this.

After Mrs. Bodil Lindqvist heard these allegations, she accepted the facts, but she refused that she was guilty of any offence.

The District Court fined Mrs. Bodil Lindqvist with 450 EUR, which made her decide to appeal the decision to the Appeal Court.

The Appeal Court decided to hold the procedures and address few questions to the European Court of Justice (ECJ) as the matter in discussion referred to the applicability of the Community Law (Directive 95/46/EC).

11.2.1.5 Questions Addressed to ECJ
Question 1
"By its first question, the referring court asks whether the act of referring, on an internet page, to various persons and identifying them by name or by other means, for instance by giving their telephone number or information regarding their working conditions and hobbies, constitutes the processing of personal data wholly or partly by automatic means within the meaning of Article 3(1) of Directive 95/46".[14]

---

[13] Case C-101/01 Bodil Lindqvist v Åklagarkammaren i Jönköping – reference to the ECJ under Article 234 of the Treaty by Götta Hovrätten (Sweden) for a preliminary ruling in the criminal proceedings before that court against Bodil Lidqvist

[14] Case C-101/01 Bodil Lindqvist v Åklagarkammaren i Jönköping – reference to the ECJ under Article 234 of the Treaty by Götta Hovrätten (Sweden) for a preliminary ruling in the criminal proceedings before that court against Bodil Lidqvist

The Court found that referring on the internet page to various persons and making them identifiable, giving their contact details, full names and phone numbers and even mentioning their hobbies, contravene to the Article 3(1) of Directive 95/46/EC because it constitutes processing of personal data by automatic means, without having permission or informing the Swedish Supervisory Authority. In other words the ECJ found appropriate the first ruling of the Swedish Court of District (the first National Instance which ruled on this case), in this particular matter of this case.

In my personal opinion, **technically**, we could consider that uploading, on your personal website, somebody else's private information and details could constitute a violation of privacy and processing of personal data without authorization. I emphasise the word "technically" because I do not think that Mrs. Bodil Lindqvist had any idea that what she was doing was representing "processing of personal data". She may have thought that what she was doing was funny and could be useful to her colleagues and also to the future candidates to her parish. On the other hand, not knowing the rule does not protected somebody against its consequences. As a summary I would like to say that every case should be considered on its own accord, not applying a general matrix without taking into consideration the human element in the equations.

"If the answer to the first question is no, can the act of setting up on an internet home page separate pages for about 15 people with links between the pages which make it possible to search by first name be considered to constitute the processing otherwise than by automatic means of personal data which form part of a filing system or are intended to form part of a filing system within the meaning of Article 3(1)"[15]?

The answer for the first question was "yes" so the ECJ proceeded to answer the next addressed questions.

Question 2

"Can the act of loading information of the type described about work colleagues onto a private home page, which is none the less accessible to anyone who knows its address be regarded as outside the scope of [Directive 95/46] on the ground that it is covered by one of the exceptions in Article 3(2)"?[16]

After examining all the relevant information and input made available from all the parties involved in this case, ECJ answered that in this case, the uploading on a personal website somebody else's private information and details represents a violation of privacy and processing of personal data without authorization, does not fall under any of the exceptions outlined in Article 8(1) of the Directive 95/46/EC.

---

[15] (6) Case C-101/01 Bodil Lindqvist v Åklagarkammaren i Jönköping – reference to the ECJ under Article 234 of the Treaty by Götta Hovrätten (Sweden) for a preliminary ruling in the criminal proceedings before that court against Bodil Lidqvist.

[16] Case C-101/01 Bodil Lindqvist v Åklagarkammaren i Jönköping – reference to the ECJ under Article 234 of the Treaty by Götta Hovrätten (Sweden) for a preliminary ruling in the criminal proceedings before that court against Bodil Lidqvist

Question 3

"Is information on a home page stating that a named colleague has injured her foot and is on half-time on medical grounds personal data concerning health which, according to Article 8(1), may not be processed"?[17]

The ECJ answered that in case of disclosure of personal data on the Internet referring in this case to an individual who had broken her leg and stayed at home on half-time medical leave, constitutes illegal traffic with personal data concerning health problems and it comes against to Article 8(1) of Directive 95/46/EC.

Again, in my opinion the ECJ ruling based on the Directive 95/46/EC, was correct but I am quite sure that Mrs. Bodil Lindqvist had no idea that she was dealing with "illegal traffic with personal data concerning health problems".

Question 4

"[Directive 95/46] prohibits the transfer of personal data to third countries in certain cases. If a person in Sweden uses a computer to load personal data onto a home page stored on a server in Sweden — with the result that personal data become accessible to people in third countries — does that constitute a transfer of data to a third country within the meaning of the directive? Would the answer be the same even if, as far as known, no one from the third country had in fact accessed the data or if the server in question was actually physically in a third country"?[18]

ECJ found that loading personal data on a personal website stored on the Internet, does not represent transfer of data to a third country as stipulated in the Article 25 of Directive 95/46/EC.

In my opinion, the ECJ ruling was fair by not interpreting the meaning of Article 25 of Directive 95/46/EC, ad literal. Why was it fair: because if following the meaning of the "transfer of data to third countries (countries outside EU and EEA)" as outlined in the above mentioned Directive, then any person using the Internet and having her own website or even a social network account could be liable for doing this "transfer". It is not sufficient to upload the data on a personal website in order to make that data available to "third countries" because somebody has to follow some steps (log in, log out), meet some requirements (geographical area), and also dispose of technical meanings (computer, Internet connection) in order to have access to the Internet where supposedly that data could be available. Even though, considering the globalization and spreadness of the Internet, it is hard to believe that somebody from the US for example would go directly to that data, which contains information referring to members of a certain parish, located in Sweden. In this case, the data was not "offered" on the Internet to someone interested in it.

---

[17] (8) Case C-101/01 Bodil Lindqvist v Åklagarkammaren i Jönköping – reference to the ECJ under Article 234 of the Treaty by Götta Hovrätten (Sweden) for a preliminary ruling in the criminal proceedings before that court against Bodil Lidqvist.

[18] Case C-101/01 Bodil Lindqvist v Åklagarkammaren i Jönköping – reference to the ECJ under Article 234 of the Treaty by Götta Hovrätten (Sweden) for a preliminary ruling in the criminal proceedings before that court against Bodil Lidqvist

Question 5

"Can the provisions of [Directive 95/46], in a case such as the above, be regarded as bringing about a restriction which conflicts with the general principles of freedom of expression or other freedoms and rights, which are applicable within the EU and are enshrined in inter alia Article 10 of the European Convention on the Protection of Human Rights and Fundamental Freedoms"?[19]

ECJ found that the National state should decide on matters which conflict between them as in this case the data protection and the freedom of expression are in conflict.

On one hand, an individual has to have protection for his personal data (Directive 95/46/EC) and also free movement of information among EU countries, on the other hand an individual has to have the liberty of expression of her religious believes for example, as provided by the Article 10 of the European Convention of Human Rights. In my opinion, here the ECJ was not very helpful by not offering a straightforward answer to the National Court. In a special situation like this, the ECJ should have given guidance to the National Court how to weight two Legislative acts, which come into conflict. The answer here would have been much simpler than to the other addressed questions, because someone cannot have granted her rights in case of doing an illegal activity. ECJ already gave its opinion on the previous five questions where it said that uploading personal data on the Internet constitutes illegal traffic with that data. Someone cannot be granted the right of freely expressing her religious or artistic beliefs when using, for example, stolen money (which was not the case here).

Question 6

"Can a Member State, as regards the issues raised in the above questions, provide more extensive protection for personal data or give it a wider scope than the directive, even if none of the circumstances described in Article 13 exists"?[20]

ECJ answered here that the Member State should provide the minimum level of protection as outlined in the Directive 95/46/EC, but it is not held liable if that level of protection goes higher, being adjusted to each Member State's needs. The answer of ECJ was fair enough because a Directive should be transposed into the National legislation by guaranteeing the application of what that Directive regulates.

A Directive does not go beyond what is necessary in order to achieve that particular objective that it was created for. But, if a Member State considers that for its national reality, the regulations that will be transposed into their national legislation from the Directive should be more rigid that will not be a problem.

---

[19] Case C-101/01 Bodil Lindqvist v Åklagarkammaren i Jönköping – reference to the ECJ under Article 234 of the Treaty by Götta Hovrätten (Sweden) for a preliminary ruling in the criminal proceedings before that court against Bodil Lidqvist.

[20] Case C-101/01 Bodil Lindqvist v Åklagarkammaren i Jönköping – reference to the ECJ under Article 234 of the Treaty by Götta Hovrätten (Sweden) for a preliminary ruling in the criminal proceedings before that court against Bodil Lidqvist.

11.2.1.6 Case Analysis

The reference that the Swedish Court of Appeal made to the ECJ was not under any obligations, it had a scope, a preliminary ruling in order to avoid differences of interpretation of EU law and its own ruling. Among other attributions, ECJ should offer preliminary rulings for cases, which come before a national court involving an interpretation of EU law, when there is a doubt as to how that EU law should be interpreted.

> The ECJ will make a decision as to how the law should be interpreted or applied and will send that decision to the national court. The national court must then apply that decision to the case before it[21]

Regarding weather the ECJ answered the questions adequately, in my opinion, the EU's view on data protection is linked closely to the privacy issues, which is not always the right approach in dealing with data protection issues. The privacy concept as outlined in Art. 8 European Convention on Human Rights refers mainly to the right for private and family life, respect of private home and private correspondence. The data protection could include privacy issues but is not limited to them. Data protection means the right of a person to know which data were gathered in regards to her person, how the data are used, how the data are aggregated, where the data are transmitted, who and how the data are protected. Also has the right to have access to that data and to modify the data. In all cases the person has to accept for that data to be used by another person, government, or entity.

In this case, ECJ have seen the issue of disclosing medical information over the Internet as being just an issue of privacy. I will go further and say it is not just about this. For example, what if somebody posting on the Internet (on a social website for example) something which it is untrue regarding another person? It is not a privacy intrusion, but making information, which is not true, available to the public could do still harm. If someone writes an article on her personal Blog with untruthful information about another person, anyone searching for information on that person for a job interview for example, could not choose her based on that untrue information. This is the reason why I am saying that anyone has the right to know any information, data referring to her person, in order to allow her to accept the information, access it and to be able to modify it. In our case, what would have been the real harm done to the person with a broken leg, if for example her employer would have found out that the person is on a medical leave because she broke her leg dancing while being drunk, instead she got injured while walking on the street?

The ruling of ECJ in this case regarding data protection (in one the first of it's kind), has important implications because it clarifies to individuals and companies that personal data has protection and no one can use it without prior authorization. Also, this case helped strengthen the position of the Supervisory Authority in data

---

[21] De Hert and Gutwirth (2009), pp. 3–44.

protection as outlined in the Directive 95/46/EC, by outlining that anyone has to consult this Authority in order to process personal data.

Question number seven addressed to ECJ and its answer shows that this Directive is rather broad and the Member States have difficulties in properly transposing it into their legislation with not much uniformity among them, because some Member States are applying it more strictly than others. The Directive 95/46/EC, if rigidly applied (through implementation of national laws) may have the effect of prohibiting what is regarded as a form of "legitimate activity".

In my opinion this was a useful warning given by ECJ to those interested in using, manipulating, accessing data, with no right or consent. At least it was a useful start, because since then more and more EU Countries used this Directive in the right direction. Also, it was a clarification given to those countries, which did not know what the Directive 95/46/EC meant by the transmitting of data to third countries. ECJ clarified that uploading personal information on a personal website, even though it could be accessible from a third country, is not qualified as transmitting data to those third countries. Based on this particular ruling, Sweden amended in 2004 its "Personal Data Act" by changing the everyday processing such as email correspondence and processing of personal data on the internet ("publication of running text on the internet"), to not fall anymore under processing personal data infringement.

This could be considered as a landmark decision[22] in Data Protection and Privacy issues as ECJ ruled on a matter which has never been addressed until then. Why is a landmark Decision? Because since this ruling took place, almost all cases involving similar issues refer to this case: **Case** C-101/01, **Bodil Lindqvist.**

Last but not least, it is worth it to be mentioned that the ECJ did not followed at all the opinion of the Advocate General Tizziano in this case (which is quite uncommon to not be taken into consideration at all).[23] Also, in my opinion, ECJ tried to make a fair balance between fundamental rights and fundamental freedoms as well. Dealing with these sensitive issues, it is always hard to take a decision regarding fundamental rights and harm fundamental freedoms and vice-versa. It is very hard to find the proper balance in ruling in these matters. One cannot acknowledge one fundamental right over another in a categorical manner. In this particular case I guess the human rights "won" over fundamental freedoms in the ECJ's view.

11.2.2 Case F-46/09: Judgment of the Civil Service Tribunal (First Chamber)

Document Date: 5 July 2011.
Application date: 05.10.2009
Form: Judicial information

---

[22] Out-Law.com. Identifying people on-line violates Data Protection laws, says European Court. Available at: http://www.out-law.com/page-4051.
[23] Tzanou (2012).

11.2.2.1 Parties

<u>Applicant</u>: V (Brussels, Belgium) (represented by: É. Boigelot and S. Woog, lawyers)

<u>Defendant</u>: European Parliament (represented by: K. Zejdová and S. Seyr, agents)

<u>Intervener in support of the applicant</u>: European Data Protection Supervisor (represented by M. V. Pérez Asinari and H. Kranenborg, agents)

11.2.2.2 Background Information

On February 27, 2006, the applicant was informed that he was successful on the selection tests for contract staff, called CAST 25 (for the 25 Member States in the secretarial field). His name has therefore been included in the database for the European Personnel Selection Office (EPSO) of successful candidates, whose validity was 3 years.

On June 2006, two DGs of the Commission expressed their intention to hire the applicant.

The applicant was called for a medical examination in order to assess its ability to exercise his function in accordance with Article 83 of the CEOS.

On 26 June 2006, the employment medical examination was held in the premises of the medical service of the Commission in Brussels (Belgium) and the applicant was examined by Dr. K.

On June 29, 2006, the applicant sent an email to MF, chief medical officer of the Commission complaining about the inappropriate behavior would have had Dr. K. towards him during the medical examination. Mr. MF. heard about this complaint in July 2006, and subsequently heard also Dr. K., who has denied the alleged facts against him.

Despite the absence of evidence regarding the allegations to Dr. K., it was decided to entrust the handling of the applicant's case to another doctor.

On September 26, 2006, the medical officer of the Commission issued a medical notice that find the applicant physical unfit.

On November 9, 2006, Mrs. S, Director in the Directorate General (DG) 'Personnel and Administration, "informed the applicant that he did not meet the physical fitness required to perform of his duties and informing him also about the possibility within 20 days to request a review of a medical board, in accordance with Article 33, second paragraph of the statute. On November 18, 2006, the applicant requested the review of a medical board. The medical board's opinion as of April 17, 2007, jointly adopted by its three members, said, after reviewing all the evidence, that the applicant does not have the skills required for the performance of his duties."

On May 15, 2007, the Commission officially informed the applicant that he does not physically fit the requirements for the exercise of his duties.

In the second part of 2008, the Applicant received a job offer as a contract agent function group II from the General Secretariat of the EU Parliament, from February 2 to August 2, 2009.

For this reason, the medical service of the Parliament sought disclosure (recorded on a note of December 9, 2008) of the applicant's medical records handled previously by the Commission.

The Parliament sent a letter to the applicant where it was stated that the offer is valid subject to the conditions of compliance with Article 82 of the CEOS and the positive outcome of the employment medical examination.

The applicant was also invited to send by fax, within a maximum of 2 weeks, the necessary documents, especially a certified copy of the original certificates of all previous employers.

On December 10, 2008, the applicant was scheduled for the employment medical examination (January 7, 2009).

On December 12, 2008, the applicant, on its own initiative, presented to the Leopold Park Clinic in Brussels to carry out blood tests. On December 12, 2008, the medical service of the Parliament received from the Commission a copy of the applicant's hiring medical record.

On December 18, 2008, the medical officer of the Parliament, after consulting the information provided by the Commission (on December 12), concluded that the applicant is physically unable to exercise "all functions in all the European Institutions." This notice is entitled "Results of medical examination of 26 June 2006 made by the Commission in Brussels" where the applicant was found unfit by the medical officer of the Commission.

On 19 December 2008, the Parliament informed the applicant that he is found medically unfit and withdrew the job offer, which was submitted on 10 December 2008.

With the same occasion, the Parliament reminded to the applicant that he had the obligation to report any other recruitment medical examinations conducted in the past with another Institution in order to facilitate the recruitment and allow the transfer of medical records held by the Institution concerned. Secondly, the Parliament stated that it had obtained the transfer of medical records of the applicant held by the Commission, knowing that he had previously worked for the Institutions.

11.2.2.3 The Case

The Applicant brought this action seeking, primarily, to cancel the decision of 19 December 2008 by which the European Parliament has withdrawn the job offer that had been presented on 10 December 2008, based on the opinion of the medical officer from the Parliament dated December 18, 2008, and secondly, seeking compensation for damages.

For sustaining his case, the applicant raises the following arguments:The opinion of the Parliament's medical officer is subjective as it is based on the documents from the Commission's medical service, dating from almost 2 years back and without any prior clinical and psychological examination of the applicant;

Secondly, he considerers that the Article 33, second paragraph, of the Conditions of Employment along with the rights to defense, were infringed as the contested decision was adopted without the applicant's right to defense or make himself heard;

Thirdly, he considered that the principle with regards to respect for privacy and private life were infringed along with the provisions of Regulation No 45/2001;

Last but not least, he identifies the existence of moral harassment.

11.2.2.4 Applicable Legislation

Article 82, paragraph 3 of the Conditions for Employment of Other Servants in the European Union;

Article 33, second paragraph of the Statute for the European Union Officials; and

Article 1, paragraph 1, and Articles 4, 6, 7, 10 Regulation (EC) No 45/2001 of the European Parliament and the Council of 18 December 2000 on the protection of individuals with regard to the processing of personal data by institutions.

11.2.2.5 Findings (Regarding the Applicant's Four Arguments)

The Court finds that the Parliament medical officer's opinion is expressed in a categorical but general terms, without examining the applicant as part of the hiring medical procedure of the Parliament and relayed just on medical tests done almost 2 years before by another Institution.

The breach of a procedural rule, including the principle of respect for the rights of defense, is likely to invalidate the decision itself to the extent that such breach has affected the content of the final decision. In this particular case the Parliament's medical examiner should have had invited the applicant and at least discussed the previous tests' result if not accepting the new one voluntarily taken by the applicant with the Leopold Clinic, but never assessed by the Parliament. Subsequently, the plea alleging infringement of Article 33, second paragraph of the statute, must also be accepted.

At the outset, it should be noted that Article 1 of Regulation No 45/2001 expressly provides that the institutions and bodies of the European Union shall ensure, in accordance with that regulation, the protection of fundamental rights and freedoms of individuals. Also, the provisions of this regulation shall not be interpreted as conferring legitimacy on an interference with the right to respect for private life as guaranteed by Article 8 ECHR.

As rightly pointed out by the applicant, the Parliament can contentious claim that the transfer would be legally based on the Article 10, paragraph 3 of Regulation No 45/2001. While this section empowers the members of the medical service of an institution to process the data necessary for the diagnosis of medical fitness of a person to exercise his functions, it has neither the purpose nor the effect of authorize a transfer of medical data such as challenged in this litigation, even if it is done between members of the medical services of the two institutions.

With regard to the Article 7 of Regulation No 45/2001, it must be noted, as rightly submitted by the applicant, that a transfer is not considered necessary within the meaning of Article 10 of this Regulation.

Moreover, it is true that the transfer at issue was made to put the Parliament in a position to check the physical fitness of the applicant to exercise his duties in this institution, obligation under articles 82 and 83 of the CEOS that can be analyzed as an "obligation in employment law" within the meaning of Article 10, paragraph 2 b) of Regulation no 45/2001, but was not established first that the transfer was "necessary" to meet this obligation. As pointed out by the EDPS, other less intrusive measures to privacy could be envisaged, allowing Parliament to ensure full implementation of Articles 82 and 83 of the CEOS. The Parliament could have particularly invited the applicant to provide certain information about his medical history and to perform medical examinations required by its own services, before asking the Commission to transfer the data. In addition, the relatively old data transferred, collected in 2006 and 2007, more than a year and a half before the contested decision, does not support the Parliament's thesis that this transfer would have been necessary, and opposes to the data quality requirements as laid down under Article 4, regulation 45/2001.

However, it is undisputed that the applicant has not consented to the transfer of the medical data from the Commission to the Parliament.

Furthermore, with regard to Article 10 of Regulation No 45/2001, it should be noted that under paragraph 1 of this Article, the processing of medical data is, in principle, prohibited. Paragraph 2 of Article 10 provides that paragraph 1 shall not apply if the person gives consent to processing or if processing is necessary to meet the obligations and specific rights of the controller in the labour field.

The Article 6 of Regulation No 45/2001, states that a change in the purpose of the collected data is permitted if expressly provided by the internal rules of the institution. In this case the change in the purpose for which the applicant's medical data were collected in 2006 and 2007 by the Commission is under no internal rule of either the Commission or the Parliament. The transfer of such data between the institutions involved is based on only a simple practice, but not on internal rules of those institutions In addition, the EDPS argued at the hearing that Article 27 of Regulation No 45/2001 requires a prior check notification if the Parliament seeks the transfer of medical data regarding a job applicant, notification that has never been issued.

However, as rightly pointed out by the EDPS in its intervention statement, the previous Court's findings do not establish that the disputed transfer of the applicant's medical data it would comply with the provisions of Regulation No. 45/2001. Indeed, the transfer must be "necessary" for the legitimate performance of tasks of the institution. In this dispute, it must first be established that the transfer was essential for assessing the fitness of the applicant by the Office of the Parliament. Secondly, the Article 7 of the Regulation expressly provides that it applies "without prejudice to Articles 4, 5, 6 and 10" of the same text.

The Article 4, paragraph 1 of this Regulation, requires that personal data must be processed fairly and lawfully, collected for specified, explicit and legitimate purposes and not further processed in a manner incompatible with those purposes. In addition, Article 6 of that Regulation provides that personal data cannot be processed for purposes other than those for which it was collected if the change of purpose is not expressly permitted by the internal rules of the EU institution.

In this case, as correctly contended by the applicant and EDPS, it is undisputed that the medical data collected by the Commission regarding the applicant, as part of the recruitment medical examinations under the provisions of Article 83 of the CEOS, had as exclusive purpose to determine whether the applicant was at the time of his recruitment, physically fit to perform his duties in the Commission services.

It should also be noted, that further processing of medical data necessary to establish the ability of the applicant to perform his employment functions with the Parliament (in December 2008), has another purpose than that for which the data were originally collected in 2006 (by the Commission). The Parliament can not properly rely on the assumption that the medical examinations carried out by all institutions would be based on the same legal basis, nor that they would be conducted in the same manner and be based on the same criteria of competence.

In this case, the various illegalities committed by the Parliament, especially the right to respect for private life and the Regulation No 45/2001 breaches, are sufficient enough to justify the award of compensation for the applicant's suffering and humiliation. The applicant is not entirely morally compensated by the cancellation of the contested decision. A fair assessment of the damage, especially in view of the seriousness of the illegality and their consequences, could indicate a moral compensation of 20,000 euros.

The Parliament is ordered to pay the applicant the sum of 25,000 euros in respect of pecuniary and moral injury suffered, all including interest.

11.2.2.6 Judgment

The Tribunal:

Annuls the decision of 19 December 2008 whereby the European Parliament withdrew the offer of employment made to V;

Orders the European Parliament to pay V the sum of EUR 25 000;

Dismisses the action for the remainder;

Orders the European Parliament to pay the applicant's costs and to bear its own costs; and

Orders the European Data Protection Supervisor, as intervener, to bear its own costs.

Conclusion

The scope of analyzing these two representatives case law is to present that in both private sector and the public sector, regulated by two different but very similar legal acts, the right to privacy and data protection is a tangible, not abstract anymore right granted to the individuals. Both decisions are considered as landmark decisions as they set forth the precedent for future issues in the filed of protection of personal data infringement.

The scope of this chapter to concretely present what personal data is in the view of EU regulators and how this could practically be enforced has been reached.

The interpretation of these two rulings aims to be as a guideline for National Courts, scholars or practitioners in the field of privacy and data protection. Concretely, the right to data protection either in the private sector or the public one, is enforceable and the breach of this right can be costly for an organization, private person or public body.

These two cases were not randomly chosen but very carefully being the one of their kind at the time of ruling. *Bodil Lindqvist* is the first case when a fine was applied to a private person for infringing the right to data protection and the *Case F-46/09* is the first one when a EU Institution or Body is fined for infringing the right of individuals with regards to data protection.

References

Council of Europe. The European Convention on Human Rights 1950.

Case C-101/01 Bodil Lindqvist v Åklagarkammaren i Jönköping – reference to the ECJ under Article 234 of the Treaty by Götta Hovrätten (Sweden) for a preliminary ruling in the criminal proceedings before that court against Bodil Lidqvist.

Tzanou M (2012) Can the balancing of fundamental rights affect fundamental freedoms? Some reflections on recent ECJ case-law on data protection. http://www.pravo.unizg.hr/_download/repository/Maria_Tzanou.pdf. Accessed 2 June 2012

Out-Law.com. Identifying people on-line violates Data Protection laws, says European Court. Available at: http://www.out-law.com/page-4051

De Hert P, Gutwirth S (2009) Data protection in the case law of Strasbourg and Luxemburg: constitutionalisation in action. Reinventing Data Protection? In: Gutwirth S, Poullet Y, De Hert P, Nouwt J, De Terwangne C (eds). Springer, pp 3–44. Available at: http://works.bepress.com/serge_gutwirth/10http://works.bepress.com/serge_gutwirth/10/

The Charter of Fundamental Rights of the European Union 2000.

The Treaty on the Functioning of the European Union. Treaty of Lisbon 2007.

Data Protection Audit: The German Experience

12

Philipp E. Fischer

> *We always take these audit findings seriously. We are always looking to improve.*
> (Steve Pierce, President of the Arizona State Senate since 10th November 2011 to date)

Abstract

As prelude, this chapter touches on definition and indicators of a Data Protection Audit. It will then describe its legal and technical prerequisites such as auditor competence, requirements of the law, requirements of ISO standards and best practice catalogs. The next sections examine the objectives of a Data Protection Audit within the corporate development and subsequently the conception of a Data Protection Audit. The final and main section draws the attention on what I named as: "Practical Guide"—that is, how to manage a Data Protection Audit "step-by-step".

12.1 Introduction

A Data Protection Audit (DPA) is a tool for data protection, which includes elements of self-regulation and competition and complements the regulatory approach to privacy: Through the possibility to advertise its data protection efforts, the data processor can be motivated to voluntarily establish a data protection management (DPM), which continuously contributes to the improvement of data protection. The DPA is a response to the increased awareness of privacy within the processing of personal data. Data protection has recently been recognized as a crucial factor for acceptance of all forms of electronic commerce and electronic government.

P.E. Fischer (✉)
SuiGeneris Consulting, Gernotstr. 4, Munich 80804, Germany
e-mail: pfischer@suigeneris-consulting.com

12.2 Indicators for a DPA

A DPA should be carried out for practical value of the data processor and not cause time burdens. Through a DPA, for example, the image of the data processor in the eyes of the citizens and especially the users can be permanently increased. However, the corresponding processor should have sufficient qualified staff in order to fulfill the necessary steps during the audit process. The DPA aims to promote "privacy-friendly" products and services (internal/external), while their data protection concept is tested and evaluated.

Various interests of the company can represent indicators for a DPA. One of these is an increased legal certainty in relation to the data protection authorities, courts, affected person and the works council. On the other hand such an audit is incentive for internal improvements to strengthen self-responsibility, competitive advantage, reducing the enforcement deficit, improving quality and reducing time and costs. Also, the positive public image of the company (increased confidence in the company) may be an important factor.

12.3 Requirements for a DPA

12.3.1 Auditor Competence

Any organisation that carries out DPA's should determine in advance, which qualifications the auditors must have. The determined level of competence must be documented appropriately within the management system and for the audit program.

12.3.1.1 General Skills
The "generic skills" include aspects such as:
- Audit implementation skills, e.g. Audit principles, audit procedures, audit techniques;
- Methodological skills, e.g. fundamentals of statistical methods, principles of test planning and testing, process control, performance measurement systems;
- Management system and—reference documents, for example document management, retention periods; and
- Interviewing skills, e.g. communication and behavior rules.

12.3.1.2 Subject-Specific Skills
The subject-specific knowledge depends on the type of audit (system audit, process audit, product audit, etc.), the derived audit criteria and the corporate sector (service providers, manufacturing, high tech products, etc.). Knowledge of company-specific management system is necessary. Management systems are always customised to the individual needs of businesses. It is therefore imperative that the auditors consider the requirements of the management system only in connection with the company that uses this system.

12.3.1.3 Education
An auditor should complete an education that allows a sufficient amount to acquire the knowledge and skills.

12.3.1.4 Work Experience
An auditor should have work experience in a technical, managerial or professional capacity. Within these, judgment, problem solving and communication skills (with other management staff or with colleagues, clients or other interested parties) are required.

12.3.1.5 Training
An auditor should have attended a training for auditors, which contributes to the development of the necessary knowledge and skills for implementing the audit.

12.3.1.6 Audit Experience
An Auditor for important audits should have gained audit experience before. This experience should extend to the entire audit process and should have been acquired under the supervision and guidance of an audit team leader working in the same field.

12.3.1.7 Personal Qualities
The personal qualities of the auditor are the basic skills to plan internal audits and to purposeful conduct them. Optimally, the auditors should be able to demonstrate the following personal characteristics (Table 12.1):

In addition, auditors should be open and receptive towards their environment to be audited, as well as possess maturity and a sound judgment. These personal characteristics are also linked to leadership skills. Thus it makes sense and is helpful if the auditor has work experience in leadership roles and knows how to move through circles of tension.

12.3.1.8 Maintenance and Improvement of Auditor Competence
Laws, standards, regulations, technologies and business processes are constantly evolving and adapted. Therefore, auditors also must maintain and develop their skills continuously. Measures are the participation in events such as internal/external training courses, seminars, etc.

Another reasonable way is an exchange of experience between auditors of different organizational units or locations where different themes, experiences and new developments should be discussed. New approaches or solutions can be developed for example in small workshops.

In smaller companies, the use of external consultants to conduct internal audits has often been proved. The conditions for the fulfillment of the duties of an external auditor can be generally assumed, while smaller companies have often failed to find a qualified internal auditor who can firstly demonstrate independence regarding the audited areas and secondly maintains and develops his qualifications.

Thus, in order to have auditors always at a high skill level, a process of continuous development and regular assessment of the auditors should be—in the

Table 12.1 Personal characteristics of an auditor

Professional ethics	The work of an auditor should comply with professional ethics. This includes good points such as impartiality, truthfulness, sincerity, honesty and discretion
Open-mindedness	Openness means being willing to consider alternative ideas or points of view
Diplomacy	Auditors should be tactful in dealing with people
Attention	Attention means for the auditor to be constantly aware of physical surroundings and activities
Fast intellectual grasp	Auditors should instinctively understand situations and can capture
Versatility	Versatility means to be able to adapt to different situations
Persistence	Auditors should be focused on persevering and achieving goals
Ability to make decisions	Decision-making means to draw conclusions by reasoning on time and on the basis of analysis
Self-confidence	Auditors act, and act independently and yet work effectively with others

best case—implemented in the management system. This can be done in the form of a process description, within which the responsible person responsible for the qualification and evaluation of the auditors is specified. Another possibility is to define the criteria in job descriptions as well as in employment contracts.

12.3.2 Requirements of the Law

12.3.2.1 Current Legislation

§ 9a BDSG[1] provides the possibility of a DPA, without detailed clarification of the requirements:

> In order to improve data protection and data security, suppliers of data processing systems and programs, and bodies conducting data processing may have independent and approved experts examine and evaluate their data protection strategy and their technical facilities and may publish the results of this examination. The detailed requirements pertaining to examination and evaluation, the procedure and the selection and approval of experts shall be covered in a separate law.

Thus, § 9a BDSG doesn't provide explicitly the possibility of a DPA, because the implementing regulations have yet to be regulated by law. It applies at the federal level, therefore, still the principle of voluntariness. Politically, however, the discussion of the "if" of a DPA, has already come to a positive end and the legislator already set a goal and indicated the manner of its fulfillment.

The wording of § 9a BDSG represents a compromise between the interests involved in its creation and therefore had some political ties effects. Through a

---

[1] Federal Data Protection Act ("Bundesdatenschutzgesetz" or "BDSG" - as of 1 September 2009), http://www.bfdi.bund.de/EN/DataProtectionActs/Artikel/BDSG_idFv01092009.pdf?__blob=publicationFile. Accessed 1 June 2012.

correct interpretation of that provision, it may also be an appropriate starting point for the implementation of the concept of a DPA.

§ 9a BDSG has two addressees and two subject areas. What matters at this point is the difference between technical institutions and data protection strategies, because the audit then requires very different approaches: for technical institutions a product audit; and for data protection schemes to be implemented by a data protection management a system audit. Therefore, the implementation of §9a BDSG would have to pursue two different strategies: the regulation of a product audit and the regulation of a system audit.

These two audit forms have to be assigned to the different target groups. The provider of data processing systems and -programs offer technical equipment that can be checked in a product audit in the way of their contribution to the improvement of data protection. For data processing bodies, it cannot be excluded right from the beginning, but it can be estimated as a rather rare case, that they also develop technical facilities as a product they want to be audited. Personal information is in fact processed by the data-processing bodies, for which a data protection strategy, that can be verified in a system audit, is crucial. But also the providers of data processing systems and programs may have designed a data protection concept for their technical facilities. As this concept in the end is implemented into the technical product, the whole data protection concept will be evaluated within a product audit and not in a separate system audit.

12.3.2.2 Future Legislation: DPA Act

The DPA Act was a proposed law with the intention that providers of hardware and software for data processing can carry out DPA's of their own data protection concepts and related technical equipment. This should be done through an evaluation and subsequent certification. Subject of the test should be whether the particular concept and the technical requirements of the provider are consistent with the applicable data protection laws in Germany. Such an assessment and certification should be done on a voluntary basis. On 3 July 2009 the German Bundestag decided for various reasons, however, not to adopt the DPA Act.

It was therein initially agreed that the different critics against the proposed Act were right:
- Not necessary but costly;
- From the formal voluntarism may arise in the private sector for competitive reasons, a de facto compulsory;
- Escapes the position of the Data Protection Officer (DPO);
- Unnecessary sixth "pillar": and
  - DPO
  - Works council
  - Data Protection Authority
  - Federal Commissioner for Data Protection
  - Courts
- Legal effect of an audit is not clear.

Until the adoption of the Data Protection Act to audit at a federal level, the normative force of facts has to be taken into account anyway. This means that data protection is now seen as a sign of quality. An Example lies in the quality management (ISO 9001). A legal provision, addressing the DPA will remain strictly necessary, because the rules, the selection and approval of the auditors are of career-limiting nature and are therefore subjected to the constitutional reservation of a Federal Act.

12.3.3 Requirements of ISO Standards

12.3.3.1 ISO 9001
The ISO 9001 demands, in addition to the assumed independence and objectivity of the auditors, in very general terms a documented procedure for the determination of responsibility and requirements for planning and conducting audits. This means that each organization has a high degree of freedom in their definition of the qualification criteria for internal auditors. Both internal and external auditors are addressed with great expectations. They must have a high degree of social, methodological and technical expertise. Requirements for auditors are stated in the ISO 19011 (see below).

12.3.3.2 ISO 19011
ISO 19011 provides guidance for successful planning and implementation of an internal audit in the company. ISO 19011:2002 is a general guide which aims to ensure that the audit is performed by a quality management (QM) system according to a specified sequence diagram. In essence, it provides guidance for the management of audit programs, the conduction of internal and external quality QM system audits as well as the qualification and evaluation of auditors.

A look at the contents of ISO 19011:2002 shows that this standard applies not only to QM systems, but is also a generally accepted standard for the audit process, the same for other audits, such as an external audit.

12.3.3.3 ISO 27001
ISO 27001 forces the organization to conduct internal audits at regular intervals. An appropriate audit program must be planned. While its implementation it has to be determined whether the measure objectives, policies, processes and procedures of the Information Security Management System (ISMS):
- Meets the requirements of this International Standard and the relevant statutory - and official regulations;
- Meets the identified standards of information security;
- Is effectively implemented and maintained and
- Is carried out according to the expectations.

An audit program shall be planned and the status and the importance of the processes to be audited as well as the areas and the results of previous audits taken into account. Criteria, scope, frequency and methods of audits shall be specified.

The selection of auditors and conduct of audits shall ensure objectivity and impartiality of the audit process. Auditors shall not audit their own activities. The officers and requirements for planning and conducting audits, and reports of the results and record keeping must be defined in a documented procedure. The responsible management for ensuring the area being audited shall ensure that measures to eliminate detected nonconformities and their causes are taken without undue delay. Follow-up activities shall include the verification of the actions taken and the report on the results of this verification.

ISO 9001 has significantly affected ISO 27001, thus ISO 27001 follows the principles of QM, as laid down in ISO 9001. This affects not only the principles of "continuous improvement" and "process-oriented approach", which form the methodological basis of management systems. Also the other principles are reflected, sometimes more, sometimes less explicitly, within ISO 27001. Many requirements in ISO 27001, which do not deal with specific aspects of information security are therefore very similar to requirements of ISO 9001. Especially for the implementation of such issues in an ISM, it is worthwhile to take a look at ISO 9001. Does an organization, that wants to implement an ISMS according to ISO build 27000, already own a certification of the ISO 9000 group, it has already given proof of an essential foundation and can meet many requirements of the ISO 27001 by using the existing QM. This is of course dependent on the degree to which the application fields of management systems do overlap.

12.3.4 Requirements of Best Practice Catalogs

Checklists of the Federal Office for Information Security ("Bundesamt für Sicherheit in der Informationstechnik" or "BSI")[2] shall be used in practice. Only if the target-performance comparison is clear, it is possible to take specific measures to achieve the desired target. The target state used in the audit must then coincide with the BSI basic protection catalog. This catalog, worked out by a working group of national supervisory authorities, represents a challenge for any data protection organization, so that a significant difference between target and performance will probably have to be assumed during the first audit.

The present method of the BSI allows the DPO without special knowledge regarding a DPA to create a strategic data protection management until a state, which can stand up to an assessment by an external auditor or a supervisor authority. Along the way, the tool measures the progress and helps to take—systematically coordinated—the necessary steps. The method is based on a total of 15 measures. The term "measure" will appear first questionable, because measures usually are only at the end of an audit, if it is clear what to do. Thus, this term has to be understood as that these 15 measures, if they all are

---

[2] https://www.bsi.bund.de/EN/TheBSI/thebsi_node.html.

implemented, are capable of achieving BSI basic protection. To determine whether a measure can be considered implemented, control questions (yes/no) shall be asked, while the answer depends on the meaningfulness of the audit. A question has to be answered "yes" only when it is actually fully met.

12.4 Objectives of a DPA

The DPA should focus on four key objectives within the corporate development:

12.4.1 Strengthening of Self-responsibility and Stimulation of Competition

The DPA should primarily be a suitable instrument to demand the personal responsibility of the data processor for data protection. Privacy is becoming an increasingly important quality feature for applications in information and communication technologies, which is understood as a competitive advantage. The DPA should enable a verifiable way to advertise data protection and data security. To ensure a high level of data, a DPM should be implemented. Its periodic review and improvement will be secured through legal rules of procedure. For the data processor it is crucial that the DPA adapts to the peculiarities of his company and opens options, to use a positive outcome of the DPA review for communication with the public and to advertise it. The DPA shall reward the data processors, which take privacy concerns into account when designing their products, and aim to give market-driven incentives for all competitors to do so as well.

12.4.2 Reduction of the Enforcement Deficit

In data protection law, there is a considerable lack of enforcement. The DPO and the supervisory authorities are overwhelmed by the global networking and the ubiquitous use of information and communication technologies. It should be the aim of a DPA to minimize these impacts. Together with the incentive for self-control created by a DPA, the deficits in compliance with applicable data protection law could be reduced. A DPA establishes new forms and instances of data protection control, by providing internal control procedures that involve external consultants and by publishing critical information to the public, which then receives control and evaluation possibilities. Since the DPA has different requirements and consequences than the official data protection control by the supervisory authorities, it can very well be a supplement, and not a replacement

12.4.3 Continuous Improvement of Data Protection and Data Security

The main objective of the DPA should be the continuous improvement of data protection and data security. Before the establishment of the DPA there were no incentives for the data processor to take its own efforts to improve data protection and data security. The DPA enables to document such efforts, to examine and award prizes, and thus creates a market incentive. It should therefore not be limited only to check the compliance with data protection laws; to meet them is required anyway.

12.4.4 DPA as a Learning System

The DPA can reach the goal of continuous improvement only if it is seen as a learning system. The regulatory focus should be on the standardization of a "learning process" within a DPM. This learning process is structured by the fact that the data processor creates a comprehensive audit to take stock of the processing of personal data and therefore compiles the relevant requirements of the data protection laws. The mere fact of an initiated multiplication and dissemination of knowledge about the organisational, technical and legal frameworks, which are involved in data processing, represents a success as such. The findings of this survey then slip into the DPM as well as positive and negative experiences with the implementation of existing data protection measures, which determine the next steps for improvement.

12.5 Conception of a DPA

Before starting the audit process, the audit objectives must be brought into a concept (Fig. 12.1).

12.5.1 Internal Corporate Requirements

In the broadest sense, the audit objectives are derived from the strategic business objectives. It is important that the defined audit objectives and the subsequent audit plans do not represent isolated solutions, but are derived from corporate strategies and relate to each other.

Management systems are basically company-specific structures that are designed to meet strategic business objectives. In order to operate these management systems effectively and efficiently, numerous interrelated processes have to be defined and controlled. Audits are a method to investigate the effectiveness of this structure as a whole or within certain areas.

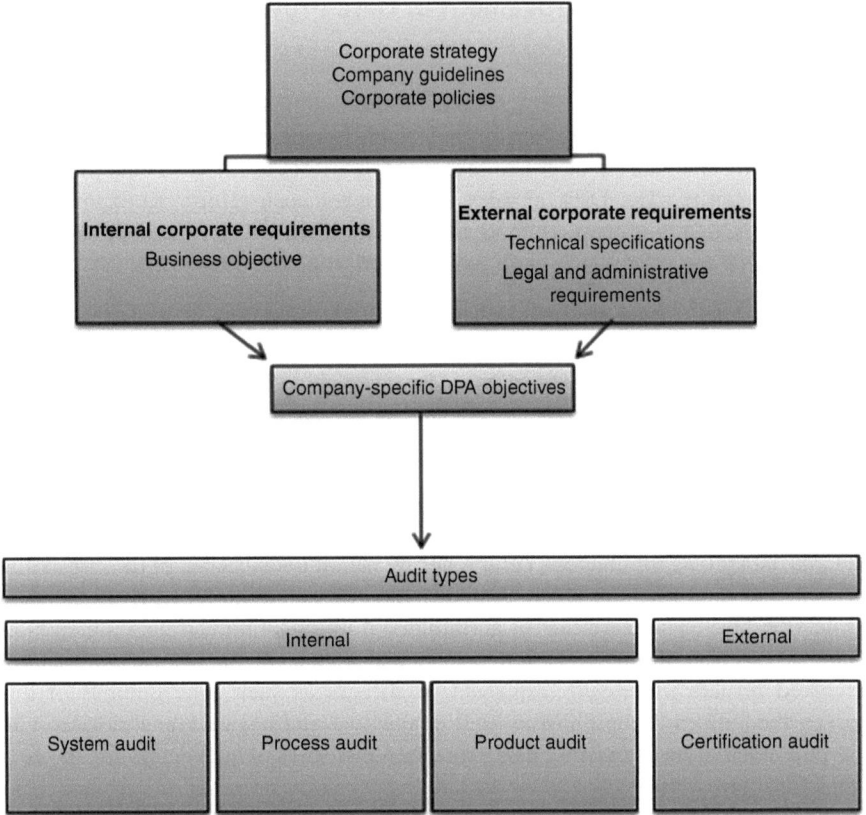

Fig. 12.1 Audit objectives

12.5.2 External Corporate Requirements

Audit objectives are not only determined by internal corporate (strategic) planning, but also by external corporate requirements:
- Requirements arising from standards or technical specifications provided by voluntary compliance of the companies: Maybe these system requirements are also audited by accredited certification bodies (Surveillance audit) and certified (Certification audit);
- Requirements resulting from statutory and regulatory provisions; and
- All other customer-specific requirements entailing internal audits and certification audits.

12.5.3 Audit Types

12.5.3.1 Overall Goals

The DPA objective influences the appropriate audit type. Objectives of higher priority that apply to all types of audits are

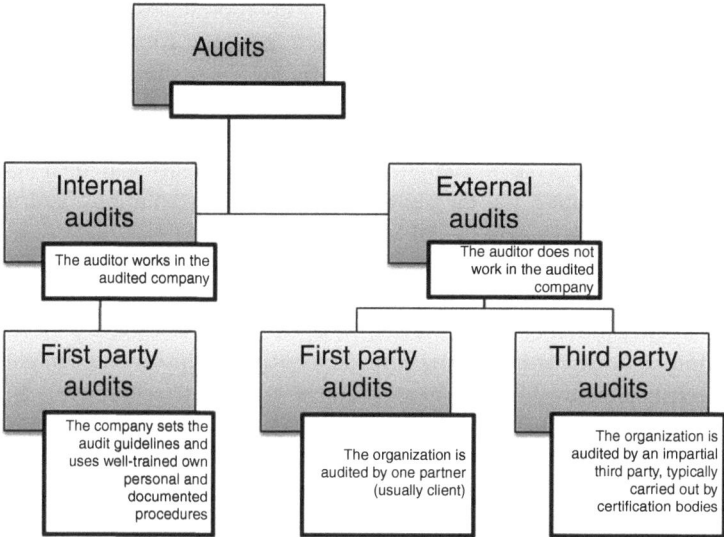

Fig. 12.2 Internal and external audits

- The improvement of actual conditions in companies;
- To provide evidence whether the proposed procedures and processes are still useful, efficient and economical; and
- Early identification of vulnerability or risk potential.

12.5.3.2 Internal/External

It has to be distinguished in principle:
- Internal audits are performed by skilled, experienced employees (DPO, employee of the revision department or of the QM department) of the audited organization itself ; and
- External audits by an independent authority (certificate authority, consulting firm) will be conducted by qualified auditors (Fig. 12.2).

12.5.3.3 Objects

The System audit is used to determine whether the whole system meets the requirements of the standard. Discrepancies or potential improvements shall be identified, and the derivation of corrections and improvements shall be passed to the head of the organization or its organizational entity.

A Process audit measures relevant processes and unstable processes for effectiveness and efficiency through assessment.

Product audits check the compliance with specified quality features/specifications and the functionality of the product. The aim is to determine a long-term quality trend.

Furthermore, there are vendor audits, which are of little significance within the framework of data protection.

Subject of a DPA is the effectiveness and appropriateness of the company's DPM. The DPA aims to use a resource that is not used for data protection yet, namely the possibility of a DPM. Accordingly, the DPA should be designed as a System audit, should be process-oriented and initiate a dynamic learning process. The DPA is not aimed at the one-time evaluation of a product, even though such may occur within a System audit (e.g. computer system) and then has to be integrated into the latter, but the ability to generate new solutions, and therefore to continuously improvement the DPM.

A Certification audit means the review and approval (certificate issue) of compliance with the standard requirements, technical specifications, as well as statutory and regulatory requirements. It is created on an external basis and is performed by a certification authority or consulting firm. Since the conditions and contents of the various certificates are not regulated within a DPA Act (see above), an almost unmanageable current market on certificates has been created.

12.5.3.4 Voluntariness

The DPA should be voluntary. For all those company representatives who have so far expressed their opinion on DPA, it is an essential prerequisite for the acceptance of the DPA. The voluntary nature could probably mean that companies might not take part in the proceedings, which consist of a large improvement regarding data processing. For a voluntary participation, however, speak mainly two reasons: First, a voluntary participation can be of a much larger space for the formulation of goals that are actually not reachable by all businesses in this specific situation. Second, a mandatory participation would be contrary to the scheme of this instrument, because the self-responsibility of the company would be weakened, not strengthened. In addition, the public will play a crucial role; the company should be forced to participate through market demands.

12.6   Practical Guide: DPA Step-by-Step

A DPA is an important tool within the so-called PDCA Cycle (Fig. 12.3):

As the audit objectives of the specific situation of a company are now set up and designed based on the corporate strategy, the audits can be prepared company-compliant. Careful planning and preparation is always the prerequisite for the success of an audit. Our steps to a better level of data protection in companies should include in the order below; our focus will particularly lie on the progress of a DPA within these 8 steps.
- Establish a data protection policy
- Inventory
- Establishment of a data protection project
- Implementation of the DPM
- Internal DPA
- Internal release
- External DPA
- Use for improvement and image advertising

12 Data Protection Audit: The German Experience

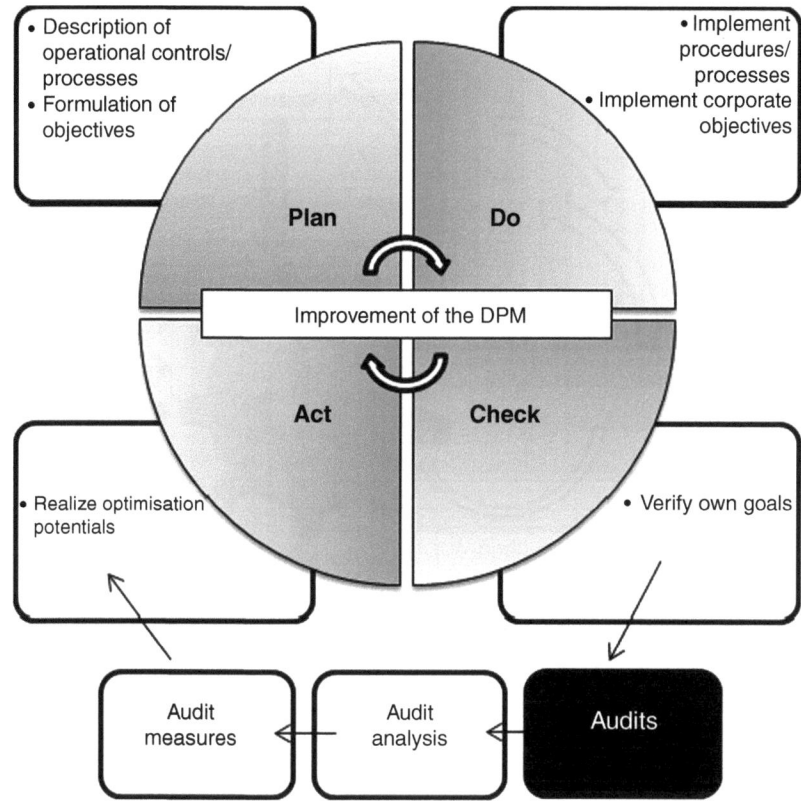

Fig. 12.3 Plan-Do-Check-Act cycle[3]

12.6.1 Planning

12.6.1.1 Elaborate a DPA Program
Definition (Fig. 12.4)
The implementation of the audit objectives is guided by a so-called audit program. An audit program is a compilation of audits and their aims carried out in the company within the next year. Audit programs may include one or more audits with different objectives and are performed separately or combined.

According to the audit objectives the audit criteria must be established: Regarding a system audit, the audit criteria can be e.g. standard requirements and the requirements of the internal management system (processes, procedures, work

---

[3] Based upon W. Edwards Deming. Deming proposed a four-step-process (plan-do-check-act), also known as the PDCA cycle. He believed that a successful quality improvement and management programme would follow the plan-do-check-act cycle of events (Deming 1985).

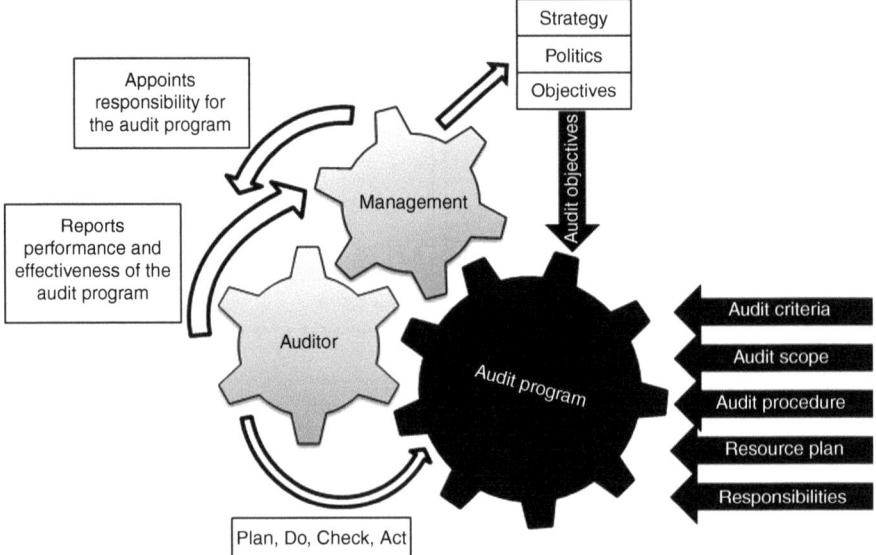

Fig. 12.4 DPA program

instructions, etc.); the criteria of a process audit may be the aims of a certain process and any customer's specifications with regard to process stability.

Within the audit program, the scope of the audit, responsibilities and the allocation of resources must be planned.

Contents of a DPA Program

The audit objectives are the basis for the derivation of the audit criteria. The audit criteria serve as a reference for the assessment and finding of conformity (or nonconformity). Audit criteria may for example be a chapter of the QM manual, a specific description of the process, laws or standards requirements.

Overall objectives of audit criteria are:
- Assessment of compliance of the management system to external requirements such as standards;
- Assess how the company's internal rules and regulations are complied with;
- Assess whether the corporate rules are effective and efficient; and
- Assess how government regulations and other external regulative are met.

The audit priorities are fixed in the audit program and can have different bases for decision. We distinguish the following four situations:
- Cross-functional business objectives as a basis for decision making;
- Specialised, task-related or other corporate objectives as a basis for decision making;
- Unplanned business objectives as a basis; and
- Corporate objectives, directly related to a process.

Table 12.2 Audit's main areas

Main area	Data	Procedure	Organization Persons
Processes	+ complete − repeated	+ complete	+ complete − repeated
Assignments	+ complete − repeated	+ complete − repeated	+ complete − repeated
Organization	+ complete − repeated	+ complete − repeated	+ complete + only once
Data	+ only once + "dead" data	− repeated	+ complete − repeated
Mixed	?	?	?

If, for example the aim is to offshore personal information into a Cloud solution, then it has to be examined, what data transfers and data processes in general take effect on data protection laws and regulations; a list of the interactions of the processes is then necessary, illustrating how they are related to each other and simultaneously illustrating the intensity with which they take effect one another.

The business objectives are practically the "starting point" for the calculation of the audit's main area and influences the way a DPA has to be carried out (complete/incomplete or once/repeated) (Table 12.2 and Fig. 12.5).

In the course of the audit program planning, the necessary resources must be identified and their availability be ensured. It should be taken into account not only financial resources for the development, implementation, control and improvement of audit programs but also the following aspects:

- Audit methods
- Procedures for maintaining the auditor qualification
- A process for improving the auditor's performance
- Availability of auditors in order to implement the audit objectives properly and professionally
- Time resources for the audit team and the employees, e.g. for the execution of audit questionnaires/interviews, etc.
- Resources for unscheduled audits; in addition to planned audits, there may be occasions that make the execution of extraordinary audits necessary; such events can for example be: change of organizational structures, increased customer complaints, introduction of new working practices, process changes, etc.

The structure of an organisation and the relationships and relative ranks of its parts and positions/jobs are of great importance. The auditor has to—at every step of the DPA—keep in mind the different responsibilities within the audited organisation.

Procedure for the Implementation of the DPA Program

The audit program procedure, which usually has an annual throughput cycle should regulate:

- Planning the audit scope
- Determining the allocation of tasks and responsibilities

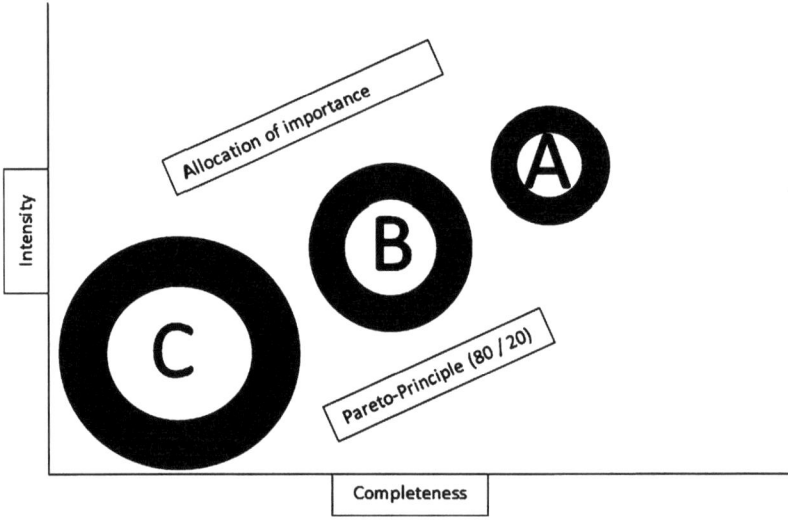

Fig. 12.5 Completeness and intensity of audits[4]

- Ensure the auditor qualifications
- Definition of audit criteria
- Resource planning
- Documentation of the audit findings (audit reports)
- Monitoring the performance of the audit program
- Development of reporting

The management must transfer the responsibility for the planning and implementation of the audit program to one or more employees. The staff should be suitably qualified (knowledge of audit techniques, general understanding of audit principles, necessary technical knowledge, etc.).

12.6.1.2 Elaborate, Approve, Publish and Announce a DPA Plan
Elaborate DPA Plan (Fig. 12.6 Chain Link #1)

First, a person responsible for the execution of the audit will be appointed as auditor, being responsible for the preparation of the audit. The appointment of the auditor is carried out by the management. Depending on the audit focus, an audit team, which possesses all the qualifications required for conducting the audit, must then be appointed. The size of the audit team is influenced by duration and scope of the audit.

---

[4] Based upon Joseph M. Juran, who suggested the principle and named it after Italian economist Vilfredo Pareto who noticed that 80 % of Italy's land was owned by 20 % of the population; gradually, the Pareto-Principle has been applied to other relationships and it is nowadays a common rule of thumb in business (Juran 1974).

12 Data Protection Audit: The German Experience

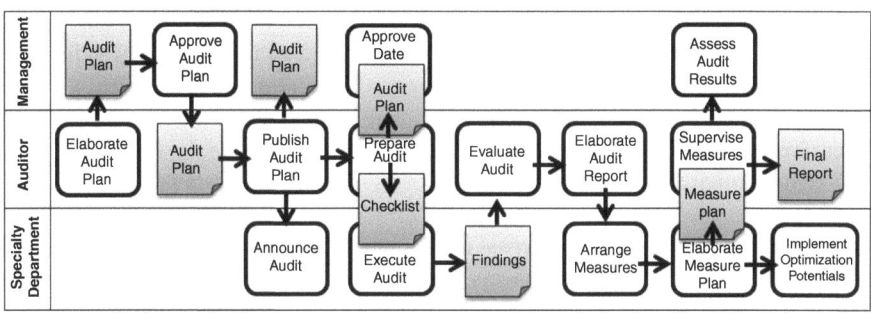

Fig. 12.6 Chain of the audit process

Another important step in the planning phase is the assessment of the relevant documents prior to the audit. Manuals, process descriptions, documents, records, work instructions, technical specifications, test reports, trend analysis, etc. have to be analyzed. It is a first compliance audit of the documentation with the audit criteria. This test also includes records of past audits (final audit report).

The preliminary examination of the documents contributes to determine whether the company's activities are adequately described in the processes and methods. This should answer the question whether the documentation is available, suitable and appropriate. The preliminary examination should be performed for all documents of the most important audit criteria. The results need to be logged. This protocol is then a useful tool for the audit. It contains information on priorities, which must be observed particularly during the audit.

In case of larger uncertainties or deficiencies in documentation, additional documents may be obtained from the respective department. If necessary, a first on-site tour (pre-audit) can be of great benefit. Through such a pre-audit can be decided whether an internal or a certification audit is possibly scheduled to early, as the audit criteria to be followed (e.g. statutory requirements) are still very poorly or not at all satisfied.

According to the audit criteria questions regarding the structure- and process organization, the processes at work, the relevant documents and records, compliance with standard requirements, customer requirements, internal or legal requirements have to be prepared in advance, compiling them in a checklist. Outstanding issues from the previously conducted document review should be incorporated as questions in the checklist.

A reasonable audit question list
- Takes into account all the standard requirements to be audited,
- Includes questions that serve to continually improve the processes,
- Serves as an audit record,
- Allows for additional questions,
- Is not only "yes/no"-oriented, and
- Not too bureaucratic.

An audit checklist can be created as follows:
- Identification of the individual claims from the text of the relevant standard
- Orientation to external audit checklists, e.g. certification of companies
- Development of additional questions that cover the situation in a work environment
- Verification of the developed audit questions regarding the relevance of installed systems

A checklist for conducting internal audits facilitates on the one hand a structured approach in which all relevant aspects can be evaluated step by step and shall—on the other hand—determine more precise expectant questions to actual problems.

It is important that the audit questions in each case meet the requirements of accuracy, accuracy, completeness and are constantly updated. The development of an audit checklist can be implemented as follows:
- Review of audit issues by the auditor before the audit or review of documents for pre-audit
- Review with the assistance of managers and professionals from the area to be audited
- Review of audit questions

The audit team leader is responsible for the preparation of the audit plan about 2–3 weeks prior to each audit. This plan contains
- Audit objective,
- Audit criteria with all reference documents,
- Audit scope (affected organizational units and processes),
- Dates, duration and type of audits, audit of the opening and final audit interview,
- Arrangements to maintain confidentiality.

Approve DPA Plan (Fig. 12.6 Chain Link #2)

For precise adjustment of the audit, I recommend scheduling a preliminary discussion between the lead auditor and the head of the audited organizational unit or the process owner. Here, the audit objective will be explained again in order to increase the understanding of the auditee. In addition, the resources needed for the audit are discussed on both sides and planned.

Publish (Fig. 12.6 Chain Link # 3) and Announce (Fig. 12.6 Chain Link #4) Audit Plan

Upon approval of the audit plan it should be published in a so-called "procedural instruction" to avoid later misunderstanding in communication. Timely notification of the audit dates and topics to all affected individuals is very important for the realization of a successful audit. No one should feel "overwhelmed". Possible questions can thus be resolved in time for the audit execution.

This procedural instruction
- Should comply with ISO 9001
- Regulates the planning, implementation, evaluation of DPAs, including the pursuit of improvement and corrective action

- What tasks must be carried out?
- What are the regulated responsibilities?
- What are the methods and procedures are used?
- What tools have to be applied?
- How and to whom the audit results must be communicated?
- How is the monitoring of improvement and corrective action?
- Is divided into sections of
  - Purpose
  - Scope
  - Other applicable documents (laws, regulations)
  - Terms and Definitions
  - Responsibilities
  - Audit plan
  - Audit implementation
  - Reporting
  - Monitoring of corrective action and change
  - Attachments

12.6.1.3 Approve Date

The exact time of the audit has to be approved by the head of the audited organizational unit or the process owner (Fig. 12.6 chain link #5). The audit is now completely prepared and ready for our next step, its execution (Fig. 12.6 chain link #6).

12.6.2 Execution

The execution of a DPA refers to Fig. 12.6 chain link #7.

12.6.2.1 Briefing

One of the most important prerequisites for successful auditing is employee acceptance for the implementation of this method. Employees may cover up anything, but the auditor should refer to vulnerabilities. Without the support of the staff high-quality audit findings cannot be made. In addition, it must necessarily be focused on the fact that audit findings might be distorted in some cases. When employees view audits as "control" or "search for a scapegoat", no objective statements are expected. For these reasons, employees should be informed (in advance of the audit and in due course) over the auditing process. This persuasion may be carried out through information sessions, staff training, or simply by personal interviews. The latter should include:

- Objectives of the DPA
- Extent, affected area, systems
- Procedures, methods, procedures, checklists, evaluation
- Required documents

12.6.2.2 Documents Review

Items
- Data protection strategy
- IT security policy
- Procedures and work instructions
- User manuals
- Organizational procedures
- Technical documentation
- Contracts with suppliers/customers
- Records of inquiries, complaints, corrective actions
- Previous audit reports

Procedure
- Review of recent DPAs
  - Problems encountered in the planning, implementation, evaluation
  - Implementation of control measures
  - Improving the potential for audit
  - Coverage/focus until the present
  - Coverage/focus in the future
- Review of the procedural instructions
  - If necessary: update
- Other material collection
  - Changes in the informational and communicational environment
  - Changes in organizational processes
  - Requests, problems, complaints
  - Current public procedure register
  - Statutory changes
  - In-plant modifications
  - Documentation for DPM

12.6.2.3 One-to-One Interviews

Employees should feel as an important partner and key knowledge holders during the audit execution. For this reason, procedure and conduct of the auditor should be directed accordingly. Auditors are moving in a very personal area of employees. They will face situations (deviations, errors) when they have to address problems that are often understood by the involved employees as a personal attack. It is therefore an important task for the auditor to recognize this behavior and to handle it with appropriate strategies. Auditors must receive prior training in basic communication and behavior rules.

Auditors should focus on factual correlations only. They should avoid emotional expressions in terms of problems that they have known outside the audit situation, which could lead to communication barriers. Communication barriers do block dialogs. Such behavior causes a limit within the employees' answers; or employees take an emotional defensive attitude that completely blocks further factual communication.

The main communication barriers can be mentioned:
- Arrange or command
- Warn or threaten
- Long-winded, monologue-like lectures
- Judge, criticize and blame
- Flatter and unwarranted praise
- Ridicule or shame
- Investigate or interrogate

Nevertheless, if the auditor observes a "defensive behavior", he must know what he can apply as a counter-strategy:
- Remain calm and objective: questioning the reason for the defensive behavior, because this must not necessarily have anything to do with the person of the auditor
- Await the auditee to finish talking: This is signaled patience and avoid a slugfest
- Ask another question: the auditor receives better starting points for his own arguments and can find out the circumstances for the true reason for the defensive behavior

It lies on the perception of the auditor to detect such situations and, at a respectful level, to respond

12.6.2.4 On-Site Inspection and Testing

A focus of the actual audit lies, in addition to the control of compliance with legal requirements and the comprehensive analysis of existing relevant documents and processes, on the review of the technical and organizational measures according to § 9 BDSG and the appendix to § 9 BDSG sentence 1.

The auditor should then examine at the spot, whether the policy of compulsory documents is properly implemented and maintained. During the on-site visits it should be carried out an extensive testing of
- Procedures, work instructions, guidelines
- Penetration Testing
- Internal security
- External security

12.6.3 Evaluation

The evaluation of a DPA refers to Fig. 12.6 chain link #8.

12.6.3.1 Verification of the Information

The collected information must now be verified. An incorrect interpretation of the facts must be avoided. Without a concrete proof in many cases no nonconformities can be found. Therefore, the information sources have to be verified, then compared and checked for plausibility.

12.6.3.2 Logging During the Audit
Audit records must be logged, e.g. through minutes of meetings, notes on the audit checklists including references to documents and records, etc. The Auditor must deal with a lot of information during the audit. Only if relevant information is collected and recorded the audit report can be elaborated detailed and credible. Even the subsequent derivation of corrective action should be based on an extensive pool of information. Basically, however, a precise tracking is required because general statements are no valuation basis.

12.6.3.3 Audit Findings
The audit evidence must now be compared with the audit criteria. The audit findings are either information about conformity or nonconformity ("deviation") in relation to audit criteria and audit objectives.

After determining a deviation (non-compliance) the auditor must necessarily clarify whether this is a random or systematic deviation.
- Random deviation: the specified standards are factually correct, but an error happened during execution; and
- Systematic deviation: the specified standards are factually incorrect. The scheduling and process planning has been done wrong and does not meet the audit criteria. Systematic deviations should be alarming to the auditor. They usually show that a system is not working properly and is ineffective. Systematic deviations from a certification audit can have such serious consequences that a re-audit must be scheduled.

12.6.3.4 Audit Evaluation
The evaluation of the audit shall be based on objective audit findings. To obtain information on the level of need for action for the nonconformance and the possibility of optimization potential, the evaluation should be very meaningful. Particular importance should be drawn at the non-conformities which have to be corrected within a reasonable time. The deviations can be categorized according to different priority levels. These priority levels must be established prior to the audit and consistently applied to periodic audits in order to get a correct comparison.

There are various possibilities to evaluate the audit findings (a combination of both is possible):
- The audit findings have been evaluated over a degree of performance;
- The audit findings have been evaluated according to their importance; and
- A combination of point 1 and point 2.

Evaluation by Performance Level
The degree of performance can be measured in several ways: via (a) scoring and (b) allocation of ratios.

Scoring
Determined for each audit finding, using the audit checklist, points are awarded. The number of points indicates the performance level of conformity. The scale of

points must be strictly adhered to, otherwise no comparisons are possible. The significance of the number of points should have been explained in the introductory discussion and will be documented in the audit report.

After scoring the degree of fulfillment of the individual QM elements is calculated (in percent) and the overall assessment of the audit leads to a classification of the audited company.

Allocation of Ratios

Every possible situation is declared using a ratio. The audit findings will be evaluated on the allocation of these ratios.

For the overall assessment of the audit criteria must be defined prior to the general evaluation, for example, via percentages. Also has to be clarified in advance exactly which audit issues may only be assessed with ratio number 1, in order to declare the audit as successful.

Rating on the Importance of the Audit Finding

As "critical", "heavy" or "major" deviation findings are called when a complete system element, or a significant portion of this element is scarce or is not satisfied, there are obvious dangers to personal data or breaches of regulatory requirements.

These non-conformities or defects can lead to significant disruptions in the processes and show that the management system is either not matched carefully to the needs of the practice or the acceptance and discipline of compliance is missing. These differences must therefore be corrected immediately.

Deviations that are rated as less critical, are referred to as "light" or "minor" deviation. An impact on the functioning of the management system or the labor and product quality cannot be excluded.

Combination of These Two Rating Scales

When the audit findings are evaluated in the first step towards the fulfillment of audit criteria, the significance of the deviation is determined. Both processing steps of this review shall be documented. This is a commonly used valuation method by certification bodies.

Crucial for a successful audit is that the evaluation scheme used in each case is systematic and continuous. This also applies to future audits. For companies or businesses with multiple locations, this is often not guaranteed for all internal audits. However, this can be implemented through consistent application of an audit which must be used by the internal auditors of any company or within the whole corporate network.

12.6.3.5 Audit Conclusions

Prior to the audit closing meeting, the audit team elaborates the audit conclusions. The focus lies on the summary evaluation of the audit findings towards the audit objective. For example, this review ends up with

- The question of whether a certificate may be issued or whether the number and quality of the deviations were too large (certification audit);
- The question if a management system is implemented effectively and continuously improved (system audit); and
- The question whether a process is effectively and efficiently (process audit).

In the derivation of all audit conclusions all identified issues and circumstances are taken into account—depending on the nature of the audit and the audit criteria usually some leeway can be used here.

At this step, the audit team prepares recommendations, such as how audit criteria can be met in the future and how the potential for optimization can be exploited. These recommendations are not necessarily directly related to internal regulations or standards, but they contribute to the improvement or maintenance of processes in the organization. Only in as "critical" assessed deviations concrete measures need to be made immediately ("immediate action").

12.6.3.6 Audit Closing Meeting

The final part of the on-site audit is an audit closing meeting. Here, in a defined group of participants, for example may consist of the introduction of the participants call, audit findings and conclusions from the auditor or audit team stated. Importance becomes the fact that the findings and conclusions are understood and acknowledged by the auditee unit. This is especially true for deviations.

It should be every attempt to reach a common understanding of the audit results. Differences of opinion should be discussed among the participants. If no consensus is found, this must be documented according to the audit report.

The audit closing meeting is very important because the areas audited should definitely get some feedback on the course. This approach increases the acceptance of the company.

12.6.4 Elaborate DPA Report

This step of a DPA refers to Fig. 12.6 chain link #9.

The DPA is completed with an audit report in which the actual state of data protection of the audited organization can be found.

- Documented:
  - Summary assessment of the company (in the area being audited) determined and practiced data protection management system
  - Individual assessments relating to data protection "issues"
  - Identification of deviations (risks)
  - recommendations for improvements
  - suggestions for optimizing future DPA
- Structure
  - Cover Sheet
  - Table of Contents
  - Executive Summary

Table 12.3 Assessment

Assessment	No. . . . . of. . . . .
Testing approach no.	. . . .
Deviation/recommendation	. . . .
Further procedure	. . . .
Executed measure	. . . .
Measure finalized on	. . . .
Measure reviewed by . . . on . . .	. . . .

- Laws, rules
- Audit scope and implementation
- Area 1 Results
- Area 2 results
- . . .
- Equipment: detailed reports on variances and recommendations for actions necessary planning dat
- Assessment (Table 12.3)
- Presentation
  - Presentation as part of a final meeting
  - Distribution written/electronic
  - Backup and Archiving
- Declaration of Conformity (Self Declaration) and Privacy Statement by Auditor

12.6.5 Corrections and Improvements Subsequent to the DPA

This step of a DPA refers to Fig. 12.6 chain links #10–12.

Careful preparation of improvement and corrective action is undertaken at a later date by the heads of the affected functional areas, departments and process owners. These can be based on the audit report that will be created after the audit closing meeting of the audit team/auditor. Corrections and improvements can concern:
- DPM System
  - Identification of reports of the DPA
  - Problem and Change messages on the fly
  - Requests, complaints
  - Changes in laws and regulations
  - Change the internal data protection policy
  - Changes in the company (structure, process, IT environment)
- Procedures for planning, implementation and evaluation of DPAs
- Procedural instructions
  Procedure of such corrections and improvements:
- Identification of corrective and improvement measures
- Assignment of implementation responsibilities
- Monitoring the implementation

Table 12.4 Perceptions

Today	Future
Privacy as a necessary evil	Privacy as an integral part of a corporate culture
Audit as a chore to attain a desired certificate	Standard proof of "compliance"
	Audit as an awareness activity
Certificate as an alibi	Award and certificate as a "flagship"
Privacy as a "troublesome" duty	Privacy as a competitive factor and a marketing tool

- Notification of completion of the Auditor
- Control
    No control
    Immediately after the completion message
    On occasion
    During the next audit

12.7 Excursus: Certification of DPM Systems

As noted above, the certification of a DPM system is based on a voluntary basis, as the BDSG still contains a discretionary provision and the Data Protection Audit Act is still not in place.

12.7.1 Motivation and Benefits

- Strengthening of self-responsibility and competition
- Reducing the enforcement deficit
- Continuous improvement of data protection and data security
- DPA as a learning system (Table 12.4)

12.7.2 Certificate Market

- Providers in Germany
    - ULD
    - TÜViT GmbH
    - UIMCert Ltd.
    - Quid! Process
    - Datenschutz Nord GmbH
    - TÜV Rheinland Group
    - DQS
    - DEKRA

- SCHUFA
- European Privacy Seal
- Customers
  - Authorities
  - Non-public entities

12.7.3 Certification Process

12.7.3.1 Seal

This is a product-oriented approach. It states e.g. that "privacy can be ensured with the tested products or the products are particularly suitable for this".

12.7.3.2 DPA

This is a process-oriented approach. Current audit reports state e.g. that "this certificate is to document that a company has taken measures to ensure the protection of personal data in accordance with the Federal Data Protection Act to ensure adequate and appropriate data protection management system is established".

References

Deming WE (1985) Out of the crisis. MIT Centre for Advanced Educational Services, Cambridge

Juran JM (ed) (1974) Quality control handbook, 3rd edn. McGraw-Hill, New York, pp 2-16–2-19

Concluding Remarks   13

Noriswadi Ismail and Edwin Lee Yong Cieh

> *As is a tale, so is life: not how long it is, but how good it is, is what matters*
> (J.K Rowling, excerpt from 2008 Harvard University Commencement speech, 5th June 2008)

You have now come to the end of this masterpiece. Although this is metaphorically the 'dessert' (concluding chapter), it does not mean you should pause exploring the ever-fascinating side of data protection. This is just a humble beginning for Malaysia, ASEAN and other Asian countries. Data protection is quite a complex subject matter, and a fairly new subject matter to many of these countries. Indeed, it will take some time to be comprehended and applied by the stakeholders.

On the other hand, the European, US and Asia-Pacific data protection development and experience is useful for Malaysia and ASEAN. We can learn from their best practices and experiences, which have been debated over, and practiced throughout, the last few decades. It is therefore pertinent that we should grasp the opportunities to understand the mechanisms of data protection, the implications arising from, and the challenges derived by, these countries' practical experience.

It's always the technology that pushes data protection reform. Owing to this, transborder data flow from one country to another is getting more sophisticated and complex. What tags along with the ease of transfer of data is the risk of losing the data, as evidenced by the many incidents where organisations have had their database compromised, resulting in the loss of huge number of their clients and employees' data. Many of these data losses were caused by lack of adequate security control and sustainable data protection governance. It's our wish and your wish that we do not want security breach to happen, ever. One should be

---

N. Ismail (✉)
Quotient Consulting, 29 Duffell House, Loughborough Street, London SE11 5PX, UK
e-mail: noris@qconsultant.com

E.L. Yong Cieh
Christopher Lee & Co, 25-2, Block B, Jaya One Section 13, Petaling Jaya 46200, Malaysia
e-mail: edwin@christopherleeco.com

cautious that a security breach will result in the organisations having to pay hefty penalty and entice potential claims/suits from individuals or organisations. It is time consuming, adding extra compliance cost and resources as well, in which the investigation may take considerable period of time to complete. To add the burden, it will also attract unwanted publicity and cause irreparable damage to one's image, brand, credibility and trustability. In light of the far-reaching implications that may arise from non-compliance with data protection, organisations should bear in mind that it is no longer 'business as usual'. Data protection should be, and must always be, the top priority. Non-negotiable.

A day in our typical life, whether inside the office or outside the office as visualised:

- **6.00am:** We wake up, immediately reach for mobile phone and enter a unique **password**;
- **7.30am:** We arrive at the office, enter the door unique **password** to gain access;
- **8.30am:** We log on to our personal computer or laptop and enter a unique **password**. Some of our intranet-based office systems require **passwords**. In order to get access to these, we enter various unique **passwords**;
- **12.30pm:** Prior to having lunch, we check our social networking sites and other online bank accounts for transactions. These require various unique **passwords**;
- **6pm:** We arrive home from work, enter a unique **password** to get into our apartment/house;
- **7pm:** We get engage with our friends and family members via other social networks. These require different unique **passwords**;
- **9pm:** We may want to update our blog. To access, we enter a unique **password**;
- **10.30pm:** We plan to book flight ticket and hotel accommodation for the year-end holiday via online. We enter various unique **passwords**, again; and
- **12am:** Before heading to bed and call it as a day, we check our personal e-mails (3 different accounts) and we enter various unique **passwords**.

Instantaneously, the flow of data in a day is unimaginable and we are obliged to remember sheer number of passwords! At times, we tend to have forgotten the passwords and recreate the new ones. If we are able to dissect the interrelationship between who's who (data user, data processor and third party) from the above, it is not an individual's responsibility. It's everyone shoulder-to-shoulder responsibility, which collectively nurtures towards accountability. This could start from home and to elsewhere.

In a commercial transaction setting, the level of accountability is obviously a must. *Demonstrable responsibility in data protection leads to demonstrable accountability.* It should start with the leadership and embedded it within the 'DNA' and culture of the company, organisation and institution. In turn, data protection dividend could be potentially yielded. As this masterpiece has had offered to readers, we hope this new addition in the data protection treatise will be able to encourage potential publication from other professionals in Malaysia and ASEAN as well. We are of the view that it's timely to publish a practical guidance on data protection and for being the first to lead. In order to be on the same page, we call upon other professionals and stakeholders to get engage with data protection by way of offering your thoughts, opinions, criticisms and consultations towards Malaysia and ASEAN's headway.

Apropos, this masterpiece is just a humble beginning of an exciting data protection journey in Malaysia and ASEAN. We aim to publish potential practical guidance of the PDPA when the time comes. Thanks very much indeed for your time in purchasing, reading, reviewing and analysing this masterpiece!

About the Editors and Contributing Authors

Noriswadi Ismail

With more than a decade of corporate counsel experience in the information communication and technology industry, Noriswadi Ismail (Noris) leads QC as its co-founder and managing consultant. Since its incorporation, Noris has provided training, consultation, and capacity building programs across a wide spectrum of industries and stakeholders.

Noris was an academic visitor in two renowned centres at the University of Oxford: Centre for Socio-Legal Studies (CSLS) and the Centre for Health, Law and Emerging Technologies (HeLEX). During the Hilary and Trinity terms in CSLS, he researched extensively on data protection in Europe and Asia (South Eastasia and East Asia) and was also involved in selected research and events of Data Protection and Open Society Project under the leadership of Dr. David Erdos, Katzenbach Research Fellow (Balliol College). During the 3 weeks of summer in HeLEX, he researched on the principles and applications of data protection within the realm of medical informatics, particularly in RFID and Hospital Information Management Systems.

In 2008, the Malaysian Institute of Management–Public Bank Berhad Young Manager of the Year Award was conferred on him. At the time, he was the Group General Counsel/Company Secretary of HeiTech Padu Berhad—a leading ICT public listed company in Malaysia, which has investments, business operations, and affiliations in Australia, the Middle East, Russia, Southeast Asia, South Asia, and the United Kingdom.

Noris is a "Majlis Amanah Rakyat" Doctoral Scholar (2009–2012) in the Intellectual Property, Internet and Media Research Centre, Brunel Law School, Brunel University, London and was previously a British Chevening Scholar (2006–2007) in Strathclyde Law School, University of Strathclyde, Glasgow, United Kingdom while studying for his LLM in information technology and telecommunications law. During his LLM year, he penned a highly commendable thesis on "Radio frequency identification technology: the internet of things that threats data protection and privacy?" His masterpieces on data protection have been published in leading global journals: *Computer Law & Security Review* (Elsevier), the *International Journal of Technology Transfer and Commercialisation* (Inderscience) and the *International Data Privacy Law Journal* (Oxford University Press, Oxford Journals).

Noris is a member of the International Association of Privacy Professionals (IAPP) Society for Computers and Law, Chevening Scholars Alumni and the Association for Technical Overseas Scholarship, Japan Scholars Alumni. As part of his pro-bono effort, Noris leads the capacity building engagement on data protection and privacy throughout Malaysian universities (especially at his alma mater—Ahmad Ibrahim Kulliyyah of Laws, International Islamic University Malaysia) and the Malaysian Institute of Management.

Since December 2011, under Noris' leadership, QC has been recognised as a global contributor of Dataguidance for Malaysia. He has provided consultation to Bristows' privacy and data protection client (the world's specialist in mobile broadband) on data protection application in cloud computing within one of the southeast Asian jurisdictions. Noris was one of the co-panelists on the international data transfers panel, to which he spoke on "Data Transfer from the Association of Southeast Asian Nations (ASEAN) to the European Economic Area (EEA)" in the IAPP Europe Data Protection Congress 2012, 14–15 November, Brussels, Belgium. On January 2013, Noris was invited and recognised by the Information & Privacy Commissioner of Ontario, Canada as its Privacy by Design (PbD) Ambassador, joining the other esteemed global esteemed PbD Ambassadors: http://privacybydesign.ca/about/ambassadors/individuals/page/5.

Noris loves travelling, writing, reading and running (he has run 6 half marathons in Blenheim Palace, Oxfordshire; Tunbridge Wells, Kent, Silverstone F1 Track and Edinburgh). At the time of profile update, he secured a ballot to run his first full Marathon in Virgin London Marathon 2013, 21st April 2013 for Cancer Research UK.

Edwin Lee Yong Cieh

Edwin specialises in telecommunications, media and technology law with special interest in privacy and personal data protection law. He also practices corporate, commercial and competition law and regularly advises on mergers and acquisitions transactions and intellectual property matters. He advises on laws and regulations in relation to protection of trade secrets and confidential information, privacy and personal data protection law, electronic commerce and online payment systems, consumer protection, product liability and product labelling, corporate and commercial transactions, as well as mergers and acquisitions. He also advises clients on issues relating to regulatory, licensing, and compliance matters under the Communications and Multimedia Act 1998 and other laws, rules, regulations, and codes of practice such as the Malaysian Communications and Multimedia Content Code and the Malaysian Code of Advertising Practice. He has experience in drafting, negotiating and reviewing commercial agreements. He has also assisted at trials in intellectual property matters and other commercial litigation matters.

Edwin holds a Bachelor of Laws (LL.B (Hons)) from the University of London, a Certificate of Legal Practice (CLP) and a Master of Laws (LL.M) from the University of Malaya under the prestigious Tun Hussein Onn Memorial Law Scholarship awarded by Kuok Foundation Berhad. He is admitted to practice in the High Court of Malaya and is a registered Trade Marks Agent in Malaysia.

Edwin enjoys reading and writing. He has published legal articles in national newspapers and law firm newsletters, and has delivered talks in conferences and appeared as a guest speaker on national television.

Eduardo Ustaran

Eduardo Ustaran is the head of Privacy and Information Law Group of Field Fisher Waterhouse and an internationally recognised expert in privacy and data protection law. A dually qualified English Solicitor and Spanish Abogado, Eduardo specialises in the legal issues that derive from the use of information technology and the Internet.

Eduardo advises on the impact of EU data protection and e-commerce law on the operational activities of all types of organizations, including FTSE 100 companies and public sector bodies. He advises a number of international clients on the adoption of global privacy strategies.

Eduardo regularly manages teams of lawyers across many jurisdictions and has assisted data protection regulators from different countries to align their positions and interpretation of the law. Named by Revolution magazine as one of the 40 most influential people in the growth of the digital sector in the UK, Eduardo is also ranked as a Leading Individual for data protection by Chambers UK and a Computerworld survey.

Eduardo advises clients in the energy, life sciences, media and entertainment, public sector, retail, and technology and communications sectors.

Eduardo has been appointed to the Board of Directors of the International Association of Privacy Professionals. He is also co-chairman of KnowledgeNet London, the editor of Data Protection Law and Policy, and a member of the Panel of Experts of DataGuidance. Eduardo is co-author of *E-Privacy and Online Data Protection* (Tottel Publishing, 2007) and of the *Law Society's Data Protection Handbook* (2004). Eduardo is a regular contributor to our Privacy and Information Law blog and has taken part in many international speaking engagements.

Eduardo regularly lectures at the University of Cambridge as part of its Masters' of Bioscience Enterprise Program on data protection law.

Eduardo speaks Spanish.

Indirani Viknaraja

Having been brought up in Malaysia, Rani moved to the United Kingdom after marriage. She dedicated the next 20 years of her life to raising her young family. While building her "career" on a part-time basis, she enjoyed an unrivalled variety of experiences in different central and local government organisations.

Having successfully seen her two children through university, she deployed all the varied experiences and knowledge she had amassed in her part-time roles as a launching pad to a full-time position in the Office of the Deputy Prime Minister. Currently, Rani works as an information management officer in Southend on Sea Borough Council.

She advises on all aspects of data protection and freedom of information risk and compliance, including data security management, handling subject access requests, audits, data sharing projects and training. Rani firmly believes that effective enforcement is the key to the success of data protection law and has led on the development of procedures and practices to increase the DP profile in the council.

Eva Rose Rahim

Graduated from Bath University, England (BSc. Computer Science & Computer Information System, 1998) and London Guildhall University, England (Distinction in MSc. IT Consultancy, 2001), Eva has more than 10 years of IT experience through her professional career. She started off as an IBM AS/400 mainframe programmer in 1999 and moved toward Web development at the time of the e-commerce boom. She has a number of commercial programming skills and vast experience in Microsoft .NET C#, MVC3, SQL Servers, PHP, MySQL, RPG/400, as well as JavaScript DOM, APIs, OOP, EPiServer CMS, social media and mobile development.

Throughout her career, Eva has been approached by many multinational leading companies such as Microsoft, MSN and LinkedIn to join them. Subsequent to joining Demand QC Global Ltd.—the world's leading social media platform provider—she become actively involved in the subject of data privacy, where she saw the extent of personal data use, in particular when integrated with Facebook,

Twitter, and LinkedIn. She has also been a director of her own Web consulting companies, Trazztech and Bella Belle Limited, in the United Kingdom.

During her schooldays, Eva actively participated in writing non-fiction articles for national magazines and newspapers, of which one was nominated as one of the five best short stories in Malaysia.

Philipp E. Fischer

Philipp E. Fischer holds LL.B. and LL.M. (Intellectual Property Law, London/Dresden).

He is officially certified as an Internal and External Data Protection Officer and Data Protection Auditor (TÜV) and was awarded as ITILv3 Expert and PRINCE2 Foundation & Practitioner of UK's Office of Government Commerce (OGC) as well as COBIT Practitioner (ISACA). Currently, he is undertaking the certification program of Certified Information Privacy Professional/Europe (CIPP/E).

Philipp is a member of the International Association of Privacy Professionals (IAPP), German-Spanish Lawyer Association (DSJV), German Association of Law and Informatics (DGRI), German Association for Data Protection and Data Security (GDD) and German Association of Privacy Professionals (BvD).

He completed his LL.M. in intellectual property law at the School of Law of Queen Mary University of London and the Technical University of Dresden. Along with attending courses in computer-, cyberspace-, e-commerce- and privacy and information law with Professors Ian Walden and Christopher Millard, he completed his dissertation, 'Will Privacy Law in the 21st Century Be American, European or International?', supervised by Dr. Julia Hörnle.

Since then, his masterpieces on data protection have been published in leading European journals. Philipp regularly gives presentations in German, English and Spanish at conferences and workshops across Europe.

After engagements at the Madrid law firm "mmm&m", "Amazon.de" and "DSB Consulting" in the Department for Data Protection Services, he worked as a research assistant at the Max Planck Institute for Intellectual Property and Competition Law in Munich and was awarded a scholarship from the German Association of Law and Informatics (DGRI).

Currently, as CEO of SuiGeneris Consulting, based in Munich, Germany, Philipp manages teams of experts at the interface between laws, informatics and economics. His firm is providing consultancy services that help companies to manage data at every step of the information life cycle. Together with multidisciplinary partners they built a think tank in order to augment privacy- and data security practice and to develop strategies to facilitate global digital information flows for today's digital economy. SuiGeneris Consulting understands data-use business models and how data flows generate profits for clients. SuiGeneris Consulting provides high-quality, total-solution services with an entrepreneurial spirit to all clients ("we think and act outside the box").

Specialties: IT Law, IP Law, Data Protection Law, Privacy Law, Privacy Impact and Risk Assessment, IT Governance, E-Commerce Consultancy, IT Security & Project Management.

Dan Manolescu

Dan Manolescu holds a master of law and technology (LLM), with specialisation in data protection and privacy, a master of arts with a focus on Internet regulations and cybercrime, and a Bachelor of Law degree (LLB).

Dan has working experience with the European Commission and the European Parliament. He is experienced in: (1) Drafting: (a) notification and documentation for personal data processing, transfer, compliance (to/with the National Data Protection Authorities); (b) notification and documentation for personal data prior-checking, compliance (to/with the National Data Protection Authorities); (c) legal mechanisms for the cross-border transfers of personal data (e.g. Safe Harbour, Contracts, BCR); (d) privacy notices and online privacy notices (e.g. use of cookies); (e) privacy impact assessments (conducting and reviewing). (2) Regulation 45/2001 (interpretation, applicability, compliance). (3) Directive 95/46 (interpretation, applicability, compliance). (4) Directive 2002/58 (interpretation, applicability, compliance). (5) Directive 2009/136 (Interpretation, applicability, compliance). (6) Data protection and privacy audit.

Since January 2011, Dan is a member of the International Association of Privacy Professionals (IAPP).

Beginning October 2011, Dan's E-Crime Expert Blog has been featured on the International Association of Privacy Professionals' (IAPP) web site and International Telecommunications Union (ITU). Since August 2011, Dan has been partnering with the International Multilateral Partnership Against Cyber Threats (IMPACT), joining ENISA, Symantec, Kaspersky, in fighting cybercrime and provide awareness.

As of January 2012, E-Crime Expert joined ITU in its efforts to establish an international collaborative network for action to promote the online protection of children worldwide by providing guidance on safe online behavior, in conjunction with other UN agencies and partners.

Specialties: Data Protection and Privacy; Cybercrime; Law and ICT; IPR: Patents, Copyrights, Trademarks and Designs.

If you have any concerns about our products,
you can contact us on
ProductSafety@springernature.com

In case Publisher is established outside the EU,
the EU authorized representative is:
**Springer Nature Customer Service Center GmbH
Europaplatz 3, 69115 Heidelberg, Germany**

Printed by Libri Plureos GmbH
in Hamburg, Germany